Hanoi Jane

Jane

**WAR, SEX &
FANTASIES OF
BETRAYAL**

Jerry Lembcke

UNIVERSITY OF MASSACHUSETTS PRESS

Amherst and Boston

LC 2010003596
ISBN 978-1-55849-815-0 (paper); 814-3 (library cloth)

Set in Quadraat, Gill Heavy, and Geogrotesque Stencil
by Westchester Book, Inc.
Printed and bound by Thomson-Shore, Inc.

Library of Congress
Cataloging-in-Publication Data
Lembcke, Jerry, 1943–
Hanoi Jane : war, sex, and fantasies of betrayal /
Jerry Lembcke.
      p.   cm.
Includes bibliographical references and index.
ISBN 978-1-55849-815-0 (pbk. : alk. paper)—
ISBN 978-1-55849-814-3 (library cloth : alk. paper)
1. Women and war.   2. Women and war—United States.
3. Feminist theory.   4. Fonda, Jane, 1937–   I. Title.
JZ6405.W66L46 2010
355.02082'0973—dc22
                              2010003596

British Library Cataloguing in Publication data are available.

CONTENTS

PREFACE

"Oh, so it's not about me?" Jane Fonda asked when I told her I was working on a book about Hanoi Jane. Right, I replied, it's the biography of "Hanoi Jane," a phrase laden with myth and legend that plays into people's memories of the war in Vietnam.

I've answered the same question many times in the years leading to this book, an experience that bespeaks how popular images of Jane Fonda the actress, activist, and philanthropist have been woven with hearsay and fantasies into a singular image so compelling that, for many people, Jane Fonda the person has become all but indistinguishable from the portrayal of her as the villainess Hanoi Jane.

The attenuated relationship between the historical Jane Fonda and Hanoi Jane makes this book less a study of her than a study of the post–Vietnam War America that brought the name into being. Of particular interest to me is the power that gendered themes of wartime betrayal dating to biblical times continue to exert in the twenty-first century, a persistence signaling the mythical qualities in Hanoi Jane embedded in the psychological architecture of humanity itself and freighted through the millennia by folktales, literary fiction, and film.

The images of Jane Fonda as the sexy space-traveling heroine in the 1968 film *Barbarella*, as the peace traveler sitting on an anti-aircraft gun in North Vietnam in 1972, and as an inspiring figure in the women's liberation movement, as players in the construction of Hanoi Jane, get their due in this book. But the usual explanation for her vilification—that her own radicalism brought it on—is balanced here by recognition that the larger-than-life if fictive Hanoi Jane works in the political culture to displace from public memory the reality that Fonda's prominence beyond the stage and screen was underwritten by mass movements for social change. In a word, remembering Hanoi Jane has helped America to forget some of the most important developments of the past half century and the many strong and determined people, like Jane Fonda, who were more products of their time than it of them.

I've written here in the spirit of the French theorist Michel Foucault's plea that we inquire into the background of the language we use when talking about matters of political and cultural importance, endeavoring to write the story of how Hanoi Jane came to be and what purpose it serves in the American conversation about the meaning of the war.

For a book that may incur the enmity of many, it's especially important to recognize its friends, those who were generous with their time and materials and personal support during the course of its writing. Sara Cooper at the Southern California Library was especially supportive, as were Marie Galbraith and Rachael Guest at the Mattatuck Historical Library. Special Collections librarians at the University of Massachusetts at Boston and librarians at the Waterbury, Connecticut Public Library, the Boston Public Library, and the Brown University library were helpful. The librarians at Holy Cross College are the best, of course, with Sister Irene and Diana Antul in Interlibrary Loan the best of the best.

In Waterbury, Marianne Vandenburgh shared her knowledge of the community and recollections of the tumultuous days in Waterbury when she hosted Jane Fonda at her lovely House on the Hill for the filming of *Stanley and Iris*. Guy Russo and the VFW members who opposed the use of Waterbury as a set for the film and boosted Hanoi Jane to national prominence might not be friends of the book but they were friendly and helpful to me. Dick Flacks, Bruce Franklin, Tom Hayden, Bob Ross, and Jim Russell, all of whom fought to end the war in Vietnam and continue the struggle for world peace and social justice, gave me help and encouragement along the way.

John Hamilton, Ann Marie Leshkowich, Virginia Raguin, and Karen Turner at Holy Cross were good sources for small details that make the book better. Lynn Barowski, a good research assistant as a student is now a friend. The writers, artists, teachers, filmmakers, and activists Nina Berman, John Connelly, Eve Gilbert, Marlisa Grogan, Mark Heberle, Craig Howes, Tony Ladd, Robbie Lieberman, Todd Paddock, Rick Perlstein, Susan Schnall, David Zeiger, and Michael Zeitlin became friends during the writing.

I am very grateful for the companionship of Jennifer Berkshire, Tim Black, Levon and Beverly Chorbajian, Bob Craig, Corey Dolgon, Mary Erdmans, Paul Fitzgerald, Colleen Fuller, Mary Hobgood, Carolyn Howe,

Molly Del Howe-Lembcke, Tom Krainz, Walter Landberg, Debora Milbauer, Jim O'Brien, Stephen Philion, Mark Santow, Richard Schmitt, Brendan Sharky, Don Unger, and Roger Walke.

It's a gift to have an agent, a publicist, and an editor who have become friends in the course of getting *Hanoi Jane* to press and beyond, and I have that gift with Laura Gross, Gail Leondar-Wright, and Clark Dougan, respectively.

Hanoi Jane

1

FROM HANOI JANE
TO OSAMA BIN FONDA
A POLITICAL TROPE
CROSSES THE MILLENNIA

In a spring term 2002 sociology course at Holy Cross College, students were engrossed in the study of the American memory of the war it fought in Vietnam decades earlier. In particular, the students were interested in why so many people believed the war had been lost because the military mission had been betrayed on the home front. The students had learned about the myth of spat-upon veterans and they had been introduced to the idea that novels, Hollywood films, and the imperfect memories of Vietnam-generation men all contributed to the widespread belief that liberal politicians in Washington and radical protesters in the streets had undermined the war effort.

Midway through the term, Marlisa Grogan, a student in the class, received an Internet posting with the heading, "Yes, Jane Fonda Did Kill Someone." Grogan was a senior navy cadet and the message had been forwarded to her by the commanding officer of the college's ROTC unit. The message began by noting that Fonda had been selected by *Ladies' Home Journal* as one of America's top one hundred women of the twentieth century and then went on to rebuke the magazine for that choice and recount the details of Fonda's trip to Hanoi, Vietnam, in 1972.

According to the message, Fonda visited U.S. prisoners of war when she toured Vietnam as a peace activist. The POWs wrote their serial numbers on pieces of paper that were slipped to Fonda when she and the men met and shook hands. The men hoped she would inform their families about their condition and whereabouts but, to their shock, she turned to the North Vietnamese officer in charge and gave him the little papers. After she left the prison, the men were beaten until three of them died. Or so the message claimed.

Introducing Hanoi Jane

The story of the POWs' betrayal by Jane Fonda is not true and yet it is one of three such stories that make up the figure of Hanoi Jane. Days after seeing the prisoners, Fonda was filmed and photographed while sitting on a North Vietnamese anti-aircraft gun looking as though she might be aiming at U.S. war planes. The images eventually appeared in the United States and have since been reproduced many times as graphic symbols of the danger she presented to U.S. pilots. According to the legend, Fonda also made speeches while she was in Hanoi in which she denounced the war and condemned U.S. soldiers. The Hanoi government broadcast those speeches to GIs fighting in the South, and Fonda's critics contend those speeches demoralized U.S. troops and lent "aid and comfort" to the enemy in the North. For some Americans, Hanoi Jane sits near the top of the list of reasons why the United States lost the war.[1]

The 1972 trip to Hanoi is the essential component in the public memory that Jane Fonda acted treasonously during the Vietnam War. But there is still more to the story. Even before that notorious journey, Fonda had co-founded with the actor Donald Sutherland and the cartoonist Jules Feiffer a traveling entertainment troupe named Free the Army, commonly called FTA. A parody of the USO shows made famous by Bob Hope's annual holiday tours of U.S. military bases around the world, FTA used music, dance, and theater to poke fun at military leaders and criticize U.S. policy in Vietnam. The troupe was banned by military authorities from performing on bases, but dissident GI groups and antiwar activists made arrangements for the group's shows at off-base sites in the United States and Pacific Rim countries. While the success of FTA endeared Fonda to thousands of GIs, it earned her the enmity of military leaders and political conservatives.

In 1974, Fonda went to Hanoi again, this time with Tom Hayden, the former leader of Students for a Democratic Society and Chicago 7 defendant whom she had married in 1973. By then, U.S. combat forces had been withdrawn from Vietnam and the last POWs had come home. On their trip, Fonda and Hayden made a film, *Introduction to the Enemy*, which treated the Vietnamese sympathetically while excoriating the United States for the ten-year bombing campaign it had waged against the North. In some of the most moving footage, the activists are shown visiting South Vietnamese peasants who were still being injured in their fields by land mines and other unexploded ordinance left behind by U.S. forces.

The war ended in 1975 when troops of the independence movement swept into Saigon, forcing the remaining American advisers to evacuate the city and compelling the surrender of the client regime the United States had put in place years earlier. The war had been the longest in American history and it was the first conflict lost by the United States on foreign soil. The defeat by a small upstart Asian nation that many Americans could never locate on a map was a hard pill to swallow. Even before the war was over, politicians and pundits began the search for scapegoats to whom the loss could be charged. Fonda's celebrity status made her an easy target for their vitriol and her continued activism in the mid-to-late 1970s kept her in their cross-hairs.

Nevertheless, the figure of Hanoi Jane began to fade by the 1980s. The 1981 film *On Golden Pond*, which Jane Fonda made with her father, Henry Fonda, had a warm, familial feel that gave her image a "good daughter" varnish. The fitness center she opened in 1979 was producing a series of "workout" books and videos that would recast her as a business woman, while her advocacy for women's health issues earned the gratitude of a generation of women entering mid life. Hayden's career in California politics, meanwhile, carried the two of them deeper into mainstream social circles as he sought supporters for his campaigns. In 1984, *World Almanac* listed her as the country's third most influential woman, just ahead of Nancy Reagan and Supreme Court Justice Sandra Day O'Connor. Fonda's 1985 film *Agnes of God*, in which she played a psychiatrist who discovers the religious world of Catholic nuns, and *The Morning After* (1986), in which she played an aging and alcoholic movie star, introduced the actress to a large segment of the film-going public too young to have known her as Hanoi Jane.

Fonda denies that she ever took a conservative turn during the 1980s but, even if the changes in her life could be characterized that way, the country as a whole was turning conservative still faster. The gap between rich and poor opened to record widths as New Deal labor gains were rolled back and social service programs were cut. In a search for explanations for their declining quality of life, millions of Americans were attracted to the demagogic rhetoric of the political Right that pointed to the defeat in Vietnam and the diminished U.S. global economic supremacy that followed as the source of the problem. We had lost the war, the spokesmen for a new generation of rightists said, because of betrayal on the home front and the erosion of our will to win by a culture of permissiveness that pervaded the lives of young people. On the eve of Desert Shield and the beginning of the Persian Gulf War that President George H. W. Bush said would shake America out of its Vietnam syndrome, thousands made vulnerable by the deteriorating condition of their work and community lives were receptive to the politics of vengeance and the appeal of a paramilitary hunt for the "enemy within." It should have surprised no one that Hanoi Jane reappeared in their sights.

America Remilitarized, Hanoi Jane Resuscitated

Had America's pretensions to imperial power remained in the abated state the Vietnam War put them, Jane Fonda might have shed the ignominy of Hanoi Jane and slid into later life as just Jane. But the times were changing again as the voices agitating for a renewed pursuit of global prominence reached receptive ears.

Trouble began three years before Desert Shield when the *Waterbury Republican* newspaper announced on November 12, 1987, that Fonda and the actor Robert DeNiro would arrive the next spring to make a film about an illiterate cook and the factory worker who teaches him how to read. Leaders of the Connecticut city, which was historically dependent on the manufacture of bullet casings and other brass products—thus, its appellation of Capital of Brass Valley—were ecstatic about the project because spending by the film company would give a boost to the community's slumping economy.

Not everyone, however, was so happy. Two days later, a letter to the paper from Gaetano "Guy" Russo, a World War II veteran and major general retired from the National Guard, promised a campaign to stop the use of Waterbury as a shooting site for the film because, as he put it,

4 Fonda had given "vocal comfort and support to the regime in North

Vietnam." The letter touched a nerve in Waterbury and the effect was felt across the country when the Associated Press picked up the story. Subsequently, all three television networks reported the controversy, running fifteen-second footage of Fonda with the North Vietnamese anti-aircraft gun in 1972.

The Waterbury aldermen voted 11 to 2 on April 25, 1988, to allow the filming of what would become *Stanley and Iris* to go on, but Russo and his supporters pledged to picket Fonda's presence. In an effort to still the troubled waters, Fonda arranged for an interview with Barbara Walters that aired on ABC's June 17 20/20 show. In the interview, Walters asked Fonda, "What were you doing climbing on that gun?" "It was a thoughtless and careless thing to have done," Fonda replied, before adding that she did not think she had been duped by the Vietnamese for propaganda purposes. Asked about the radio broadcasts she made to the men on the aircraft carriers from which the raids on North Vietnam were being launched, Fonda implied that she was only trying to get them to think about the consequences of their actions. Of her 1973 statement that claims by former POWs that they had been tortured were "lies," Fonda said she had "popped off and shouldn't have said it." In guarded tones, Fonda went on to say that her intention had been to help end the killing, not to hurt the POWs or make their situation worse, and that she wanted to apologize to the men and their families.

The 20/20 apology created enough space for *Stanley and Iris* to be completed but it didn't satisfy Fonda's critics. Being sorry for the hurt to individual veterans was not enough when what they wanted was a broader political apology for the damage they said she had done to the military mission in Vietnam. For them the issue was treason, not thoughtlessness, and her failure to apologize for betraying the nation confirmed their belief that she was, and always had been, a menace to America. As it turned out, the 20/20 apology that might have buried Hanoi Jane breathed enough new life into the aging icon to carry it into the next century.

Hanoi Jane and the Persian Gulf War

Stanley and Iris came out in 1989. It was Fonda's last film of the century and its moving story line may have coupled with her divorce from Hayden in the same year to temper her negative public image. As it turned out, neither the political nor the personal would leave well enough alone. The Gulf War revived concerns about national security, and Fonda's marriage to the owner of CNN, Ted Turner, in 1991 created new fodder for the anti-Fonda crowd.

In August 1990, Iraq sent troops across its border with Kuwait. The conflict was about the definition of the border and the oil beneath it, but President George H. W. Bush alleged that the incursion was a prelude to an Iraqi attack on Saudi Arabia; with that, he dispatched forces to the Gulf region in defense of U.S. oil interests. By late fall, the administration was threatening to bomb Iraq itself and possibly invade the country to overthrow its leader, Saddam Hussein. U.S. peace activists mounted a sizeable antiwar movement in response.

As a counter to the movement, pro-war pundits and conservative columnists likened the protesters to sixties-era activists whose actions, they said, had demoralized the troops in Vietnam and robbed the nation of victory in Southeast Asia; opposition to Bush's war plans was tantamount to betrayal of the soldiers themselves, a form of spitting on them, just as protestors had spat on soldiers returning from Vietnam. By the time the bombing of Iraq began on January 17, fanciful tales of Vietnam veterans abused by protesters pervaded the discourse over whether the bombing should be supported or not, making the war in the Gulf, in some minds, as much about Vietnam as Iraq.[2]

The image of the spat-upon Vietnam veteran, and the subtext of betrayal that it conveyed, converged with other Vietnam-war legacies to create a climate of near hysteria as bombing began. On January 19, the Hussein government ordered all the foreign news media except CNN and one Spanish journalist to leave the country. CNN gave Peter Arnett, its ace war reporter, permission to continue broadcasting amid the falling bombs.

Arnett stayed and his decision was met with suspicion. The fact that Saddam Hussein allowed CNN to remain in the capital raised questions about Turner and Arnett's loyalty: Maybe they were trading with the enemy? Had they cut some kind of deal whereby Hussein let them stay in return for their producing news stories that were sympathetic to the regime? Or perhaps the boys from Atlanta were actually "soft on Saddam." Arnett's work as a young reporter who was often critical of the

United States' conduct of the war in Vietnam was dredged up as a prior record; his wartime marriage to a Vietnamese woman providing confirmation for some skeptics that he was, indeed, capable of sleeping with the enemy.[3]

The reappearance of loyalty issues and the invocation of Vietnam War history as a way to animate them for public consumption were almost certain to reinvolve Jane Fonda—and they did. Turner had begun dating Fonda just before the Gulf crisis and, once the bombing was under way and Arnett's reporting from Baghdad had linked Turner and CNN with Vietnam-era images of treason, it was almost inevitable that the right wing would invoke Hanoi Jane in an effort to further discredit Turner and CNN. That's what happened, with the added consequence that Hanoi Jane had yet another incarnation.[4]

Throughout the 1990s, military writers blasted CNN for its role in war coverage, reiterating the Arnett-Vietnam-Turner-Fonda axis. David Hackworth, recalling that he had met Arnett while serving as an officer in Vietnam, wrote that the journalist had been "from the school that 'Ho Chi Minh has got to win'" but that, "to his credit, he didn't climb into a Red gun position for a photo op as did Siamese twin 'Hanoi Jane.'" Now, Hackworth claims, Arnett was protected from firing by CNN because "he's still connected ideologically at the left hip with Jane Fonda-Turner," a reference to Fonda and Turner's being married.[5]

Ladies' Home Journal Jane

The irony is that Fonda's separation from the leftist Hayden and marriage to one of the country's richest and most powerful men might have moved her well off the margins of social status and into the mainstream of American respectability. But it didn't, and the irony was amplified when the conservative Ladies' Home Journal inadvertently stoked the passions of her enemies by bestowing "woman of the century" honors on her in 1998.

One of many best-of-the-century lists compiled by entertainment and literary organizations in the late 1990s, the Ladies' Home Journal "best" were women who, according to the journal editor Myrna Blyth, "have made contributions to our culture that influence women today and will continue to influence women's lives into the coming millennium." The selections, made by a panel of academic women, were announced in the October 1998 issue of the magazine. Simultaneously, the journal published a glossy coffee-table volume, 100 *Most Important Women of the 20th Century*, that includes a foreword by Barbara Walters and photographs and biographical sketches for each of the women.[6]

Fonda's appearance on the list was interesting. At first blush, it seemed a reach for the stodgy *Journal* to be feting a sixties-generation radical like her, but the inclusion of the rebel-rocker Janis Joplin and the civil rights pioneer Rosa Parks on the same list made Fonda's presence less conspicuous. Moreover, the editors downplayed her activism, emphasizing instead her role as "workout guru," which they said had popularized the idea of fitness for a mass audience. She had become "America's personal trainer," according to the text printed alongside the inset cover of her 1981 publication *Jane Fonda's Workout Book*.

With the *Ladies' Home Journal*'s makeover, Fonda may have passed muster with mainstream American women as one of the twentieth century's "best," but the political Right looked right through Workout Jane and saw Hanoi Jane. Controversy over her selection was extended with the renewed interest in the war brought by the twenty-fifth anniversary of its end in 2000. With debates reengaged over how the United States had gotten into the war and why it lost the war, journalists and conservative commentators resuscitated the home-front betrayal theory for the defeat and, with it, the image of Hanoi Jane.[7]

"Kabul Jane"

Hanoi Jane is a name that symbolizes behavior and expressions that many Americans consider threatening to national security and their own beliefs, and so it was no surprise that it would find its way into conversation after the attacks of September 11, 2001. On October 6, less than a month after planes hit the World Trade Center and the Pentagon, the *Waterbury (CT) American-Republican* ran an editorial with the title "Kabul Jane?" Referring to an interview Fonda had done with an Atlanta radio station, the editorial said she had "insinuated the United States was to blame for the September 11 terrorism." It went on to ask whether she would soon be sitting on an anti-aircraft installation in Afghanistan, broadcasting anti-American propaganda over Radio Kabul, or posing for pictures with U.S. prisoners of war. Waterburians were never fond of

Hanoi Jane, the writer concluded, but they will not like "Osama bin Fonda" any better.

That a small-city newspaper would so quickly and spontaneously seize on internal loyalty as a pertinent matter in the wake of 9/11 and link that concern, through the image of Hanoi Jane, to the Vietnam era testifies to the depth and authenticity of American unsettledness about the war in Vietnam and the degree to which the nation's understanding of current events continues to be filtered through memories of it. The Waterbury response dovetailed with speculation that someone within the government may have known the attacks were coming and failed to take the appropriate steps; downstream, those rumors mixed with attempts by some academic writers to understand 9/11 as a kind of blowback, (re) payment-in-kind from the unhappy recipients of decades-long U.S. military and economic policy.[8]

He's like . . . She's like . . . Hanoi Jane

Even before 9/11, Hanoi Jane was used as an analogy to characterize another person. When Barbra Streisand produced a 1998 movie for NBC that contained material the National Rifle Association thought was contrary to its position on the constitutional right to own guns, their spokesman, Charlton Heston, labeled Streisand the " 'Hanoi Jane' of the anti-gun movement."

The apprehension about national security after the attacks, however, increased the frequency of Hanoi Jane brandings. In October 2002 the syndicated columnist George Will criticized congressional representatives Jim McDermott and David Bonior for visiting Iraq. "Not since Jane Fonda posed for photographers at a Hanoi antiaircraft gun," Will wrote, "has there been anything like Rep. Jim McDermott saying Americans should take Saddam Hussein at his word, but should not take President Bush at his." A few days later, a letter appeared in the *New York Post* tagging Representative Bonior " 'Baghdad' David Bonior," while another warned McDermott that he "might go down in history as the Hanoi Jane Fonda of our war against terrorism." Scott Ridder also got the Hanoi Jane treatment. Ridder is the former U.N. arms inspector who decided the inspections were actually part of a phony effort by the United States to vilify the Iraqi regime. When he spoke out he was ridiculed as "Ritter of Arabia" and "Hanoi Jane."[9]

The spike in Hanoi Jane's popularity with the post-9/11 punditry had hardly receded when John Kerry announced his candidacy for President. Surely there was a role for an already auditioned figure of un-Americanism on this stage. Within weeks, photos appeared—one real and one manufactured—juxtaposing the antiwar activist John Kerry with Hanoi Jane's evil twin, Jane Fonda. True, Kerry had returned from Vietnam to oppose the conflict and help establish Vietnam Veterans Against the War as a major force for peace in the early 1970s. But the spinning of those biographical details into a tale of his having betrayed the well-being of other men still in harm's way and thereby contributed to the loss of the war was an exercise in myth-making that boosted George W. Bush's bid for the White House and kept Hanoi Jane on the tip of the nation's tongue.

Jane Fonda's memoir *My Life So Far* came out in 2005 to bestseller sales, critical acclaim, and public appearances by her that packed arenas from coast to coast. But it also lengthened the life of Hanoi Jane. When Fonda signed books in Kansas City, a man bought a copy and stood in line for ninety minutes before stepping to the table and spitting on her. While speaking at the Bushnell Auditorium in Hartford, Connecticut, a few weeks later, Fonda was picketed by the same group of veterans from Waterbury who had tried to stop the filming of *Stanley and Iris* eighteen years earlier.[10]

By this time, too, Fonda was proving the rumors of her turn to conservatism unfounded by coming out publicly against the wars in Iraq and Afghanistan. When the documentary *Sir! No Sir!* about the Vietnam-era GI antiwar movement was released in 2006, there she was as historical Jane in the archival footage of FTA and newly taped Jane reprising the meaning of the past for opponents of the current conflicts. At a large January 2007 antiwar demonstration in Washington, DC, Fonda took the stage to say that silence was no longer acceptable, while conservative counterprotesters associated with the on-line journal *Free Republic* hoisted a Fonda effigy with a sign reading, "Jane Fonda; American Traitor; Bitch."

The endurance of Hanoi Jane for thirty years speaks to its qualities as a trope that communicates something deeply felt in the American psyche. Tropes, however, are literary devices with provenances, biographies with points of origins and paths of development that can be traced. Tropes are created in particular contexts and kept in use by individuals and groups for whom they serve identifiable purposes. Tropes, in other words, help tell stories and yet have their own story to tell. The following chapters tell the story of one of America's most potent political tropes, Hanoi Jane.

"THIS IS JANE FONDA . . . SPEAKING TO YOU FROM HANOI"

When told of my interest in how Jane Fonda came to be vilified as Hanoi Jane, most listeners express surprise. Why would an academic writer be interested in the obvious: Didn't Fonda do it to herself? Didn't she ask for it by encouraging GIs to resist the war, befriending the North Vietnamese, sitting on the gun, and criticizing the POWs? And isn't her celebrity status reason enough to explain why she, and not someone else, became the lightening rod for criticism?

The claim, though, that Fonda's own behavior and public personae destined her for the Hanoi Jane role can stand up only if what she did was distinguishable enough from the actions of others to warrant the hostility she inspired. Were who she was, and what she did, really so different?

For people hearing about it for the first time today, the mere fact that Fonda went to Hanoi and met with North Vietnamese leaders at a time when U.S. policy forbade such travel probably sounds like eccentric and risky behavior. And in a way, it was. To begin with, travel to Hanoi from the United States was an arduous, weeklong undertaking. Itineraries went through Europe and Asia with several stops and no certainty that U.S. bombers in the skies over the North would delay or even cancel the final leg into Hanoi. Hotel accommodations were scarce. Nighttime blackouts left visitors feeling their way by flashlight and, when the bombs dropped, joining their Vietnamese hosts in shelters that were cramped and poorly ventilated.[1]

Returning to the United States, activists faced recriminations from the government, discrimination from employers, and indifference, if not hostility, from the press and public. Some of the first to make the trip had their passports confiscated on their return. A young history professor at Yale, Staughton Lynd, was denied tenure after the university president declared statements made by Lynd in Hanoi "irresponsible." Ethel Taylor recalled being ridiculed and ostracized when she returned home. Measured by the degree of difficulty and discomfort the trip entailed, and the potential for unwanted personal and professional consequences that awaited her return, what Fonda did was certainly remarkable.[2]

Left at that, Fonda cuts an adventurous figure, appearing heroic to some observers, foolhardy to others. But the outsizing of Fonda's presence in the events of the day by her critics helps displace from public memory the large and mass-based social movement against the war that had grown steadily after the first regular U.S. ground troops arrived in Vietnam in 1965. Opposition to the war gained momentum until the fall of 1969 when the Moratorium Days brought business as usual to a halt in some cities and turned out tens of thousands of mainstream Americans in support of peace. In *Vietnam Wars*, Marilyn Young recalls that resistance to the draft resulted in more than three thousand prosecutions by 1968, a development that was blending by then with resistance within the military and the organization of Vietnam veterans opposed to the war.[3]

Nor was Fonda a pioneer on the peace trail to Hanoi. By the time she went in 1972, more than three hundred other American peace activists had already been there. Indeed, pilgrimages to Hanoi had something of an aura about them, a credentialing experience necessary to establish one's authority as an opponent of the war. The first American peace activists, Mary Clarke and Lorraine Gordon, members of Women Strike for Peace, landed in Hanoi two months after the first marines went ashore to defend the Da Nang airfield in 1965. Clarke and Gordon had attended a peace conference in Moscow where they met with North Vietnamese women who had invited them to attend. In Hanoi, they co-planned with their hosts a five-day conference to be held the following July in Jakarta, Indonesia.[4] In the fall, four members of the W. E. B. Du Bois Club made the trip and became the first American peace activists to meet with a U.S. POW, Air Force Captain Robert Daughtrey, who had been shot down a month earlier. By the end of the year, a third group, which included Tom Hayden, was in Hanoi.[5] From then until formal U.S. involvement in the war stopped in early 1973, the list of U.S. peace supporters going to Hanoi grew longer. With hundreds of other opponents of the war having preceded her, there was nothing politically notable about the fact that Fonda went to Hanoi in 1972.[6]

The Importance of Celebrity

Even if the trip itself, however, was not exceptional, what of the claim that Fonda's celebrity made it important? Henry Holzer and his wife, Erika, compile the strongest case against her in their book "Aid and Comfort": Jane Fonda in North Vietnam. They say her activities were all the more deplorable because of her notoriety, contending that, had she been tried for treason at the time, "a jury could have concluded that her status, by itself, was sufficient to provide aid and comfort to the North Vietnamese."[7] But was the social distance between her and her fellow travelers really so great? And could the perception of her higher social standing have been so persistent over the years to account for the attention her trip continues to get in the twenty-first century?

Status is an elusive quality, and so it is not clear that anyone could make a case, thirty years after the fact, either for or against the importance of Fonda's prominence in the matter of her trip. Any measure of social status will have its limitations, but the number of times an individual appears in mainstream news sources provides one indication of her importance. Not all sources of news from 1972 are still available to us, and many of those are not sufficiently indexed to be useful to researchers. The New York Times, however, has for decades been meticulously indexed and the volumes of those indexes are widely available to researchers using public and campus libraries. Moreover, the attention paid to an individual in the pages of the Times, the nation's "paper of record," would have carried over into the amount of coverage given that person by news organizations across the country, making the Times index the go-to resource for research of this type.

By counting the number of entries in the *Times* index for Fonda and others who went to Hanoi, we can compare their visibility as public figures. Making that comparison, we see that the "celebrity status" explanation for why Fonda becomes Hanoi Jane is pretty weak. For 1972, the year she went to Hanoi, Fonda was the subject of thirty-three *New York Times* stories, five of which were film reviews. Former Attorney General Ramsey Clark, who went a few weeks after Fonda, was covered in fifty-nine news stories that year. Fonda's prominence was more comparable to that of Cora Weiss, leader of Women's Strike for Peace, who also went to Hanoi and was mentioned in nineteen news stories in the *Times*, or that of the singer Joan Baez, who was mentioned in seventeen news stories, many of them about her opposition to the war and the draft. A year later, 1973, Ramsey Clark was still more newsworthy, with thirty-one *Times* stories to Fonda's twenty-two.

Another way of making the comparison is to see how much attention the press gave the actual trips. In Fonda's case it was negligible. A small, twenty-five-line, story, "Jane Fonda Appeal Reported by Hanoi," appeared on page 9 of the *Times* on July 9. It was accompanied by a still smaller story reporting that the U.S. State Department rebuked her for going. A photograph of her at an anti-aircraft site, but not on a gun, appeared in the July 16 edition, with a caption noting the State Department's "distress" over her reported antiwar broadcasts on Radio Hanoi. The next story, again very small and on page 9, did not come until twenty days later.

Time and *Newsweek* magazines ignored the trip until Fonda returned, and then they made little of it. In its July 31 sidebar "The War in Indochina," *Newsweek* ran a United Press International photograph of her standing on a North Vietnamese dike with an accompanying caption saying she had gone on Hanoi radio to denounce U.S. "war criminals." A week later, the magazine included a twenty-four-line note about her return from Hanoi on its "Newsmakers" page, reporting that Fonda received a mixed greeting of cheers and the epithets "Hanoi Rose" and "Red Pinko" at her landing in New York City. Two congressmen were said by *Newsweek* to have branded her a traitor. *Time* did not mention the trip until August 7. Then, far from lampooning her radicalism, the editors actually cited her as a credible (if not impartial) eyewitness source for a story about U.S. bombing of irrigation dikes, thereby establishing a benchmark in her public image from which we can measure the evolution of Hanoi Jane.[8]

The New York Daily News treated the trip as an election-year story. Under the headline, "Jane: POWs Want McGovern," the paper reported on the July 25, 1972, press conference she gave in Paris where she said seven POWs being held by the North Vietnamese had asked her to tell their parents and friends to vote for Democratic Party candidate George Mc-Govern. If Richard Nixon stayed in office, she said, the men "fear they will be prisoners forever." Filling the news hole of the movie page and positioned just above the ads for Parades, a film about the breakdown of military discipline, and Deep Throat, the breakout pornographic film that celebrated oral sex, the story about Fonda's travel to Hanoi barely registered as news.[9]

Television news gave some attention to Fonda's trip but mostly by working their reportage of it into other related stories. On July 21, for example, CBS Evening News reported not on her trip but on Representative Fletcher Thompson's call for her to be investigated for treason. Four days later, ABC and NBC used her, much as Time had done, as an eyewitness source on the controversies surrounding the bombing of dikes in North Vietnam.[10]

Other prominent people got far more press attention for their treks to Hanoi. When Harrison Salisbury went in 1966, for example, he was the assistant managing editor of the New York Times and had already won a Pulitzer Prize. The U.S. press was more interested in his trip than it would be in Fonda's and his dispatches from Hanoi actually had an impact on Pentagon policy, an effect that Fonda could only have hoped for.[11]

A line of famous Americans followed Salisbury's path to the North. In 1967 the Black Power leader Stokely Carmichael went with greater visibility in the press than Fonda would have five years later. Indeed, the manifest of travelers was so star-studded during the weeks and months surrounding Fonda's trip that the significance of her efforts hardly stood out. At least forty-two Americans went to Hanoi in 1972, including the Nobel Prize-winning biologist George Wald in March, Ramsey Clark, and Peter Arnett, the Pulitzer-holding journalist. In December, Joan Baez and Telford Taylor, the chief prosecutor for the U.S. government at the Nuremberg war crimes trials, witnessed the Christmas bombing of Hanoi from ground level.[12]

Ramsey Clark was more interesting to the press than Fonda, who left Hanoi about the time he arrived. His father had been a U.S. Supreme Court Justice and he, U.S. attorney general for Lyndon Johnson. Clark's denunciations of the U.S. war were carried over Radio Hanoi, and when he returned home he criticized the bombing of the dikes and linked the release of POWs to the U.S. willingness to end the war. *Time* devoted several paragraphs to his criticism of U.S. bombing raids and his visits with U.S. POWs, who he said were humanely treated, "unbrainwashed," and healthy. The news magazine ran a half page of photographs showing him in North Vietnam, one with Clark surrounded by smiling North Vietnamese. In an August 17 editorial, the *New York Times* said Clark had used "poor judgment" in criticizing American war policies while in North Vietnam but called his intentions "humane" and his observations about the mass suffering being inflicted on the Vietnamese by the bombing "correct."[13]

There is no gainsaying that Fonda was a popular public figure and that the familiarity of many Americans with her name gave the memory of her time in Hanoi some durability. But other travelers had their own celebrity cachet, and who would remember today that the writer Susan Sontag, the singers Judy Collins and Pete Seeger, or even Ramsey Clark also went to Hanoi as peace activists during the war? So if her fame, such as it was at the time, is an insufficient explanation for Fonda's canonization as Hanoi Jane, what else could account for it? The easy answer is that it was not Fonda's trip to Hanoi in itself, or even who she was, that etched her into public memory but rather what she did while she was there.

Been There—But Done *That?*

A useful assessment of Fonda's activities in Hanoi can be made only through comparison with what others did while they were there, and by interpreting what she did in the context of the times. Many of the individuals and delegations that made the journey went with so little attention from the government and press that their efforts are virtually lost in the historical record. Indeed, researching the news coverage of U.S. activists in Hanoi, one notes how dismissively they were treated by major papers, such as the *New York Times*. With Fonda's trip, there is a striking disparity between how little attention was paid to it in the newspapers of the day and how large it looms in the American memory of the war decades later.

Medical Relief

Coming near the end of an eight-year string of war opponents journeying to Hanoi, Fonda's trip had some strong competition for "the most radical" award. In 1966 a Quaker group requested passport validations from the U.S. government to carry medical supplies to the North. Permission was denied, but the group went ahead with a publicity campaign against the war and a fundraising effort for a hundred boxes of pharmaceuticals and surgical items. On March 22, 1967, a crew of eight loaded their humanitarian goods on the ketch *Phoenix* and sailed from Hong Kong to Haiphong in North Vietnam, knowing they faced imprisonment and fines when they returned to the United States. In Hanoi, members toured the city and met with officials, civic leaders, and the Vietnamese press. The group explained the American peace movement to the Vietnamese, delivering what one crew member, Elizabeth Boardman, called a "Quaker lobbying pitch."[14]

Prisoner Releases

The most controversial delegations to Hanoi were those attempting to end run formal governmental channels and carry on their own private negotiations for the release of prisoners. The first of those came in November 1967 when a group of American activists met in a "seminar-style" conference with representatives from North Vietnam and the South Vietnamese National Liberation Front (NLF) in Bratislava, Czechoslovakia. Following the conference, a smaller group, which included Tom Hayden, traveled to Hanoi, where they spent two weeks touring bomb-damaged areas and meeting with POWs. In Hanoi, Hayden was informed by an emissary of the NLF that a prisoner release could be arranged through its Cambodian embassy in Phnom Penh. Hayden traveled alone to Phnom Penh where, for four days, he worked out the details for the release and made travel plans for himself and the three freed prisoners, James Jackson, Dan Pitzer, and Edward Johnson.[15]

The release came on November 11, Veterans Day in the United States, a coincidence that could hardly have been better for public visibility. The next day's *Sunday New York Times* covered the holiday on its front page, along with a large photo of Hayden and the liberated GIs in Phnom Penh. And then there was the news of the war itself, which could not have been more dramatic. A major confrontation between U.S. and North Vietnam forces was under way at Dak To in the Central Highlands, one of a series of "border battles" that preceded the Tet Offensive in early 1968, which would prove to be the turning point of the war. The contrast between the war news and the antiwar news of the release was striking: the *Times* kept the NLF release before the public for two more days with a large profile of Hayden the next day and a November 14 story alleging that Jackson, Pitzer, and Johnson had been brainwashed.[16]

The first release of POWs held in the North came early in 1968. North Vietnamese leaders contacted the U.S. pacifist David Dellinger in January, inviting him to arrange for the reception of freed prisoners by a representative of the peace movement. Dellinger asked the Boston University history professor Howard Zinn and the Jesuit priest Daniel Berrigan to go to Hanoi for the turnover. After a week there, Zinn and Berrigan were handed Norris Overly, Jon Black, and David Methany, all pilots. The five left Hanoi on February 16 and made their first stop in Vientiane, Laos, where they were met by U.S. ambassador William Sullivan. Sullivan took charge of the prisoners and transferred them to an embassy flight.

The release occurred during some of the heaviest fighting of the entire war: the battle for the city of Hue was raging, the weeks-long siege of Khe Sanh was ringing up its toll in lives and material, and the second wave of the Tet Offensive was rocking Saigon and other cities. But the dramatic photos and reports from the multiple battle lines in South Vietnam did not push the story of the liberated POWs off the front page, and the controversy surrounding the itinerary of the home-bound flyers kept the story before the public for several days.[17]

Private Negotiations

Independent missions to the North went on until the end of the war and some of them involved interventions at high levels of both governments that could have ended the fighting sooner. George McT. Kahin, a Cornell University professor of Southeast Asian studies, went in September 1971 to "establish what the actual negotiating position of North Vietnam was," thinking that he might be able to facilitate talks between the North and the United States. From the North Vietnamese negotiator

Ha Van Lau he learned that a peaceful settlement might be possible if General Duong Van Minh could win the presidency in the upcoming elections in the South. Kahin's findings were conveyed to Senator J. William Fulbright, chair of the Senate Foreign Relations Committee, and then to the State Department, where they were distorted and then "leaked" to the press to discredit the senator as "dovish." The administration supported the reelection of the Thieu-Ky regime in Saigon and the war continued.[18]

Making Friends with Foes

The strongest accusation against Fonda is that she gave "aid and comfort" to the enemy by leading them to think they had friends, like her, behind (their) enemy's lines. It is an indictment that goes beyond the distastefulness with which more moderate critics hold her time in Hanoi, alleging that she demoralized U.S. troops and POWs through her radio broadcasts, and that her pose for photographers on the anti-aircraft gun lent legitimacy to the North Vietnamese air-defense efforts and its imprisonment of U.S. pilots who had been shot down. The more strident plaintiffs charge her with "overt acts" that constitute treason; the acts they name include the tours she took of a museum, a hospital, irrigation dikes, and a textile center, always accompanied by North Vietnamese officials. The implication of the charge is that these were collaborative behaviors that gave encouragement to the North Vietnamese. In retrospect, it does seem possible, on one hand, that fraternizing of that sort could have been a morale booster for the North. On the other hand, decades of struggle for independence had hardly left the Vietnamese wanting for the good cheer of an American movie star.[19]

Whether Fonda's schmoozing with the enemy was treasonous, in a legal sense, is somewhat different from how those activities played into the creation of Hanoi Jane. The portrayal of her as "touring" with the communists works as a disparaging element in the betrayal narrative only if it is forgotten that hundreds of other Americans and visitors from many countries had been treated the same as Fonda. In 1965, the Phoenix crew made similar tour stops and the skipper, Earle Reynolds, enjoyed a sumptuous meal catered aboard the boat by a Haiphong hotelier. Anne Weills, who went in 1968, recalled having "toured the North Vietnamese 'banquet circuit,' making speeches and meeting individuals from all levels of North Vietnamese society."[20]

It appears, in other words, that the kind of mixing that Fonda did with the North Vietnamese had become the routine for visitors to the North by the time she went in 1972. Moreover, some of those who arrived before her would seem to have lent even more support to the enemy than she did. By taking medical supplies to the North, the crew of the *Phoenix* had given "aid and comfort" to the enemy in literal ways not even approached by Fonda. Those who negotiated for the terms of prisoner releases were, in effect, conducting their own foreign policy in clear violation of the spirit, if not the letter, of U.S. law—Fonda didn't do that. Early travelers who cued the North Vietnamese about which Americans they could work with had seemingly breached security in a way that could have affected the outcome of the war; whereas whatever Fonda may have done in that regard was far too late to have been of any help to Hanoi. Likewise for the general socializing with political and civic leaders that most of the peace travelers did by accepting tours, special meals, and other favors. To have had any effect on the way the war would end, they would have had to have been done in the early years, not six months before the fighting stopped.

Fonda is also accused of having used her radio broadcasts from Hanoi to encourage GIs to desert or even mutiny. That charge was first made in an analysis done of her trip by the propaganda specialist Edward Hunter for the September 1972 House of Representatives Committee on Internal Security. Hunter's brief claimed that Fonda had appealed to GIs to "disobey orders . . . desert, and generally take the side of the enemy." But she had not, and when she faced her first news conference in Paris on her return from Hanoi, she emphasized that she had not urged servicemen to disobey orders. Eventually, the government's release of its own transcriptions of the broadcasts revealed that Hunter was, at best, exaggerating what she had said.[21]

Fonda had indeed addressed one broadcast to GIs in South Vietnam, but there is nothing in its transcript that substantiates what Hunter said she said. She did describe the in-service protests against the war and resistance to military authority that had grown widespread years before and she truthfully reported that desertions had increased dramatically since 1969. She also noted that some U.S. officers were "being killed, fragged" by their own men, but, she added, "in America we do not condone the killing of American officers." While not encouraging rebellion

21

in the ranks, Fonda did repeatedly call for U.S. soldiers to think for themselves.[22]

The seriousness of Fonda's "offense" in appealing to GIs to think for themselves is diminished still more when viewed with a comparative perspective. Joseph E. Thach, research analyst for the House Committee on Internal Security, said in a September 5, 1972, memo that eighty-two broadcasts had been made from Hanoi by U.S. visitors, including the MIT linguist Noam Chomsky, the activists Sidney Peck and Ann Froines, and Pete Seeger. Some of the statements aired contained words that were incendiary compared with Fonda's. On September 20, 1970, for example, the Reverend Philip Lawson, a Methodist minister associated with the Black Panthers, called on his "black brothers" to "disobey all racist officers" and "join the . . . Vietnamese forces" in order to be welcomed back to the United States as "true black men."[23]

Fonda addressed herself to pilots in nine of the eighteen broadcasts attributed to her. At the time, most of the U.S. flyers were stationed on off-shore aircraft carriers. The critics of those broadcasts say they were demoralizing to the pilots because she accused them of atrocities that were punishable as war crimes. But did she? The transcripts reveal that she actually chose her words carefully on that point, making a distinction between the civilian and military leaders who were giving the orders for the bombings and the soldiers carrying them out.

In one broadcast she used words similar to what other visitors to Hanoi had used to describe the destruction from bombing raids and then said, "I don't know what your officers tell you that you are dropping on this country. . . . But one thing you should know is that these weapons are illegal. . . . The men who are ordering you to use these weapons are war criminals, . . . and in the past, in Germany and Japan, men who were guilty of these kinds of crimes were tried and executed." In another broadcast she accused the Nixon administration of lying to the troops and the American people about the conduct of the war and then spoke to "the men in the cockpits of the Phantoms, in the B-52's, the F-4's: If they told you the truth, you wouldn't fight, you wouldn't kill."

Some of her broadcasts to pilots recounted aspects of Vietnamese history and culture that underscored the tenacity of the Vietnamese people when facing foreign invaders. She recalled the insurrection of

AD 40, led by the Trung sisters, which threw the Chinese out, and the Vietnamese defeat of the French at Dien Bien Phu in 1954. In a talk dated July 25, 1972, she said:

> You must understand that the people of Vietnam are peasants. They live with the land—the land is a part of their lives, as it has been for thousands of years. Every time you drop your bombs on the heads of these peasants it becomes clearer to them who the enemy is. . . . How can we continue to rain this kind of terror on these people who want nothing more than to live in peace and freedom and independence?

On August 15, Fonda's prerecorded impressions of a July 19 meeting with captured U.S. pilots was broadcast. "They all assured me," she reported, "that they have been well cared for. They listen to the radio. They receive letters. They are in good health. They asked about news from home."

Radio Hanoi: Who Heard? Who Cared?

Like so much else related to Jane Fonda's 1972 trip to Hanoi, the significance of her radio commentaries cannot be separated from the times in which she made them. There are, first of all, questions about who, if anyone, heard what she said. Despite the image that many Americans now have of GIs sitting with their ears glued to a transistor radio listening to Fonda sweet talking them into despair, there are curiously few veterans who claim to have heard her. Don Poss maintains an Internet site called "War Stories," the type of place where one might expect to find occasional postings from Vietnam veterans who listened to Fonda. As of January 2005 there were five archived postings at that site that make critical mention of Fonda's broadcasts, but none of the writers claims to have heard them.[24]

The few veterans who do claim to have listened to Fonda are less than persuasive. One who posted at "War Stories" makes a passing reference to having heard "Jane Fonda-Ho's broadcasts from Radio Hanoi" in 1971—at least a year before she was even in Hanoi. The author of a posting on another Web site claims to have heard her during the Tet Offensive of 1968—four years too early to be true. In 2005 I ran a classified advertisement in *Vietnam* magazine asking to hear from veterans who had heard the broadcasts. A woman responded that her father had heard

Fonda and that he had photographs he had taken of her when she was in South Vietnam—Fonda, however, was never in the South.[25]

In some ways, it makes sense that she would not have been heard. Almost all U.S. combat troops had been withdrawn from the South by the time she arrived in July 1972, and, just days after she returned home, the very last fighting units were gone. Moreover, most historical accounts of the propaganda war in Vietnam note that Radio Hanoi and Liberation Radio (Giai Phong), the voice of the NLF in the South, were regularly jammed by the United States and the South Vietnamese government.[26]

If Fonda's words had reached the ears of troops in the South, what would they have heard that they did not already know? Even if they had been in-country for a full year at the time, they would have had years of previous exposure to the antiwar movement at home before even entering military service. Many would have witnessed the widespread demonstrations of the fall Moratorium Days of 1969 as high school or college students and, perhaps, been personally affected by the dramatic events of spring 1970, when the shootings at Kent State and Jackson State closed universities across the country. It is unlikely they could have come through basic training during 1970 or 1971 and not become familiar with the antiwar GI coffeehouses just outside the gates of their bases, or remained unaware of Vietnam Veterans Against the War, whose presence was often made known inside the gates through underground newspapers. It is even less likely they would have gone through training and on their way to Vietnam without exposure to the culture of resistance that permeated military life during those years.

Nothing Fonda said in her broadcasts was news to the few GIs left in the field. Military personnel stationed in Southeast Asia got their news from *Pacific Stars and Stripes*, a civilian newspaper authorized by the Department of Defense and distributed free to them. In a twenty-four-page format that included comics, sports, entertainment news, "Dear Abby," and feature stories, the paper presented condensed versions of wire-service reports on the war from the Associated Press, United Press International, and other news organizations. *Stars and Stripes* also carried the same news of the antiwar movement as the papers back home. On October 15, 1969, for example, the paper reported on the stateside Moratorium Days against the war with a five-column front page headline that read, "Hundreds of Thousands in Mixed Moratorium Day." Two days later it carried a page 4 story on a platoon of the Americal Division that had worn black armbands on an operation near Chu Lai to support the Moratorium on the war. The story quoted the platoon commander, 1st Lieutenant Jesse Rosen, saying, "Personally, I think the demonstrating should go on until [President] Nixon gets the idea the every American should be pulled out of here now."[27]

On July 4, 1972, just days before Fonda arrived in Vietnam, a dramatic five-column heading, "Hijacker Slain in Air Drama; Tried to Take Jumbo to Hanoi," announced the paper's report on a South Vietnamese student, Nguyen Thai Binh, a recent honors graduate of the University of Washington, who had commandeered the Pan Am flight from San Francisco to Saigon as a protest of the U.S. war effort. While Fonda was in Vietnam, the July 12 edition reported that Vietnam veterans were joining other groups for protest at the Democratic National Convention in Miami Beach.

Reports of GI dissent in Vietnam were not uncommon. The September 8, 1972, edition of *Stars and Stripes*, for example, ran a page 2 story, "Death Penalty Ruled Out in 'Fragging' Trial," telling of the case of Private Billy Dean Smith, who had been accused of "detonating a fragmentation grenade in an officers barracks at Bien Hoa Army Base in Vietnam on March 15, 1971." Two officers had been killed. Rumors of defection were even reported, as in a September 13 Associated Press story, "Report 3 GIs Aid VC fight," about supposed turncoats known as Salt, Pepper, and Porkchop.

It is more likely that pilots and personnel stationed offshore on aircraft carriers would have heard Fonda. Surrounded as they were with electronic gadgetry and technical wizardry, they could have pulled in anything they wanted to hear—or blocked the reception of what they did not want. It seems unlikely, though, that pilots would have gone out of their way to tune into Radio Hanoi (with or without Jane Fonda), and their doing so would contradict the claims that those broadcasts were unwelcome and demoralizing. On a more mundane level, the former POW and war historian Mike McGrath suggests that "sailors had watches to stand, duty stations to work at, and little time to go out on deck to try to find the Hanoi Station." Other than "as a lark," he speculates, they would not have been interested enough to listen and wouldn't have been demoralized if they had.[28]

And why would they have been? *Stars and Stripes* printed her remarks almost as soon as she made them. The July 17 paper carried a page 4 story headlined "U.S. Bombs Dikes, Jane Fonda Says." It was a straight-up Associated Press news story without commentary or criticism, the same matter-of-fact report that was appearing in papers across the United States on that day. Datelined Moscow, where the broadcast had been monitored, the story was accompanied by a photo of her visiting an anti-aircraft gun site. It reported her July 14 broadcast from Hanoi in which she observed that irrigation dikes essential to the livelihood of Vietnamese peasants had been bombed. The story quoted her address to pilots: "All of you in the cockpits of your aircraft, on aircraft carriers, all those who load bombs, repair aircraft, work on the ships of the 7th Fleet—think about what you are doing."

The ironic fact that Fonda's words more likely reached U.S. fighters through the pages of the military's house organ than the enemy's airwaves greatly dispels the aura of duplicity that decades later surrounds her image as Hanoi Jane. The reality was that there was plenty of discouraging news for U.S. pilots in 1972, and they didn't need Fonda to tell them. Her inference that the bombings may have been illegal by international law may have been upsetting to pilots, but its significance paled in comparison with what *Stars and Stripes* was putting on their minds. Headlined "Assessing the Bombing: Freeing POWs—or Making More?" a story in the paper's September 15 edition began:

> The American effort to compel a Vietnam settlement and free the [U.S.] prisoners of war by the sustained bombing of North Vietnam has resulted in a major increase in the number of POWs.
>
> With the loss of an Air Force F4 Phantom and its two crewmen in North Vietnam Monday, the U.S. command listed a total of 100 American Airmen missing in the North since the resumption of bombing more than five months ago, on April 6. That's an average of more than four men a week.
>
> Thirty-seven of the fliers have been reported captured. Many of the others were probably killed.

What would have been more demoralizing—Fonda's humanitarian plea to stop bombing dikes, the hard cold fact that bombing runs over the North were producing prisoners faster than peace, or the obstinacy of military leaders who were prolonging the imprisonment of those already shot down while putting at risk those still flying? The same story quoted a Radio Hanoi broadcast by the recently captured Air Force Major Edward K. Elias as saying the bombing was better at filling the North Vietnamese detention camps [with U.S. flyers] than ending the war. Whether or not military personnel heard Elias's broadcast or those of the twenty-some other pilots who made antiwar broadcasts is beside the point: the crews still flying didn't need to tune into clandestine radio to get the word—the daily papers stacked beside the water cooler would do just fine.[29]

POWs: The Captive Audience

The charge that Jane Fonda lent aid and comfort to the North Vietnamese rests in large part on the supposition that Radio Hanoi's broadcasts of her words hurt the morale of U.S. soldiers and undercut the discipline of combat units. Sensing the weakened condition of their enemy, the communists were thereby encouraged to continue the fight. But with so little evidence that any active-duty personnel heard the broadcasts, why does this accusation, and its implication that Fonda's time in Hanoi was a factor in the outcome of the war, continue to ring true for so many Americans?

The answer seems to be that American public memory has conflated the history of the war itself with representations of the POW experience. Whereas there is considerable doubt that fighting troops heard Fonda, the claims by former POWs that they heard her are more believable. In the first place, we know that prisoners in Hanoi listened to Radio Hanoi and heard the broadcasts of antiwar activists. On September 13, 1972, for example, NBC Nightly News aired a segment of film made by Swedish television in which Captain William Byrns, shot down and captured in May 1972, said he had heard Ramsey Clark on the radio the night before. It also makes sense that the North Vietnamese would have wanted their news about the war to reach the prisoners, and that Radio Hanoi would have been able to reach nearby prison camps without U.S. electronic interference.[30]

It is likely, though, that the number of POWs who heard Fonda is far smaller than is now commonly believed and that the negative impact of her words on them has been greatly exaggerated. In spring 1972, about 220 of the pilots were moved from Hanoi to a prison the Americans called Dogpatch, a few miles from the China border. The prisoners were kept there until January 1973, when processing began for their repatriation to the United States. Mike McGrath was one of the captives dispatched to Dogpatch where, he recalls, "there was no electricity and, thankfully, no Radio Hanoi, Hanoi Hannah, Jane Fonda, John Kerry, et al."

So how many POW ears were left in Hanoi to be offended by Fonda? There were 462 prisoners returned from Hanoi in February and March 1973 and about 60 of those were shot down after she was there. Adding those to the 220 in Dogpatch, there were at most 180 prisoners in Hanoi at the time who could have heard her and many of those, we know, had declared their own opposition to the war.

For those who did hear her, Fonda's statements would not have been any more shocking or dispiriting than they would have been to troops still in the fight. Most of the captive shootdowns were officers with college educations who were familiar with the rhetoric, tactics, and personalities of the antiwar movement through the news. By 1972, there were prisoners with family members and friends involved in the opposition to the war. Major Floyd Kushner's wife, Valerie, seconded the nomination of the antiwar senator George McGovern as the Democratic Party's candidate for President in 1972. Some of the younger flyers would have encountered first-hand the antiwar movement on their college campuses or had a chance to see FTA, the antiwar entertainment troop that Fonda and other celebrities toured to military bases in the United States and Asia during 1971.[31]

Pilots and sailors, ironically enough, because of their otherwise insular lives on aircraft carriers, may have been among the Americans most aware of the rebel movement within the military. In his book *Vietnam and Other American Fantasies*, the cultural historian Bruce Franklin recalls that by 1971 dissent had coalesced into a coherent movement on the gigantic aircraft carriers USS *Coral Sea* and USS *Kitty Hawk*, both crucial to the air war over Vietnam. In 1972, several more carriers, including the *Midway*, *Ranger*, and *Forrestal*, had their missions to the Tonkin Gulf interrupted by acts of sabotage and attacks on officers. Fifteen hundred crew members of the USS *Constellation* signed petitions demanding that FTA be performed on board. Moreover, through *Stars and Stripes* and the regular press, flyers would have known long before they were shot down that antiwar activists were deeply involved in prisoner-release activities.

The idea that their innocence was shattered by Fonda's voice on the camp intercom is itself rather naïve.[32]

For other reasons, the POWs who had been held the longest were also unlikely to have been greatly affected by Fonda's presence. From what they tell us in their memoirs, speeches by visiting activists had become routine long before 1972. In *A P.O.W.'s Story: 2801 Days in Hanoi*, Colonel Larry Guarino, captured on June 14, 1965, wrote about hearing the famous baby doctor Benjamin Spock, as well as Stokely Carmichael, Joan Baez, and Pete Seeger on the camp radio when they were in Hanoi in 1967. In fact, POWs may have been better versed in the pros and cons of the war than many other Americans. In his memoir *Black Prisoner of War*, James Daly recalled that the *Pentagon Papers* were serialized over the camp radio with excerpts being read by the POWs themselves.[33]

The controversies surrounding Fonda's broadcasts from Hanoi and who did or did not hear them are less important than the way they construct the Hanoi Jane that mediates American memories of the war. False memories of having heard Fonda broadcasts, or even having seen her in South Vietnam where she wasn't, demonstrate not that people's memories are bad or even less that they are making things up. Rather, the stories demonstrate the power of an iconic figure like Hanoi Jane to shape public memory, a power that we can see at play even in the work of professional historians.

In *Honor Bound: American Prisoners of War in Southeast Asia*, Stuart Rochester and Frederick Kiley tell how dispiriting the broadcasts of American peace activists were for the men held in Hanoi. To enliven their point, they recall for us that POW "Fred Cherry heard Jane Fonda's voice over a camp public address system in October 1967 as he was in the midst of an extended torture siege."[34] The historical facts are that Fonda was in France at the time, not Hanoi, that her transformation to political life was still ahead, and that it would be five years before her voice would be heard over Radio Hanoi. We cannot tell from the citation where the authors got that story but the sourcing of it is not the point—I doubt that the authors made it up or, for that matter, that Cherry did either. The point, rather, is that Hanoi Jane is the enemy Other in the mythology of the prisoner *at* war, which compels her presence at the time and place of battle: 1967 when according to the hard-line account the torture was most severe. And so large and commonplace was Hanoi Jane in the American sense of the war by the 1990s when Rochester and Kiley wrote that they apparently never thought twice about the details in the story—from wherever or whomever they got it.

"Saigon Laura"—Why Not?

There are, finally, those images of Fonda's visit to an anti-aircraft gun installation, which clearly played a powerful role in her eventual demonizing. Visuals are the currency of television news, so it is not surprising that U.S. networks picked up the Japanese-shot footage of Jane at the gun site. Still, only CBS used the film for evening news, and then only as an accompanying visual for their report that Representative Thompson was accusing her of treason. The increased importance that has attached over the years to that brief segment, lasting fifty seconds, along with the still photos that were taken at the time (or lifted from film frames) may confirm the adage that a picture is worth a thousand words. But the fact remains that, at the time, the Jane-on-gun story was barely newsworthy.

Like so much else about her trip, the pictures of Fonda in the gun pit have to be placed in their proper historical context. In January 1973, the ABC correspondent Laura Palmer accepted an invitation to meet two women soldiers of the NLF near Saigon. Wearing a communist pith helmet, Palmer draped her arm around one of the enemy fighters as the news cameras clicked and whizzed. Hours later, the United Press International beamed the image around the world with the caption, "East Meets West in Saigon as a Viet Cong Woman Soldier Admires the Bra-less Look of ABC Correspondent." The incident did not deflect Palmer's career, since she went on to work for NBC and write for *Time* and *Rolling Stone*. By the next century, who would know? Who would care?[35]

Palmer evidently had the same questions on her mind when she recalled the experience in *War Torn*, a 2002 book about women journalists who covered the war in Vietnam. Sensing that readers a quarter-century removed from the war might not find the anecdote interesting, she played the I'm-like-Jane card, likening her photo-op with the guerrillas to the notoriety of Fonda's photo on the gun. What gives Palmer's reach for a place in history its real poignancy is its confirmation that we remember those years through Hanoi Jane and not "Saigon Laura" and that it is not so clear why that is so.[36]

Whatever the impact the treks to Hanoi by Fonda or other activists may have had on the morale of POWs, it is hard to see the connection between those facets of the Vietnam era and the outcome of the war. Critics claim that the war and confinement of the POWs was prolonged by her and the other peace travelers, but there is little logic to their point or support for it from independent scholars. An argument can be made that the U.S. failure to launch massive and early ground attacks across the 17th parallel and into Laos short circuited any chance for a quick war. But that plan was scrapped for reasons having to do with military strategy and the politics of Vietnam, not the influence of the antiwar movement at home. And besides, when those decisions were made in 1965, opposition to the war was nascent and Jane Fonda was playing a wholesome former schoolmarm in *Cat Ballou*.[37]

In reality, the creation of Hanoi Jane as a betrayal figure may derive less from anything the real Jane Fonda did in Hanoi than from the needs of those who constructed the image and kept it alive. Belief in that mythical construct helps to displace American recognition that the air war was a strategic failure and that it was the war planners who put the flyers at risk by underestimating the will and skill of the Vietnamese people. Hanoi Jane is a scapegoat for those failures and a face-saving device for the chagrined "top guns" tackled in the wrong end-zone. The story asks us to believe that the fighting capacity of the POWs was undiminished by their capture, that they not only continued "the mission" but did so to a degree that was significant to the war effort, and that the war would have ended sooner had their resolve not been sapped by Fonda's treachery.

To believe this, though, we are also asked to redefine the war. For some purveyors of Hanoi Jane, the enemy was communism, a phenomenon that for them was less important as a historical movement with political and economic consequences than it was an ideological force with religious meaning. They saw communism as the Antichrist, the devil incarnate, the battle for Vietnam just one front in a war for the soul of mankind, a war with battle lines that ran through the hearts and minds of captured pilots as surely as anyone else's.

The war that Hanoi Jane constructs goes beyond loyalty to flag and country; it's about fidelity to ideals, values, and faith, with the captives on the front line the way they had never been before they were captives. It is a war that didn't end for the GIs and pilots when they were captured and it didn't end when they were released. When the warriors in the Hanoi Jane myth were repatriated, they merely redeployed their assets to the war on the home front, a struggle that had emerged from the streets and campuses of America during late 1960s and early 1970s but was morphing into a divisive culture war by the time of their return.

3

PRISONERS AT WAR

HANOI JANE'S MYTHICAL

OTHER

Myth is about more than veracity. Many stories are false but not all false stories are myths. When an aging professor who never got off the bench as a college basketball player tells students about his buzzer-beating shot that won the big game, he is not telling the truth, but that does not make his story a myth. A myth is a group's story, a story of indeterminate origin and truth that has consequences for the group. A myth matters for the group as a whole.

A story is a myth, or not, depending less on its truth than its meaning for the people who tell and hear it. In fact, the common expression that myths are made of something suggests that myths often have a basis in fact. The power of a myth can be enhanced by its plausibility—it could have happened the way the story says. The idea, for example, that Jane Fonda's broadcasts from Hanoi could have demoralized GIs fighting in South Vietnam, thereby insuring the victory of the communists, is consistent with the facts that her words were broadcast, there was a serious morale problem among GIs, and the United States did lose the war.

The obscurity of their origins and provenances, however, is also what imparts a mythical quality to some stories. A story that cannot be proven true is even more difficult to prove false. The paucity of evidence that any GIs heard Fonda's broadcasts is not evidence that none did, a fact that leaves some minds open to claims that her time in Hanoi was decisive to the outcome of the war.

In their most generic forms, myths pair figures of good and evil. Often the story is about an evil person, group, or thing that tells us whom to beware of and what acts should not go unpunished. The same stories tell us what is good, if sometimes only by inference—the opposite of bad, we can assume, must be "good." But some story-telling forms link good and evil more structurally. In the Bible, for example, the prophet Isaiah tells believers they will recognize the Messiah as the one who is persecuted by his opposite, Satan. When Jesus' disciples Matthew and Luke write in the New Testament about his betrayal, the story is intended as a fulfillment of Isaiah's prophecy and a sign that he is the Christ.[1]

The Hanoi Jane story works on both these levels. She is the historical figure representing the antiwar movement and, as such, puts in a bad light those who protested the war—they are thought of, by some Americans, as being a traitors, just like her. But she also works in a more structural and complex way to help construct her mythical opposite. Hanoi Jane is a betrayal figure and to believe in her is to believe in the verity of those she is alleged to have betrayed. On a broad cultural level, she is said to have betrayed the military mission in Southeast Asia and, by extension, the United States itself. But the betrayal of the POWs is the core chapter in that larger narrative because, as it turns out, it resonates with the mythology of captives that has been critical to the construction of American identity for three hundred years.

A Captive Nation

A people's narrative is the story they tell about themselves, the story of how and why they came to be what they believe they are. The American narrative braids together religious and secular themes for a story about the "good people" threatened by powers that could destroy the group from the outside and the weakness of those on the inside who might betray the group. The religious strands of that story are as old as Genesis where Eve is unable to resist the fruit of the tree of knowledge forbidden to her by God. From the Garden of Eden on, the plight of humankind is a series of God's tests that winnow the weak from the strong, the true believers from the pretenders to Grace.

Many of God's tests involve deception. In the New Testament, God's people are fooled into following the false prophets of Antichrist, the Beast, because he masquerades as Good and promises relief from earthly miseries. Antichrist is revealed in governments and social policies that promise peace, justice, security, and happiness, when, in fact, these goals are achievable only through loyalty to God, not government. As a project begun by Puritans in the seventeenth century, the young America was lulled with images of its place in the biblical narrative.[2]

John Smith and Pocahontas

The first literature produced by colonial America was the so-called captivity narrative, stories written by Americans about themselves or others who had been captured by Indians. In her 1999 study of that genre, the anthropologist Pauline Turner Strong writes that American identity took form through representations of "struggles in and against the wild: struggles of a collective Self surrounded by a threatening but enticing wilderness, a Self that seeks to domesticate this wilderness as well as the savagery within itself."[3]

John Smith was captured in December 1607, six months after the founding of Jamestown. His captors were warriors of the Pamunkey tribe, led by chief Powhatan. Spared from death by Powhatan's love-struck daughter, Pocahontas, Smith negotiated his release, receiving land for Jamestown in return for his promise of cannon and a grindstone for the Indians. By this account, Smith saved Jamestown. Smith was a hero.[4]

But subsequent interpretations of what "really" happened during his captivity render it the stuff of myth. Strong, for example, suggests that when Pocahontas "saved" Smith by casting her body between his head and the Indians' clubs, she was actually playing a role in a rebirthing ritual designed to transform Smith into a Pamunkey. In short, Strong says, Smith was probably submitted to an adoption ceremony, not an execution.[5] In this anthropological light, we are led to consider that the captivity experience may have confronted him with his own "inner savagery" and his vulnerability to Pamunkey paganism. Had Smith conjured the story of his near-execution to disguise, even to himself, the appeal that conversion to "Indianism" had had to him? And was the hint of Pocahontas's seductiveness a story-telling ploy to divert questions about his own attraction to the sexuality of the Indian girl and the impotence of his own faith as a restraint on him in that situation?

These questions were only implicit in Smith's story, but they gained prominence as new chapters were added to the captivity canon during the Indian wars at the end of the century. The narrative of temptation, punishment, and redemption became more complex after several instances of captives, apparently giving in to the same temptation Smith may have felt, choosing to remain with their erstwhile captors. Those stories, in the hands of early eighteenth-century preachers, gave the captivity literature the qualities it needed for an interface with the POW narrative coming out of Vietnam 250 years later.

The Other on the Inside

King Philip's War during the 1670s subdued Indian resistance to English expansion and opened new lands for settlement. As Puritans moved out of their fortified environs into the "wilderness," memberships in established congregations dropped and church leaders' concerns rose that the physical distance between preachers and believers might have a spiritual counterpart. Recalling that the missionary John Eliot warned of "wilderness temptations," Strong writes that religious authorities feared their followers might abandon "the lawful and godly order of Puritan settlements to embrace the individualistic anarchy presumably characteristic of heathen life."[6]

The wars of 1689–1713 pitted the English settlers against the Catholic French and their Indian allies, allowing Puritan preachers to use their captured parishioners as examples of what happens when followers stray too far into the woods—and beyond the influence of the established community of believers. The captures were interpreted as signs that God was displeased with the settlers' pursuit of worldly gain, their bondage an act of retribution for their backsliding. Cotton Mather preached that God was punishing not just the captives but the entire community of believers for, as Strong puts it, "transgressing the boundary between a godly, orderly, disciplined Self and a wild, untrustworthy, and insubordinate Other."[7]

Whereas other preachers held up previous captives, such as Smith, as exemplars of strength, Mather used women in a new generation of war prisoners to show the consequences of weakness. One of his examples was Hannah Swarton, whose Puritan Self proved permeable in the presence of what Mather called the "bloody, popish, and pagan" enemy Other. The more well-known case, preached by John Williams, involved his own daughter, Eunice, who became a Mohawk after her capture in February 1704.

It would be hard to overstate the importance of the captivity narratives in the formation of American identity. As the country's first literary form, it constructed the dialectical tensions that defined what was American and what was not. At one pole, the image of "them," a racialized figure with a nomadic, libidinous, matriarchal, and pagan way of life, the attraction to which forced Puritans to recognize the "them" in themselves. At the other pole, was "us," a godly but fearful people besieged by the beasts beyond the gates and beset with doubt about the Puritan will to resist the wild within. The ultimate threat to the settlements was on the inside, the inability to ward off Indian encroachments, but, as well, the failure to suppress the impulse to Indianism from within its own hearts and homes.[8]

The America birthed by this narrative was born embattled, and the American born with the values of discipline, self-denial, austerity, and subordination to authority inscribed in his genes was born a warrior—hard and male.[9]

Korea, Vietnam, and the Renewal of America's Captivity Narrative

The captive Self and the captivating Other, as Strong puts it, are the oppositional poles between which American identity is formed. That process of identity creation went on well into the nineteenth century as the ongoing conquest of North American Indians reproduced the need of Americans to see goodness in themselves and evil in others. The great and victorious wars of the twentieth century—the "War to End All Wars," 1917–18, and the war against fascism, 1941–45—did not tax that self-identity unduly, but the return of U.S. expansionism in the post–World War II years did. A crisis of legitimacy that began with the war in Korea grew to dangerous levels during the Vietnam War years, requiring nourishment for the American images of Self and Other.

As if scripted by History, those two wars also produced timely new generations of captives with stories that would reinvigorate the nation's collective narrative. The potency of claims that U.S. prisoners held by communists in North Korea were "brainwashed" carried over into public imaginings about what was happening to U.S. pilots imprisoned in North Vietnam. The facts of the Vietnam War's widely perceived illegitimacy and its loss would bequeath the Vietnam chapter an intensity the captivity literature had never had, spawning a search for the enemy within, and the contrivance of that enemy in the absence of the real thing.[10]

Hanoi Jane was conceived in that renovation of Americanism. Far more than a symbol of the military mission betrayed, Hanoi Jane represented the antiwarrior latent within the culture, the self-indulgent and rebellious underbelly of America that could, and did, turn hard men soft and cost the nation its victory in Southeast Asia. Hanoi Jane was female and sexual, a representative of the unrepressed Other deeply embedded in the culture and psyche of the disciplined male Warrior that surfaced, most troublingly for conservative supporters of the war, in the POW camps themselves. The new chapter of the "captive America" narrative that the POW experience of the Vietnam era would write, then, had, like the previous chapters, as much to say about America itself as its enemy.

Gooks: The Asian Other Racialized

The representations of the POW experience in Southeast Asia did say a great deal about the enemy, and much of it followed in the tradition of racial disparagement characteristic of the three-hundred-year-old captivity stories. By the time the war began, moreover, that tradition had been given an Asian twist by the war against the Japanese during the 1940s and the Korean War of the early 1950s. In both those conflicts, U.S. propaganda produced caricatured images of Asians with exaggeratedly slanted eyes, buck teeth, and sloping foreheads. In *North Korea: Another Country*, Bruce Cumings reports that the *New York Times* military editor Hanson Baldwin described Koreans as "barbarians," primitive peoples," "armored horde," and "invading locusts." Other U.S. leaders and publications called them "half-crazed automatons" and "wildmen with arrested development." This "nauseating stew of racial stereotypes," Cumings writes, stirred diverse peoples into a nameless sludge that accumulated under one name: "gook."[11]

The term *gook* was carried over from its Korean use, becoming the appellation of choice for Americans referring to the Vietnamese. By the late 1960s, GIs arriving in Vietnam were quickly introduced to that word and its extended lexicon of *slants, slopes, zips,* and *dinks* that diminished the people they were ostensibly there to support. Flyers too adopted that language for their memoirs. In *Before Honor,* Eugene McDaniel described one of his guards, who was about five feet ten inches tall, as "the world's tallest gook"; about another he wrote, "savage, and that said it all." Larry Guarino wrote without apparent sarcasm that Vietnamese "brains functioned on different frequencies from ours." "So I gave up any thought of reasoning with them," he said, "and declared them to be 'just gooks.'" Ralph Gaither recalled being driven from Camp Dogpatch to Hanoi by "a bunch of gooks."[12]

Racist portrayals of the Vietnamese color most of the POW memoirs and in some instances the writers use descriptions of deviant behavior and local customs to make their point. Gaither, for example, describes what he saw from Dogpatch:

> The guards made horrible sport of butchering their food. When they killed a pig, they first punched its eyes out so that it would stand still, then they beat it to death. Cows suffered a like fate. They tied them with ropes strung all over like a spider web, and then beat them to death with an ax. The women killed the dogs for meat by hanging them in a grotesque position and then beat them with sticks. All the while the guards and women laughed as though they were at a sports event.

From that, he concluded, "You could not generate much respect for such people as that. We prisoners could not expect much better treatment than they gave their animals and that's about what we got."[13]

One may take at face value the accuracy of Gaither's report and still question his use of it to describe the treatment of POWs. Cruelty to animals might predict cruelty to people, but we would have to know more about the cultural practices of the people and circumstances surrounding the events he witnessed before accepting the analogy he constructs. Using the treatment of animals as an indicator for the national character entails an even greater leap. Even though U.S. treatment of prisoners was as bad as or worse than that dished out by the North Vietnamese, one could make little sense out of that record by having witnessed, say, U.S. soldiers shooting elephants from helicopters for sport. For that matter, Vietnamese prison guards are likely to have been a small and select portion of the population, from which, whatever their behavior, it would be dangerous to generalize about the nation's people as a whole.[14]

From Refinement to Confinement

The ubiquity of the terrifying Oriental Other in the Vietnam POW narrative is based less on America's continuing need to believe the worst about the Vietnamese than on the way that image helps construct what Americans want to think about themselves. Not only are "we" not like "them" but our POWs proved that Americans would not forsake themselves or their nation even under the extreme conditions of imprisonment by the enemy. And there is indeed much in the historical record to justify that pride in the strength demonstrated by the POWs.

Even under the best of peacetime conditions, mid-twentieth-century life in less-developed countries like Vietnam lacked the safe drinking water, sanitation systems, balanced diet, and electrification that most Americans were accustomed to by the 1960s. And Vietnam had not enjoyed peacetime conditions. After decades of exploitation by the French, the country had fought wars against the Japanese occupation of the 1940s and the French attempt to recolonize it after World War II. Basic physical infrastructure had been destroyed, rebuilt, and destroyed again while the people's meager resources were repeatedly conscripted for military service. Even before the United States inflicted ten years of bombing on its roads, bridges, and harbors, chemical defoliation on its agricultural land, and an economic embargo on medical supplies, Vietnam was an economically battered country.

The deprivations suffered by the Vietnamese inevitably extended into the conditions of prison life for captured Americans. The centerpiece of the camp system that held U.S. prisoners was Hoa Lo prison, built by the French to punish resisters to its colonial rule in the late nineteenth century. Located near downtown Hanoi, where wartime privations had made sanitation and water drainage tenuous, the prison was infested with rats, mosquitoes, and other vermin that made life miserable, even fragile, for the prisoners. The prison was dank and, in the winter months, cold. Electricity for lights was limited because of fuel shortages in the city and irregular because of U.S. bombing. The diet for prisoners was sometimes near subsistence level and offensive to American tastes. Rice was the staple, and it was supplemented by watery soup with a few vegetables and an occasional head or foot from a chicken. Memoirs written by the POWs commonly tell of dirt in the rice that they suspected of being fecal material from rats or mice; many POWs suffered diarrhea, probably contracted from dirty water used for cooking; pails in their cells that the men dubbed "honey buckets" and emptied themselves sufficed for toilets. Medical care for the POWs was minimal. Men needing attention could be neglected for days and eventually treated with primitive methods and medicines of questionable quality. And yet, as bad as it was, there are Hanoi residents who would complain thirty years later that their suffering during the war was worsened because "the best" was going to the POWs.[15]

The deplorable circumstances of confinement the POWs suffered left an indelible imprint on their bodies and psyches that can be read years later in their memoirs. It is impossible to read those accounts without putting one's self in their shoes and using their experiences as a measure of one's own character—and find the comparison very reassuring. Notwithstanding the misery faced by the POWs, the perception of deprivation many of them felt was magnified by the social distance between the privileged backgrounds they came from and the degradation in which they sat in Hanoi. Many of the early shootdowns were high-ranking middle-age professional military men. Commander John Stockdale, shot down in September 1965, was a forty-year-old alumnus of the Naval Academy who had done graduate work at Stanford; Larry Guarino was a forty-three-year-old air force major when he was shot down in June 1965; George "Bud" Day was a forty-two-year-old air force major with a law degree and a master's degree in political science when he was captured in August 1967; Gerald Coffee was a thirty-one-year-old UCLA graduate and nine-year veteran of the U.S. Navy when he was shot down in February 1966; John McCain, whose grandfather and father were both navy admirals, could have been considered upper class.[16]

The relative privilege of college educations, admissions to service academies, and high social status defined their lives right up to their last takeoffs. Air Force Major Jay Jensen described his last hours at Korat Airbase in Thailand before being downed in February 1967:

As I shaved with my electric razor and then showered in nice warm water, I thought to myself, "for a combat situation we have it pretty good. This is the way to fight a war. A clean comfortable bed, white sheets, a large air-conditioned (when it worked) room, cleaned up by a maid. A nice warm water shower and clean latrine—not bad." We had a really great Officers Club and dining hall, probably the best in Southeast Asia, and soon they would have the swimming pool completed. I enjoyed playing tennis and racquetball too.[17]

A few hours later, Jensen was on the ground near Vinh in North Vietnam, where, he wrote, an old peasant woman, standing about ten feet away, "dipped her hand into a slimy rice paddy, coming up with great gobs of mud and throwing them at me—and she wasn't missing." A rough truck ride away from Hanoi, he was shortly in solitary confinement in Hao Lo prison, lonely and depressed.[18]

For some of the POWs, their separation from home, family, and even other prisoners was as hard to endure as the material reality of camp life. The time under lock and key ranged from eight years to a few weeks and, for months, those taken captive early in the war had no way of knowing whether family members, or even military leaders, knew that they were alive. The accumulation of days, weeks, months, and years became a test of faith in their family, friends, and government that they would not be forgotten or forsaken for political expediency. For some, the social isolation, which at times meant even limited contact with their English-speaking fellow prisoners, became a test of their sanity.

In the Hanoi Jane story, however, the forgotten POW is not the central character. The prisoner betrayed by her has not been sidelined by his capture and then forgotten; he is a prisoner who is still in the fight, a warrior engaged with the enemy, whose role in the outcome of the war gets compromised by the treachery of visiting peace activists. The prisoners in the Hanoi Jane legend are prisoners *at* war.

Authenticity and the POW Story

In his book *Prisoners of Culture*, the social critic Elliott Gruner interprets the POW story of the Vietnam era as an extension of the early-American captivity narrative. In that light, the POW memoirs appear at first glance to be rather conventional forms of hero construction, telling of the prisoners' continuing loyalty to the mission and the comrades still fighting it. Many of the accounts record the resistance of the downed flyers to Vietnamese efforts at extracting militarily sensitive information in return for medical care, food, and early release. When they defied their interrogators, the captives were subjected to painful beatings, relief from which was then offered in exchange for information. The hero-prisoner is a holdout, he sacrifices his own well-being, takes one for the team so to speak, rather than divulging information that might increase the risk to his buddies and the security of his homeland. The prisoner at war was the dominant narrative in what scholars have dubbed the "official story" that emerged from Hao Lo prison; the hero-prisoners in that story are, like John Smith, still fighting the good fight.[19]

Not surprisingly, though, questions linger about the struggle waged inside the walls. Movies like *Hanoi Hilton* that came out in the 1980s created the impression that all the POWs were routinely tortured, and that impression has been sustained by the activism of individuals and groups who believe that some American personnel still missing from the war remain imprisoned in Vietnam or Laos. Indeed, much of the rhetoric and imagery that makes up the Hanoi Jane figure invokes and evokes those same impressions: emaciated captives, shackled, hanging by their arms from ropes, or locked in bamboo cages. But the historical record is more complex than that, revealing a lot of variation in the allegations of who was mistreated and the reports of when and how they were.

To begin with, a comprehensive account of the POW experience is elusive. The North Vietnamese have never admitted to using torture, and yet with the political realignments, defections, and emigration that have characterized Vietnam in the thirty years since the war ended, we might expect that at least one individual who worked as a guard or staff would have corroborated the charges of the POWs. Instead of corroboration of that type, we have an October 25, 2008, London *Times* story for which the reporter sought out Tran Trong Duyet, the former prison director, to ask about the presidential candidate John McCain's claim that he was tortured while a prisoner in Hanoi. Duyet said, "I never tortured or mistreated the POWs nor did my staff." Nguyen Tien Tran, another director, confirmed Duyet, saying, "We had a clear code of taking care of the injured. Why would [McCain] say he was tortured?" Those disavowals can be dismissed as self-serving, of course, but in the absence of verification 43 that torture did happen, the only "records" of camp life we have—the ones carried as memories by prisoners themselves—tell a different story but one no less encumbered by self-interest.[20]

And even that version has variation. Almost all accounts agree that there was no torture after 1969, which means that any of the 156 flyers shot down after January 1, 1970 (about one-third of the POWs returned in February and March of 1973), is marginal to the prisoner-at-war story that is conventionally told. There is a similar marker on the early years: the twenty-three pilots shot down during the first year of the air war over the North reported that they were not tortured until September 1965, after which time, a few say they were, some say they were not, and most have remained silent on the issue. That discrepant pattern continues through the fall of 1969, raising questions in some minds about the reliability of the reports and providing an entry point for inquiries about the reasons for the variations in the memories of the prison treatment, however harsh it was.

There is also the glaring disparity in the memories of POWs from different branches of the service: of the seventy-five army POWs who came home in 1973, all captured before 1970, forty tell their stories in the collection *We Came Home*, edited by Barbara Powers Wyatt, but none describes having been tortured. That is not to say that some of them were not mistreated. PFC Gustav Mehrer, for example, described being bound and hung by his arms during interrogation, but his report was exceptional and he did not refer to it as torture. Army Major William Hardy made a point of saying he had not been tortured. George Smith, whose story is not included in the Wyatt volume, wrote complimentarily in his own book, *P.O.W.*, about the treatment he received from the National Liberation Front in the South. At the very least, this variegated picture dispels widespread beliefs that all the POWs were tortured—a notion fostered by statements like that of George Coker, who wrote in the Wyatt collection, "Like 95% of the POWs, I was tortured many times"—and contradicts a central claim of the official story that torture was a systematic, day-to-day policy of the North Vietnamese.[21] Because the popularly believed story of widespread torture is based on the subjective and conflicting accounts of the POWs themselves, questions about its authenticity are hard to answer.

As part of a peace delegation that visited Hanoi POWs in 1967, Carol Cohen McEldowney wrote in her journal that the "decent treatment" of the prisoners had been verified and was no longer an issue. McEldowney's observation is significant because it was made five years before Fonda was there and well within the period when the official story claims the torture was the worst. Moreover, McEldowney had been in Hanoi two weeks by then and had grown suspicious of what she was hearing from her North Vietnamese escorts. Calling some of their presentations on non-POW matters "bullshit" and "propaganda," she was, if anything, inclined to believe the opposite of what her observations led her to conclude about the POWs condition.[22]

The objective data bearing on the treatment of the POWs, scant though it is, tends to support what McEldowney recorded in her journal. A 1975 Amnesty International report indicates that the mental and physical condition of the released POWs was "really good" when they arrived at Clark Air Base in the Philippines, an observation consistent with studies reported in 1978 that found former POWs to be in better health than a control group of noncaptive Vietnam veterans. Most interesting was the finding of the latter study that Vietnam-era POWs had lower levels of physical and psychological health problems than POWs from previous wars.[23]

The Captive Self in Hoa Lo Prison

The origin and provenance of the official story add to the air of legend that surrounds the prisoner-at-war narrative. In his 1993 book *Voices of the Vietnam POWs*, Craig Howes says the story was actually the product of a power struggle between POWs over how they should behave as captives. Article IV of the Code of Conduct for U.S. military personnel extended the code to troops held as prisoners of war and provided for the senior-most officers among the prisoners to establish a command structure that replicated regular military hierarchy. Inside Hao Lo, then, a chain of command emerged within the prison population that had the majority of prisoners under the control of older and higher-ranking U.S. officers. In late 1970, the Vietnamese consolidated prisoners who had been held in small camps scattered in and around Hanoi in Hao Lo, a change that resulted in larger numbers of prisoners falling under the control of fewer senior ranking officers, or SROs, as they came to be called. As these

POWs who had had little prior contact with one another came together and began sharing their personal experiences, the officers arranged the pieces into a version of events that was then retold to newly arriving prisoners as a way of orienting them to camp life and culture. According to Howes, this version of events was an "administrative history" assembled for training purposes and designed to legitimate the SROs' control over the other prisoners. Howes says that this virtual curriculum for the subordination of POWs to their own officers was committed to memory by a few senior officers and then recalled later for John G. Hubbell, who turned it into the six-hundred-page book *P.O.W.*, published with help from the Pentagon by Reader's Digest Press in 1976. Over the years, Hubbell's book has become known to most Americans as the official POW story.[24]

The official story, however, was a highly selective version of the total POW experience. In the first place, the figures of civilians who had been captured were all but erased, while those of enlisted men taken in the South were treated diminutively as weak in body and character, leaving the navy and air force officers who had been shot down over the North to dominate the story. The official story also downplayed the amount of resistance there really had been to the authority of the officers and disparaged the motives and reputations of those prisoners who had broken with the imposed discipline. Most important, the canonized account featured the SROs in the role of heroic warrior-prisoners in order to credential them as worthy of deference from the men they sought to command: they were the toughest never-say-die guys who had kept faith with their comrades on the outside by keeping military secrets on the inside and paying the price of painful torture for having done so. This element in the story in turn provided grist for the postwar mythology that the real war extended into Hao Lo, behind whose walls there were real warriors to be betrayed by Hanoi Jane.

The general narrative of the authorized account is that the Vietnamese altered their prison practices as required by the resistance of the prisoners, changes in the domestic or international political environment, or developments on the war front itself. Thus, the abrupt cessation of torture in late 1969 is variously attributed to the death of Ho Chi Minh or to the early release of a few prisoners whose public testimony on torture sparked a letter-writing campaign by the POWs' families that put pressure on the Hanoi government to lighten up—an explanation supportive of the idea that the struggle of the prisoners, and, by extension, their families, was meaningful.[25]

Other explanations for the softening of the prison regimen in late 1969 are more political, but they disagree about whether it was acts of peace by the United States or acts of war that brought positive changes to the POWs. By the "dove" reading of history, the improvements for the prisoners may have been Hanoi's in-kind reciprocity for recent U.S. bombing halts and the Nixon administration's announcements of troop withdrawals. This reasoning runs counter to the views held by "hawks" that the Vietnamese were a racial Other lacking the civilized sensibilities that peacenik naïveté imparted to them. The prisoner-at-war story, moreover, required belief that the prisoners were masters of their own fate, which made their improved conditions and eventual repatriation explainable as byproducts of war, not conciliation and peace.

Thus it was, a decade or so after the peace accords were signed, that a revisionist version of history emerged with the contention that the United States had actually won the war and that the improvement in the conditions for POWs even before it ended were the spoils of that impending victory. The individuals and groups promulgating that view argue that the failure of the communists to achieve an out-and-out victory through their Tet Offensive of 1968 equated to a victory for the United States that essentially ended the war then. Recognizing their defeat, the Hanoi leaders feared they would be tried for war crimes by the United States and its allies and convicted for the mistreatment of prisoners as well as other wrongdoings. In this version of events, the post-1969 prison reforms were a public relations move by the communists trying to save themselves from the gallows.[26]

Critics of the official story, however, including some former POWs, wonder whether the greatest change in 1969 was in Vietnamese's prison practice or in the story told by the SROs about the pre-1969 conditions. Was it just a coincidence that conditions changed at Hao Lo and other northern camps at the same time the first large group of GIs captured in the South arrived or was their arrival the trigger for a change in the story the SROs needed to be told? Is it possible, in other words, that the disparity between the pre- and post-1969 conditions looks so great because the SROs constructed a kind of "bad ol' days" mythology that exaggerated the tough times they had been through in order to impress and establish authority over the newly arrived prisoners?

The suggestion of a political subtext to the official story implies that there was a kind of one-upmanship being played by the SROs who were sensitive to the weakness of their own credentials as hero holdouts. By almost any measure, the prisoners who had been taken in the South had had it worse. Held in small and temporary jungle camps that did approximate the Hollywood images of bamboo cages, starvation diets, menacing wildlife, and forced marches, the mostly army POWs actually longed for an upgrade to the permanency and hard-shell shelter of a real prison and the medical and dietary amenities that the urban environment of Hanoi could afford them. When Frank Anton, a chopper pilot downed and captured on January 5, 1968, in the northern part of South Vietnam, arrived in Hanoi after months of captivity in the South, Hao Lo, he reported, looked "like a Holiday Inn." To him and others from the South, it was a relief to be there; to the SROs, the new arrivals from the South were a threat to the prisoner-at-war image that was in the making.

Torture, Punishment, or . . .

There are also competing interpretations to be made of the rough interrogations that the captives were put through. A central claim of the prisoner-at-war narrative is that the holdouts were heroes because the information they refused to give up was militarily significant—but some of the POW memoirs suggest otherwise. Everett Alvarez, for example, recalls that in his first days of capture he rebuffed his interrogators' inquiries about his unit, the plane he had flown, and his family. He was particularly sensitive about his family, lest the Vietnamese be able to harass his wife and parents and thereby diminish the morale of other military families. A week after his capture, however, Alvarez was confronted by a guard he called Owl: "You are Everett Alvarez, Jr. You are twenty-six. We know you live in Santa Clara, California. And we know your parents live at 2168 Bohannon Drive, and your wife's name is Tangee. . . . You were on U.S.S. Constellation. Your commander's name was Bolsted. Your Admiral was William Guest. You were member of attack squadron 144." Alvarez was devastated. What, he wondered, did the Vietnamese want from him if they could get all the information they needed through other means, and what point could be served by his continued resistance? [27]

Alvarez's experience was not exceptional. Bob Shumaker was brought to Hao Lo in February 1965 and was shortly shown maps with his targets and routes that the Vietnamese had recovered from his downed fighter. Air Force Colonel Theodore Guy, shot down March 22, 1968, says he gave interrogators false information until they showed him an organizational chart with his name on it. By the time Robinson Risner, also an air force colonel, was shot from the sky in September 1965 he had already been featured on the cover of Time magazine as a Korean War "ace" who was now engaged over Southeast Asia. That story revealed that he was squadron leader of the "Fighting Cocks" the Air Force 67th Tactical Fighter Squadron, that his $2.5 million F-105 could carry twelve 750-pound bombs or eight pods of nineteen rockets each with a six-barrel twenty-millimeter cannon that could fire four thousand rounds a minute. Loaded, the craft could top speeds of 1,660 miles an hour. Risner, according to the report, had grown up in Oklahoma, was forty years old with a wife, Karen, and five sons, all of whom lived in Okinawa, where he had been posted before duty in Vietnam.

For the kind of propaganda purposes the POW mythologies allege the Vietnamese were pursuing, it is hard to imagine what more they would have wanted from him than what the Time story told them; if they did want more technical information about the planes, carriers, and munitions, it would have been more easily obtained through trade journals and the military intelligence apparatuses of the Soviets, Chinese, and other allies of the Vietnamese. With decades of their own intelligence-gathering experience, the Vietnamese would have known as well as anyone that information extorted from prisoners was unlikely to be reliable enough for decisions on military operations.[28]

The motivation for the treatment meted to the POWs is important because whether or not they were tortured depends in considerable degree on what it was that the North Vietnamese intended. Some of the POW accounts, such as that of Captain Stephen Leopold, who arrived in the North in November 1968, mix together the language of torture with descriptions of camp life. Leopold wrote:

Our new camp . . . was a real hellhole. I lived in a small, black-washed cell with a wood bed on the floor. The camp routine consisted of getting up at 5 a.m. (you had to follow this schedule or be punished), 49 folding up your blankets and sitting on your bed until 7 a.m. when a guard took you to the well to wash and empty your chamber bucket, returning to your room and sitting on the bed until 11 a.m. when lunch was served . . . laying down for two hours after lunch, getting up and going through the same routine until the 4 p.m. meal.[29]

What Leopold described sounds unpleasant but hardly consistent with most people's image of a "hellhole," much less the kind of conditions one would expect to find under a camp commander whom he described as "extremely sadistic—in brief an Oriental Eichmann eagerly awaiting the 'final solution' to the American POW problem." In fact, a lot of Vietnam-era veterans would recognize the routine of predawn revelry followed by hours with nothing to do but evade the harassment of their officers and NCOs as life in the U.S. Army as they knew it. As for tending to his own "chamber bucket," enlisted men in Vietnam were often punished for minor infractions by being ordered to "burn shit," the standard means for disposing of human excrement on military posts—a task normally assigned to Vietnamese civilians working on the posts and one that officers like Leopold had no experience with. In that sense, much of the abrasiveness of confinement felt by Leopold—a magna cum laude and Phi Beta Kappa graduate of Stanford—can probably be better understood as relative deprivation suffered by officers from privileged backgrounds, not torture.[30]

Most accounts make clear that the treatment of some of the POWs was at times bewilderingly brutal. In an effort to get at the reasons for that, however, the official story is very quick to demonize the Vietnamese and dismiss the reality that Hao Lo and its satellites faced the same challenges for managing a large population of inmates as any other prison system. In short, there were rules to follow and consequences for breaking the rules. It is common practice, for example, for prison administrators to control communications among the prisoners lest they foment plots for breakouts or rebellions, and the North Vietnamese system was no exception to that practice. Isolation from other prisoners was often the sentence for attempts to communicate within the prison population, but "isolation," in those instances, was sometimes confinement in one's own cell. Eugene McDaniel, for example, told of Ron Mastin's being in "solitary" for six months "a few rooms down from my own."

McDaniel, shot down in September 1967, was nevertheless able to make contact with Mastin, for which McDaniel himself was in turn blindfolded, put in irons, and deprived of sleep for thirty-six hours.[31]

Risner's story read similarly. For the first month or so after he was captured, his treatment in Hao Lo was unpleasant but otherwise unremarkable. He established communication with other prisoners by tapping on the walls, but finding that to be "too slow and unsatisfactory," he began drilling holes in the wall; he drilled so many holes that he remembered the "wall looked like a piece of Swiss cheese." When other prisoners saw his handiwork, Risner passed them the metal rods he had used for tools and they punched through their walls, "until every room was connected up and down the hall." Caught shortly thereafter, Risner was locked in leg irons and denied food, water, and toilet privileges for four days.[32]

One can condemn the excessiveness of the Vietnamese response to the resolve and ingenuity of Mastin, Risner, and the others who subverted the prison rules while yet seeing how, from the Vietnamese side, the response is better understood as punishment than torture. For that matter, even a cursory knowledge of American prison culture conjures some frightful images of what would befall civilian prisoners if they drilled holes in their cell walls!

. . . Corporal Mortification?

The most fascinating accounts of torture, however, come from POWs who openly admit to having consciously provoked the Vietnamese to torture them and at the time even inflicting physical injury on their own bodies—essentially torturing themselves when the Vietnamese would not do it. Like Everett Alvarez, other pilots captured during the first year of the air war had quickly recognized how little was at stake in the interrogation sessions and given the Vietnamese useless information to avoid physical coercion. That changed, however, with the arrival in Hao Lo of what Howes calls "the triumvirate of great leaders" in the late summer of 1965.

The "three" were Risner, Stockdale, and Navy Rear Admiral Jeremiah Denton, all older senior officers with what proved to be unrealistic commitments to the literal interpretation of the Code of Conduct. Denton came in July and declared himself in charge of the other captives, some

51

of whom had been there for nearly a year: "Follow the Code," he ordered, and plan for escape and resistance. As it played out, Denton's order was a dangerous act of provocation by which, he admitted to the press years later, "we forced them to be brutal to us." There was a sadistic inflection in that approach, moreover, because Denton ordered all those POWs who had already "failed," by cooperating with the interrogators, to "bounce back" by confessing their weaknesses to him or other SROs and then return to interrogation sessions wherein they could then "succeed" in resistance and have another chance to endure torture. The threat for not repeating the cycle was that SROs might bring charges, years later, after release, against the insubordinate underlings, who had been "broken" by the Vietnamese. Had that part of Denton's order been put into words for the press, it might have read, "We SROs forced the North Vietnamese to be brutal to our lower-ranking fellow POWs."[33]

Stockdale and Risner followed Denton into the prison system a couple months later. For them, as for Denton, torture was not something to be avoided, but a test of will and faith to be passed. Reversing the conventional logic whereby torture was the consequence befalling the prisoner for failure to give the Vietnamese the information they wanted, the three leaders posited war as the normative relationship between the POWs and their captors, with torture being the form that combat took in those circumstances. For these hardliners, the cycle connecting interrogations and torture began with torture: to be "at torture" was the natural state-of-being for the American POW. Like any form of warfare, torture was painful; it took men to their limits and required periodic retreats—a return to the interrogations. But warriors bounce back, they return to combat. And the prisoner at war, Howes explains in *Voices of the Vietnam POWs*, uses the interrogations as the road to take back to the "front lines" where he belongs—in the stocks, under the lash, and in the ropes.[34]

The fact that senior officers among the POWs actually provoked mistreatment by the Vietnamese has always been an asterisk on the torture stories that POWs told on their return. But, as a segue to the religious subtext that makes the Vietnam-era POW stories resonant with the early American captivity narrative, the accounts coming out of Hanoi of self-inflicted bodily pain are still more poignant. In January 1969, for example, Stockdale began fasting to protest Vietnamese attempts to extract what even he knew was useless five-year-old information from him about his unit. Then, fearing that they might try to film him for propaganda purposes, he battered his own face with a stool and cut his scalp to create wounds that would appear to have been inflicted by his captors. Stockdale's self-mutilation became a kind of theater that he "staged" to assuage his anxiety and self-doubt, he said, with his most effective prop being the "puke balls" that he formed by swallowing soap and then vomiting. This abuse of himself went on for days, with self-delivered "early morning bashings" that turned his face and hands into mashed flesh. "It really became a test of self-discipline," he recalled later.[35]

Risner tells a similar story. Also fearing he might be photographed or filmed for propaganda purposes, he says he first considered killing himself and then thought about cutting the tendons in his hands. Without explaining what purpose crippled hands would have served in that context, he goes on to tell us that the Vietnamese really wanted his voice. Since he was a high-profile captive, an American hero even in the eyes of his fellow prisoners, his voice heard reading news or information over Radio Hanoi would lend credibility to North Vietnamese broadcasts; so it was his voice that he would deny them.

Recalling that drinking acid or striking the throat could damage the voice, Risner knelt and prayed. "I said, 'Lord, is this the right way to go? Should I cut my wrists? Should I try to destroy my voice?'" In the end, he went for the throat: "I began pounding my throat as hard as I could. My eyes watered and sometimes I saw stars. I gave frequent chops to the throat. . . . I choked and struggled to get my breath. My neck swelled up, but it did not affect my voice. . . . I could still talk." Risner turned to the acid treatment, counting on his soap to have enough lye in it to damage his throat.

> I took my cup and filled it with a third cup of water, and part of a bar of lye soap. I crumbled; mashed and stirred it into a mushy, mucky substance. Then I began gargling with it. It burned the inside of my mouth like fire, almost cooking it, and I accidentally swallowed some. The taste was enough to make me vomit. To increase the effect of the acid, I decided also to try to damage my vocal cords, I held a rag or towel over my mouth and screamed as loud as I could but at the same time compressing the air I was expelling so there would not be much noise. I continued this for three days and nights, staying awake

as much as possible. By the third day, I could not whisper. I tried to talk, then tried to sing. I could not do either. It had worked! I was now a mute.[36]

It had not worked and Risner was not mute; one good cough the next day and his voice was back, leaving him with nothing but diarrhea for his effort.

At War, But with Whom?

For Denton, Stockdale, Risner, and other hardliners, torture became a way to confirm their worth as American warriors. Evidence of physical damage from torture, they hoped, would be evidence, upon their release, that they had remained at war during their imprisonment. When the torture they wanted from the Vietnamese was not forthcoming, they provoked it; when that did not work, they inflicted their own damage. As Stockdale puts it in his memoir, he prayed that his binge of self-flagellation would "make Syb [his wife, Sybil] and those boys of ours proud."[37]

The story of prisoners at war is the official story, but it is the story of only a few of the hardcore SROs and it is not always so clear that the war being fought within Hao Lo was the same as the one being fought outside the walls. It appears on reexamination, for example, that SRO demands that prisoners resist interrogations had little to do with military strategy and a lot to do with SRO control over the prison population and the sense of self-discipline that some SROs, such as Stockdale, needed to have validated by being tortured. Likewise, the resistance of senior officers to what they considered their exploitation for propaganda purposes probably had more to do with the war in the United States than the war in Vietnam. Risner's futile effort to disable his voice lest he be forced to read something over Radio Hanoi that the other POWs might hear is a case in point.[38]

Risner does not say what he would have had to read nor does he date the time of his struggle with that issue, but it occurred about the time of a similar incident Stockdale describes in his memoir. Stockdale objected to prisoners' being used to "read the news" because he had learned in a course at Stanford, Comparative Marxist Thought, taught by "an old Kremlinologist who knew all [the Marxist strands]," that the use of prisoners that way could be manipulated for brainwashing. The point had been driven home for Stockdale by tapes made by psychologists who had studied the POWs from the Korean War.[39]

But is that what was going on in Hao Lo? By Stockdale's own account (dismissed by him as communist trickery), the Vietnamese wanted an American to read the news because their interpreters did not have sufficient skill in English to be understood by the Americans. And what was the news they wanted read? Stockdale recalled that it was *New York Times* excerpts from the paper's assistant managing editor, Harrison Salisbury, who had recently returned from his fact-finding trip to Hanoi. True, Salisbury had come back to the United States critical of the Johnson administration's Vietnam policy, but if there was a credible source to be had from the U.S. side of the war, he was it.[40] He was, moreover, having an effect on government policy makers, a status that one could say entitled him to be heard by all Americans—civilian, uniformed, or imprisoned. Stockdale nevertheless put out an order that participation in the readings should stop and twenty years later, in his memoirs, stuck to the cold war line that Salisbury's *Times* report was "loaded with what we had all been getting for months as the [Communist] Central Committee's propaganda line."[41]

Taken at face value, Stockdale's denial of the news to the POWs appears to be due to his fear that the ideological war beyond the walls of Hao Lo was more than "his men" could handle—best to protect them from it. Led by the reinterpretations of other captivity stories made by Strong and Gruner, however, we have to ask whether what Stockdale feared more was the enemy inside the walls, indeed the enemy within the hearts and minds of the POWs themselves.

The SROs' fear that their underlings might defect, and evidence for the legitimacy of that fear, can be found in the memoirs. By the early 1970s there was open rebellion against the SRO leadership. Some of the discontent was fomented by the newly arrived POWs from the South who had survived jungle confinement for months and years before arriving in the Hanoi system. Their experience made them skeptical of SRO "authority" that was based on the officers' claims to having suffered abuse between 1965 and 1969.[42] Comments to the effect that Hanoi was like the Holiday Inn compared to the jungle camps, and the southern captive Floyd Kushner's post-release statement to the press that he was "damned glad to get to North Vietnam" are indicative of the tension that pervaded relations between senior officers and the others. Moreover, the key to survival in the South had been individual resourcefulness tempered by a form of mutuality that had supplanted rank-based hierarchy with time in captivity as a measure of authority. By Hao Lo standards, the jungle POWs brought an anarchist culture into the system that was discordant with the authoritarianism of the three "great leaders."[43]

Although there was more to the dissent than struggle over the distribution of power among the prisoners, that issue is a cue to understanding the Vietnam-era prisoner experience as an extension of the American captivity narrative. The resistance of rank-and-file POWs to the control of their own officers was accompanied by emotional sentiments that aligned them with the enemy Other. Many of the memoirs reveal sympathy for the suffering of the Vietnamese, some even with expressions of guilt by the writers for their participation in the bombings. Jensen, for example, later reflected on the anger of the peasants who captured him, writing, "When you think about it, their behavior was understandable. They had been bombed by our aircraft for a long time. Their homes had been destroyed, their crops and animals destroyed, and perhaps some of their family members killed. It was no wonder they were angry." John Young says, "We felt sorry for the Vietnamese because they had suffered. We felt guilty about what had happened to them."[44]

In more than a few cases, those kernels of humanism sprouted critiques of the United States' war policy and more explicit identification with the Vietnamese. James Daly, who became a conscientious objector while in Vietnam, read the *Pentagon Papers*, Felix Greene's *The Enemy*, and antiwar plays performed in the United States provided to him and his mates by the prison administrators. Daly also studied the classical writings of Marx and Lenin and remembers, "The learning was exciting, just knowing what these political and economic teachings were." Since the war in the minds of the SROs entailed an ideological struggle with communism and socialism, the attraction of the Marxist classics to some of the men was a troubling form of "going native."[45]

And just as Cotton Mather had worried about Puritans who settled in the woods beyond earshot of the preachers, so too did senior officers like Risner, whom Howes likens to an "evangelist" compelled to lead and teach, worried most about the rank-and-file POWs who were or had been free from SRO oversight. That concern may or may not have reflected an inflated sense of how influential the officers could be in the lives of imprisoned comrades, but the fact is that some of the most intense expressions of affinity for the Vietnamese side of the war came from the Americans who spent most or all their confinement in the South. Army Sergeant George Smith, for example, was captured near Hiep Hoa in 1963 and held for two years. Upon his release, Smith returned to the United States and became a celebrated figure within the antiwar movement when he wrote P.O.W.: Two Years with the Viet Cong, a memoir that, in Howes's words, reflects "how a POW comes to recognize the justice of his captors' cause."[46] As a measure of how porous the cultural boundary was between the Hanoi POWs, the GI antiwar movement, and the influence of the Vietnamese captors, the prison administration made Smith's book available to the POWs.

The social distance between the SROs and the enlisted men was also a good predictor of who would be a dissident. One dimension of that distance was an artifact of the military's hierarchy. Referring to the prison population, Young recalled that "many of the enlisted men opposed the war," a footnote to which could read that by the early 1970s the enlistees in the Hanoi system were a cross section of the enlisted men in Vietnam who were growing restive about the war. Correspondingly, the enlisted men in Hanoi were almost all army soldiers or marines who had been captured in the South and held in jungle camps for months before being moved north. The officers, by contrast, were air force and navy pilots shot down over the North. The more interesting dimension, however, derived from the disparate class backgrounds of two groups. The enlisted men were likely to be from poor or working-class families with little stake in the war, whereas the pilots, and the SROs in particular, were often from middle-class or even upper-class families with, if nothing else, military and political careers that hinged on the outcome of the war.

Those social-status differences were intensified for the prisoner-at-war narrative by the greater contact that enlisted men had with the Vietnamese before their capture and during their days in jungle camps. Whereas officers, particularly those flying off aircraft carriers, had never seen, much less interacted with, any Vietnamese before being shot down and meeting their enemy under the extraordinary circumstances of being prisoners, the enlisted men are likely to have initially seen Vietnamese in quite ordinary roles: street vendors, civilian employees on army bases, bar girls, or even girlfriends. In-country for more than a few days, a ground soldier probably knew at least one Vietnamese by name and within weeks may have known something about his or her family and even seen where that family lived. Depending on the circumstances, of course, those encounters could have reinforced racist stereotypes that GIs brought from home or confirmed their fears that every conical hat hid a terrorist. But, whatever the quality of the exposure to the Vietnamese that GIs carried into their prison experience, it lent an element of humanity to the faceless and nameless "V" that the SROs were unable to see beyond, even years later in their memoirs.[47]

The conditions of jungle captivity, adversarial though they were, deepened the acquaintance that most enlisted POWs had with Vietnamese life and the hardships of the people. Captured in the South, GIs endured weeks of being marched from one village to another, spending nights in the grass-woven huts of peasants where their encounters with the people produced stories much more nuanced than the demonizing portrayals of the Vietnamese painted in the memoirs of the bomber pilots. Frank Anton, the chopper pilot downed and captured in January 1968, for example, described one occasion.

> Much of the next day was spent crossing paddies and creeks. In the afternoon we stopped at a hootch owned by a woman who looked to be about sixty but was probably younger. . . . I took off my boots. She saw that my feet were wet. She removed my socks and dried my feet with a rag. She left and returned in a moment with a pair of clean white socks belonging to her. She pulled them very gently on my feet and hung mine up to dry. Other villagers had hissed and thrown rocks at us as we passed. But this act of kindness was unexpected and I was touched.[48]

Unlike the Hanoi prisoners, the men held in the South had seen that they ate the same food as their captors, indeed sometimes being forced to gather what they ate from the jungle, just like the guerrilla fighters, and cut thatch and bamboo for the huts that housed them. Like the POWs in the North, they also coined nicknames for their guards, but they were more likely to know their real names—Huong and Qua (a Montagnard) among them—and remember others respectfully years later as, say, Mr. Ho or Mr. Hom.[49]

It was the humanizing of the Other that the SROs seemed to fear because recognition of the humanity in "them" meant recognizing an element of them in "us," an acknowledgment of the enemy within—the enemy within the hearts and minds of their own rank-and-file. The real fear, as Howes puts it, was of the "white Gook," the POW underling who would give in to the urges of his inner Other, and become, in a sense, an Other. Believing that "enlisted men collaborated [with the enemy] almost instinctively," SROs viewed with alarm any behavior that looked Vietnamese to them—squatting or eating from a bowl—as signs that one of their men might be crossing over. As a prophylactic to cultural contamination, SROs enforced their own segregation of POWs from the Vietnamese, prohibiting, for example, their learning of the language.[50]

Meanwhile, senior officers battled uncertainties about their own Selves that the prison experience amplified. Just as they feared the attraction that Vietnamese culture and communist ideology might have for their men, so too did they feel the tug toward the Other on themselves. Navy Lieutenant Commander Charles Plumb's greatest worry was, in his words, "becoming a different person." Some of that fear was induced by cold war images of the brainwashed Manchurian Candidate, but the gendered anxiety about the stability of their masculinity is most pronounced in the memoirs. With the impertinence of schoolboy locker-room talk, the memoirists tell us, first, how attractive the Vietnamese women found them and, then, how they resisted the temptations of the flesh and maintained their manly bearing. But it wasn't just women with the hots for the fighter jocks. "The guards in Dogpatch were homosexuals—to a man," Ralph Gaither reported, "and they liked to stare at us when we were in the shower." One former POW told a London Times reporter during the 2008 presidential campaign that John McCain routinely addressed his captors as "slant-eyed cocksuckers." No matter the sexual orientation, the Right Stuff was off limits to Vietnamese hands—gratification was deferred until release.[51]

Execution or Conversion?

Questions about Vietnamese motivations have bedeviled interpretations of their harsh treatment of the POWs for years. The interpretation supported by the "official" prisoner-at-war story is consistent with Orientalist views that Asian culture is inferior to Western with regard to its respect for human life and dignity; for many of the returned prisoners and the Americans influenced by the stories they told, the Vietnamese were simply crude and cruel people. Mary Hershberger dissents from this view, concluding that the bad treatment is best understood as punishment meted out for the POWs' resistance to camp rules. Howes goes between those positions, arguing that torture is indeed the proper characterization for the way the POWs were treated but that the motivation for it was control.[52]

Howes avoids a racist otherization of the Vietnamese by seeing what they did as a form of coercion that was thoroughly modernist. Europeans, he points out, had taken torture to new and higher levels during the nineteenth-century colonial period in an effort to extract total subjugation and citizenship from their minions. Their vulnerability to revolt led to a kind of "institutional hysteria" and the adoption of techniques that wrenched body pain to such levels that it could alter the minds and emotions of rebels and political dissidents. As an agency of a socialist state, Howes argues, the Vietnamese Prison Authority is a modernist manifestation rather than an expression of premodern primitivism, but that it was torture, nevertheless, and its objective, contra Hershberger, was to "display the Camp Authority's power," not to get information.[53]

The discernment of Vietnamese motivations is less important, however, for understanding the origins of the Hanoi Jane mythology than is the POWs' perception of what was happening to them. With the abundant inconsistencies in the accounts of torture handed to us by the official story, and the numerous references in the POW memoirs to their fears of the white Gook within themselves, or their comrades, it seems likely that, as much as for John Smith, the attraction of the Other is what scared some POWs enough to mask their vulnerability with a counternarrative about the terror that the Vietnamese visited on them. In short form, it is possible that it was not the extinguishing of (them)Selves that they feared—execution in the Smithian legend—so much as their conversion to the ways of the Vietnamese and the righteousness of their cause.[54]

Reflecting on his own interrogation experience, Army Captain John Dunn turned over the same stone that obscured the Pamunkey side of history for centuries when he wrote that his prison commander "seemed more interested in conversion than [in] . . . the application of torture to obtain information." Dunn's insight wasn't just imaginative. Many of the POWs described the education programs the Vietnamese provided for them, the content of which seems to have differed little from what was being taught in U.S. college classrooms by the late 1960s: the history of Vietnamese struggles for independence, the details of the Geneva Accords that had ended the French occupation and artificially divided the country, and basic political economy. From what we know, there was little in the Hao Lo "lesson plans" for POWs that is not today the accepted wisdom of what the war was about. That being so, the claim by one of the Vietnamese interrogators that the prisoners were being given "the right to rebirth" seems all the more plausible, all the more sincere, all the more resonant with take two on the John Smith legend.[55]

BARBARELLA
AS PROLOGUE

There is a lot of sexual feeling involved in it. All these people
expected her to be a certain kind of person . . . and when your
fantasy life is threatened, and Barbarella becomes a revolutionary,
it's very upsetting.—Tom Hayden, 1990

Gender has long been a theme in the narratives of war-time betrayal, making it predictable that in the wake of the lost war in Vietnam figures of female treachery would take root in American culture. The prominence of women in the U.S. antiwar movement may have increased the likelihood that one of them would be held accountable for the defeat; what was less certain was that Fonda would be that one. She was not the most radical of the many women activists of the day; nor was she the only woman to go to Hanoi.

Within a few years after the war's end, however, other female radicals slipped from public memory while Fonda became a national preoccupation. During the war in Vietnam, the condemnation of Joan Baez for encouraging young men to resist the draft and Angela Davis for encouraging acts of armed revolution as an acknowledged member of the Communist Party probably exceeded any criticism of Fonda. But Baez, Davis, and other women were never held singularly responsible for the loss of the war, as Fonda came to be. And even if their behavior of others was deemed traitorous at the time, it was soon dismissed as simply that and forgotten along with most everything else related to war.

Unlike other female protesters, Fonda seems to have stirred something deeper in the American psyche. It was not just the military cause that she allegedly sold out, or the health and well-being of the POWs that she supposedly compromised. There was something more basic to American identity that she offended, something that transcended Vietnam for which the issues surrounding the loss of the war were merely the vehicles for expression. Hanoi Jane, in other words, works the way it does in American culture for reasons having less to do with Hanoi and what Jane did there than with the crisis of masculinity wrought by the American defeat in Southeast Asia. The tale of Hanoi Jane is undeniably about betrayal, but the story it tells resonates beyond the accusations about who undermined the U.S. mission in Vietnam or assumptions of national and racial supremacy that were shattered by the Vietnamese victory. In the end, Hanoi Jane is a myth not only because it misrepresents what Jane Fonda was about as an antiwar activist but because it also derives from her starring role in the 1968 film *Barbarella* and the distortion of her image as a sex symbol.

Eroticizing the Betrayal

Men whose masculinity is bound up with an eroticized sense of womanhood feel let down, manipulated even, when they are confronted with the reality that their fantasies have masked. For many men (and some women), the images of women projected by the entertainment media are constituent elements of a dream world that becomes "real" to them. Coming to the screen at a time when the dominant sex and gender identities in post–World War II American life were beginning to be questioned, and fantasies of space travel were becoming reality, *Barbarella* the movie, with its underdressed superwoman and technology that was futuristic even by contemporary standards, could have titillated some young male imaginations in the late 1960s.[1]

In many ways, however, late-1960s real life overtook the fantasy world of films. The liberalizing of Church doctrine that followed Vatican Council II in 1965 combined with the development of oral contraceptives to loosen sexual mores; the New York City Stonewall movement for gay rights normalized sexualities long considered deviant; and women in the civil rights and antiwar movements challenged their roles as coffee makers and bed partners assigned to them by men, constructing in the process their own agency as political activists. The occurrence of the first moon landing a year after *Barbarella* crossed the screen, moreover, probably had many boys who, a few years earlier, imagined themselves as Buck Rogers now dreaming of being the next Neil Armstrong. Left at that, *Barbarella*'s importance in the story of how Jane Fonda the actress became fodder for a betrayal narrative for the lost war in Vietnam is diminished. But there's more to the story.

As time passed, the Barbarella-Fonda linkage may have receded from public consciousness in general, but as her second husband, Tom Hayden, points out in the epigraph to this chapter, her coming out as a political activist soon after the film's release stuck in some minds as a kind of betrayal in itself. Unlike other film stars of that era who went into their postscreen lives still known as the seductresses they played, Fonda, at a young age, stripped away the fantasy by renouncing the provocative figure she had cut in *Barbarella*. By doing it on her own, Fonda set herself up to be reviled for being the actress who first perpetuated the fraud and then the messenger who pulls off the mask as if to say, "Ha, fooled you?"[2]

As it turns out, though, the sex-bomb character that some Americans still associate with Fonda and that she too scorned in later years may itself have been a creature of media misrepresentation that grew larger and more seductive in the post-Vietnam years. While the full story of Hanoi Jane's creation entails a campaign of criticism for her 1972 trip to Vietnam and the gendered subtext of her betrayal of her image as Barbarella, a closer look at the movie character she played reveals that the first level of myth making was the mythologizing of Barbarella as a sex kitten, a distortion that proceeded apace as the vilifying of Fonda took shape in the 1970s.

The Deconstructed *Barbarella*

The totality of the Barbarella figure cannot be separated from the subtext embedded in it, the story-within-the-story that can be brought into view by looking at the French comic-book series that inspired it. Written by Jean-Claude Forest in the mid-1960s, *Barbarella* is a postmodern graphic novel that combines the science-fiction imagery of next-century space travel with adaptations of classical Greek characters, such as Medusa, the medieval settings of castles and moats, and modern themes of human emancipation and sexuality. The stories told are basically political, with each episode featuring an oppressed population that Barbarella sides with in some sort of struggle for liberation. The Earth girl is never portrayed as a savior figure, however, because of her own circumstances of being marooned or held captive; her position with respect to her allies is always one of mutuality.

The comic's opening panels show Barbarella piloting an astroship as it approaches the planet Lythion. Lythion appears to be an uninhabitable desert until she sees a giant greenhouse nestled in a volcanic crater. Smashing through the glass roof, she crash lands the ship in the strange land of Crystallia, where Dianthus and his sister Knautia recognize the astroship as friendly and set out to free Barbarella from the thicket of rose bushes she has fallen into. It's a campy beginning to a series of exploits, each of which has the slapstick character of this one and representations of power that tease our sensibilities: is Barbarella entrapped or embraced by the anthropomorphized thorns of the rose bush? And is the man who has saved her named for the Roman goddess who protects women—or just a pink flower?

The uninhibited sexuality and identity blending only hinted at here gets more graphic as the story progresses, providing the complexity for the filmic Barbarella scripted for Fonda a few years later. Joining the Crystallians for battle against the rival Orhomrs, the galactic warrior woman "drains" the power of enemy soldiers through sex in order to escape capture, has a fling with an enemy soldier, Ahan, and then declares the triumph of Good over Evil before hitching a ride on the first flower-bearing cargo ship leaving town—piloted, with luck, by Dildano, a "handsome captain." The Earth girl rockets off Lythion bound for Sogo, a pariah city where a perversion a day is said to be invented. On her way, a series of mishaps lands Barbarella in bizarre places inhabited by characters and creatures that challenge the conventions of the 1960s Earth-bound world she has come from. She escapes the bondage queen Medusa and the sadistic hunter Strickno, only to be recaptured by the kinky princesses Stomoxys and Glossina, whose idea of fun is to bind her with rope and turn loose a collection of mechanical toy soldiers and dolls that attack, biting her ankles and thighs. That episode ends with the king's arrival to administer a bare-butt spanking to one of his twisted daughters.

Arriving at the aptly named Sogo, Barbarella learns that anyone entering the city and resisting its depravities will be thrown into a labyrinth from which only Pygar, the last of the Ornithanthropes, has the capacity to escape. Using a crude map to wend her way through Sogo's back alleys, she is met by a voluptuous "one-eyed slut" who makes clear her desire for the Earth girl. The nameless harlot turns out to be the queen of Sogo herself, who throws Barbarella into a giant cage of birds that leave the space traveler's body thoroughly pecked. An androgynous robot, Dictor, rescues Barbarella, satisfies her sexually, and returns her to battle.

Barbarella reenters the fray, only to be captured by the guards and hooked up to the Excessive Machine, a contraption with the power to pleasure its victims to death. Barbarella, however, is freed when she offers to subdue the eye-patched queen by entering her dreams, whence the two engage in a sequence of plots against each other. The story, and the series, race to an apocalyptic ending when the queen orders her end-of-time creation, the Beast, to spew venom that will kill everyone. As the queen faces demise in the evil of her own making, her only hope is escape from Sogo and, for that, she needs the space-traveling heroine. When the Queen of Mean agrees to take a "good sound spanking" from Barbarella "whenever the need arises," the Earthling enlists Pygar to carry them both away from the collapsing kingdom of perversion.

On the face of it, *Barbarella* the movie plays into the creation of Hanoi Jane because Barbarella the character, played by Jane Fonda, sexualizes Fonda's image and violates the masculine identity commonly derived from the male-warrior role—women are not supposed to be soldiers, except in comics. For that reason, it follows for some students of post-Vietnam culture that men are threatened by her and adopt the Hanoi Jane epithet to express their dislike. Certainly those elements are at work, but this rereading of *Barbarella* allows us to identify still more potent elements, whose qualities, because they are only implicit, shed light on just why the Barbarella-Fonda linkage is so disturbing.[3]

These are political stories with gendered relations of power using the aesthetics of magical realism to deconstruct the interpenetration of sex and violence, deterritorialize sexuality, and explore the boundary between the conscious and subconscious narratives found in future Fonda productions and performances—sometimes subtly, sometimes not.

Barbarella's attraction to Pygar's impotence, for example, anticipates her relationship with Luke, the Vietnam veteran in the 1978 film *Coming Home* who helps her to her first orgasm despite his paralysis from the waist down. The sadomasochistic imagery in the print version of *Barbarella*—How many adult spankings can there be in one comic?—meanwhile, points to those same Freudian-themed story lines that reappear as Gloria's death wish in the character Fonda plays in *They Shoot Horses Don't They?* (1969) and the dialectics of sexual desire appropriated by Bree for personal empowerment in *Klute* (1971).

Most of the plot turns on Barbarella's access to futuristic weaponry and the exercise of her sexual prowess. In situations where it really counts, she enters an alliance with men (Dianthus, for example), defeats men with sex, or guns them down with exotic fire arms. Submission to men is reserved for after-battle downtime and, even then, the balance of power is not always clear. In the first place, the sexual orientation of the characters is often ambiguous—Barbarella herself keeps us guessing. In the first story she doesn't hesitate to climb into the cab with Captain Good-looking for a ride home but after that things get more confusing. When Medusa tells Barbarella, "Men don't interest me," the Earth girl whips off her shirt and asks, "What about me?" Medusa's face is turned away from Barbarella at the moment so the scene is mainly a tease for us, the readers. A bit later, though, after Barbarella has hogtied the evil one, she says she "can't bear the thought of hurting her." In the story's last panels, Barbarella and the queen move toward a sensual embrace but, due to Medusa's makeover by then as Barbarella's clone, we are not offered homoeroticism so much as excitation at the boundary of homo- and autosexuality. In Sogo, Barbarella's identity is really put to the test by the horny queen who cannot keep her hands to herself: Barbarella's resistance is consistent but unconvincing, leaving us wondering whether and when the two will hook up. They don't. But when the queen dismisses the threat posed by the Beast, saying, "Anyway, I prefer other games . . . Come with me," the Earth girl's eyes are lovingly fixed on the rose covering the queen's crotch.

Barbarella's most satisfying sex is with Diktor, the robot of indeterminate gender, and her attraction to Pygar, the blind birdman, if not Platonic, certainly unsettles the phallocentric mind. The other hetero hunks could be poster boys for New Age masculinity. With a name like

Dianthus, her flower-growing first-friend is cast as the sensitive type—and, on that score, he doesn't disappoint; Ahan, who is more peacenik than soldier, shares his bottle of "Skiawolf" with Barbarella. But as they position themselves for lovemaking, she's on top.

From the Comic Pages of Jean-Claude Forest to Roger Vadim's Script

Most Americans know Barbarella only through the 1968 film by the same title. In most respects, the movie resembles the print version. She crash lands in a crystalline winter land, where she is met by two naughty little girls who cuff her hands before unleashing their mechanical dolls with razor-sharp metal teeth that tear hunks of flesh from her legs and arms. The main characters from the comic book, including Pygar and the sexy queen, make reappearances here, although the roles of some, like Dianthus, now "rotating president of the Sun System" and speaking with a lisp, have been rescripted; Dildano is the bumbling leader of a revolutionary movement against the tyrant queen; Barbarella is still a warrior woman, this time on a directed mission rather than haplessly falling into situations as she did before—and she is still fighting the good fight for galactic freedom and justice.

The movie has a unified story line but nonetheless lacks the drama of the comic; its sexuality, while more explicit because it involves real actors, is less erotic. Besides the opening striptease scene in which Barbarella appears fleetingly bare breasted, there are six situations in the film that could be qualifiedly classified as "sex scenes." A hairy rescuer repairs her spaceship and offers to "make love" to her, an expression she finds old fashion, since Earthlings have not done "it" that way for centuries. Today, she explains, when the "psycho-cardiogram readings" of two Earth beings are in "perfect confluence," they take "exhalelationtransferance pellets" and touch hands until "full rapport is achieved." This avoids what she calls the "distraction and danger to maximum efficiency" represented by the old way. He convinces her to try the "old way"; but as they approach each other, the camera diverts to an animated outdoor scene.

Sexy? Not really—nor are the other would-be sex scenes. When Barbarella meets the birdman Pygar, he informs her that he has "lost the will to fly," an expression we understand metaphorically when he sails away after having, ahem, showed Barbarella his "nest." He's flying and she's smiling, but the scene is innocent enough for a PG rating.[4] Arriving on the dingy streets of Sogo, the birdman and his Earth friend are ogled by its degenerate denizens, but it isn't clear who is interested in whom or why. Barbarella's first encounter with the queen is loaded with titillation, yet when the eye-patched seductress delivers her "Wanna come 'n' play with me?" line, the space warrior betrays not a hint of interest and sprints off. In the scene that follows, the sexually charged head-of-state pushes Pygar to the floor and mounts him, only to be told by him, "Angels don't make love, they are love." With that, she orders her guards to dispose of the "winged fruitcake"—Barbarella isn't in the scene. Barbarella has one last pellet-driven, fully clothed, and upright "rapport" with Dildano, the inexperience rebel, and then blows the fuses of the "excessive machine." But that's it for sex in *Barbarella* the movie.

True, the film is salted with scantily clad men and women, hetero- and homosexual innuendo, and sado-masochistic references, but Barbarella, credentialed by the Sun president Dianthus as his "only double weighted astronomic aviatrix," comes off mostly as an intergalactic warrior woman, cartoonish but with good politics. (The box cover of my copy describes her as, "a female James Bond, vanquishing evil in the forms of robots and monsters.") Viewed superficially, she might appear to be male dependent, since she is rescued twice by men and transported to Sogo in the arms of Pygar. But the sightless feather-man needs her to see the way, and it is she who guns down the queen's air-defense forces on the flight to the kingdom of twist. Once there, Barbarella does the saving, pulling the angelic Pygar from the clutches of the Great Tyrant on two occasions.

Fonda's Barbarella is undeniably zany but, whereas that image might give her some late-life embarrassment, it works against the claim that *Barbarella* bequeathed her a sex-kitten legacy. Indeed, the reviews that followed the film's release were too varied in their description of Fonda's portrayal of Barbarella to conclude that the content of the role itself accounts for the sexualizing of Fonda's image. In a review for *Newsweek*, Paul Zimmerman, for example, called Barbarella "a pure innocent"; he never used the word *sex* even once in the entire review. Writing for the *New Republic*, Stanley Kauffmann called Barbarella's space suit–doffing in the opening scene a "spoof on stripping" and noted the film's inventory of "late-adolescent gags and gadgets about sex, the worst of them tedious, not offensive, and the best of them bright." Renata Adler's entry in the *New York Times*, entitled "Screen: Science + Sex = 'Barbarella,'" highlighted the sexual in the film but complained about its misogyny, apparently missing the point that its only sadist was a woman.[5]

Charles Fager's review in the *Christian Century* probably captured the essence of *Barbarella* best. He called Fonda's character "a cross between James Bond and Batman who zaps around the universe in the year 40,000, saving a disarmed earth from interstellar evil." He noted that "lots of miscellaneous female flesh is displayed" but that that feature "failed to hold even this male reviewer's attention." Fager went on, recalling the talk-show host Johnny Carson's remark that "his youngsters had seen the movie and had not noticed anything unusual or provocative about it." Its sex, Fager concluded, would "probably bore even a lecherous old man."[6]

The fact that the filmic Barbarella was an inauspicious point of origin for the sex-bomb image that came to surround Fonda means that the post-sixties cultural spin given the film had as much to do with the construction of that image as the film itself. Sexiness is a matter of taste, of course, and tastes are fashionable; what is a turn-on for one generation of men might be enervating for another. Taking the measure of Barbarella's heat isn't all that hard, however, since there is a consensus standard to use and she's Marilyn Monroe.[7]

Jane Fonda: No Marilyn Monroe

In his 1990 biography of Fonda, *Citizen Jane*, Christopher Andersen said, "She had probably done more than anyone since Marilyn Monroe to sustain the image of women as little more than objects of sexual gratification." Following Andersen's cue, Claire La Fleur wrote that Fonda is remembered as "a voluptuous space-age sex-toy who captured the attention of the most virile men in the galaxy."[8]

Andersen's likening of Fonda to Marilyn Monroe is hard to sustain. To begin with, Marilyn Monroe was a kind of performance act by someone born Norma Jean Mortensen who merged her on- and off-screen identities. Fonda, by contrast, never lived as Barbarella and never adopted the persona of a Hollywood sex symbol. Fonda successfully played serious roles in *Cat Ballou* and *Hurry Sundown* before *Barbarella* and in many films after, some of which, like *Klute* and *Coming Home* were recognized as major contributions to women's liberation. To write that she was the successor to Marilyn Monroe's throne as Hollywood's sex queen, Andersen had to erase the likes of Jayne Mansfield and Mamie Van Doren, who scorched the screen long after Monroe's death in 1962.

La Fleur's remembering of Fonda is another exercise in cultural revisionism. Barbarella was not voluptuous and her men were not virile. The Fonda who filled the film's space suit reportedly carried a 35-22-37 figure on a 5-foot-7-inch, 110-pound frame. If anything, she was a svelte study in contrast to the Marilyn Monroe that Marge Piercy describes: "She swayed. She was ripe and succulent. If she had bones, they were buried in flesh. She was flesh itself made luminous. Muscles, bones, sinews, they were there but unimportant in the message of flesh and skin."[9] As for Barbarella's virile men, the hirsute hero who wants to do "it" the old-fashion way passes the testosterone test. But what about the gelded Pygar? Or the pratfallen politico, Dildano, who wants to do "it" the pharmacological way? The whole point of the movie's sexual theme is that the world has evolved to the year 40,000 by leaving behind sex as the 1960s knew it, because, as Barbarella lectures the hairy hunter, other means of "ego-support and self-esteem" had made it pointless—an apt put-down of mid-twentieth-century machismo.

Some chroniclers recall the off-screen use made of Fonda's youthful nudity as a justification for her sex-symbol reputation. But the context and use made of those images suggest the difference, not similarity, between her and the Monroe-type expressions of early 1960s sexuality. The November 13, 1967, *Newsweek*, for example, adorned its cover with an above-the-waste side-to-back still photo of Fonda/Barbarella that suggested nothing more about her front side than a rib cage. The story for which the photo was presumably a come-on was about the new permissiveness in American society. It was a liberative trend, according to the article, driven by a new generation that was breaking free from Victorian repression and hypocrisy, wanting "to strip away all the sham and all the cant of their elders and to strive instead for truth and honesty." The new permissiveness that Fonda was being used to (sex) symbolize was, in other words, a departure from sexual mores that were as restraining as Monroe's costumes—sexy she was, but sexy in an anti-Monrovian way. A comparison of their respective appearances in *Playboy* reveals a similar asymmetry: whereas Fonda did everything in her power to keep the unauthorized shots of her out of *Playboy*, and sued when they did appear, Monroe had willingly exposed herself for the magazine's historic first centerfold.[10]

Another difference is that Monroe's films are as atavistic as *Barbarella* is futuristic. Set in the 1950s, films like *The Seven Year Itch* were a reaction to the home-to-workplace migration of women during World War II, as thousands of women filled places of men mustered for military service. The government-sponsored political campaign to legitimate the use of theretofore homebound labor in factories had to be reversed in the postwar years, and films celebrating the redomestication of women fit that agenda. Fonda's Barbarella, in contrast, commands her own spaceship and zooms around the universe thousands of years in the future. *Barbarella* asks us to imagine a world that is yet to come, whereas Marilyn Monroe's roles ask nothing from our imaginations, because they are stamped from a world we have left behind.

There is one way that the equation of Fonda to Marilyn Monroe works, but, interestingly, it works against the logic of those who make the comparison to denigrate Fonda. Monroe's characters were sexy and everything else that the wartime propaganda figure Rosie the Riveter was not, but they were really not the boy toys that popular memory would have us believe them to be. Most of them were wily teasers who used their sexual prowess to get what they wanted. In the *Seven Year Itch*, for example, The Girl (as she is called) remains oblivious to Tommy's advances while fueling his fantasies and exploiting his desire, hoping to escape New York City's summer heat through invitations to his air-conditioned apartment. Like Fonda's Barbarella, The Girl seems unconscious of her sexuality, making Tommy the character who is hostage to his own libido. If we strip away the costuming of Barbarella and Monroe's characters, and look solely at the gender politics embedded their roles, Fonda and Monroe both get high marks for their representations of male-female relations. What is important is that this—the only way in which Fonda and Monroe were alike—ends up in the circular file when the comparisons go to press.

Barbarella: A Cult Classic—but Not for the *Hamburger Hill* Crowd

Early in the research for this book, I mentioned to Fran Hoffmann, a sociologist, that I thought Fonda's sexualized image had something to do with the demonizing she has endured as Hanoi Jane. Told that I was going to look into the role of Barbarella in that process, she said, "Oh, Barbarella. Sure that's popular again, kind of lesbian cult classic." It was an interesting comment, because if the film were truly more than an item on the filmographies of movie buffs, and its popularity girl- rather than guy-driven, the lie would be given to claims that Fonda's sex-kitten image at the turn of the century is the byproduct of her role in Barbarella.

It didn't take me long to confirm the film's popularity—it was available at my small neighborhood video store—and doubt about its cult status was dispelled when *Entertainment Weekly* (May 17, 2003) ranked it number 40 on its list of top 50 cult movies. When my Google search turned up 104,000 links to Internet sites, I knew that *Barbarella* was a twenty-first-century phenomenon.[11]

The content of the Barbarella sites are clearly female-identified. One of the first links is to the "Barbarella Festival," an all-girl effort to stage an annual rock 'n' roll/garage band concert in Uppsala, Sweden; they signed their early press releases "the Barbarella movement." Other sites bring the movement to fans through clubs, memorabilia sales, film reviews, and shared historical/interpretive information. Notably, the Internet interest is purely in the fictional character Barbarella, with one "Barbarella Headquarters" site even stating that its purpose is "not meant to honor Jane Fonda or her political views." On one personal Web site, a blogger calling herself Barbarella posts her diary.

The lesbian appeal of the film was equally apparent on the Internet. A Google search for "Barbarella + lesbian" yielded six thousand links. The first was to the "Renaissance Lesbian Film Review," which features a 2001 essay by Agnes Vega that begins, "I remember watching *Barbarella* . . . and being really impressed [by Fonda's] cute face and her impressive tits." Seven links later, there was "Barbarella and Her Lesbian Lover," a porn site where sexually explicit photos of straight and lesbian couples were displayed. There were commercial sites for porn videos starring the actress Barbarella and advertisements for product designs with Barbarella (and Rosie the Riveter) likenesses. The blogger Barbarella's diary turned up again in this search, as did blogger-authored short stories and essays that reference in one way or another Barbarella/*Barbarella*.

Jane Fonda's relationship to the character she played in *Barbarella* is clearly a complex phenomenon involving more than one layer of mythology. On one level, the creation of Hanoi Jane entails the belief that, by her political work, Fonda betrayed the very sex-kitten image that she had helped to promote. Belief in the existence of beautiful and sexually available women is a staple of masculine culture, a fantasy that materializes in the figures cut by attractive entertainers like Fonda. When Fonda stepped out of that role and emerged as a major political figure, she, in effect, became real, thus dispelling the mythical female Other on which the very identity of some of her male fans rested.

In *Citizen Jane*, Andersen writes, "To American servicemen with Jane Fonda pinups taped to their lockers, it was as if [the 1940s screen star] Betty Grable had begun making Nazi broadcasts from Berlin." But that can't be true. As a chaplain's assistant in an artillery unit I saw the insides of more bunkers and hooches than most GIs and I remember the *Playboy* centerfolds that adorned lockers, not *Barbarella*, or any other images of Fonda. Memory, mine or anyone else's, is not a good source of evidence, of course, and material sources bearing on the question are bound to be scarce. Nevertheless, I bought an advertisement asking for photos taken by GIs of pinups displayed on their lockers in Vietnam. I got only one response and, while I can't testify to all the images in it being *Playboy* centerfolds, none of them appears to be Fonda.[12]

On a second level, the image of Fonda as a Marilyn Monroe–like sex bomb has to be understood as a post hoc cultural construct that functions mainly as an accoutrement in the mythology of *Hanoi Jane*. Going back to the supposed point-of-origin for that image—*Barbarella*—there is no way the character played by Fonda was sexually charged enough to have indelibly typed her as a real-life sex object. Nor did critics of the day see the role that way. Moreover, the sexology of Barbarella has a fascinating duality: running parallel to the heterosexual Barbarella who anchors the Hanoi Jane mythology is the bisexual Barbarella who excites the imaginations of her lesbian fans.

Although there is room for differing interpretations of *Barbarella*, it is worth noting that *Barbarella* fans have a primary relationship with the object of their affection in the sense that they are not using the film or its leading character to say something about Fonda. They have a realistic assessment of the film's quality—the blogger Barbarella calls it "one of the worst films ever made"—but an appreciation for its boundary-busting sexuality. They have little interest in Fonda but nevertheless value the film because of its marginality to mainstream gender culture. The reverse is true for those who disparage Fonda as Hanoi Jane. With *Barbarella* remembered as it is by Haddad-Garcia as "a vivid relic of the younger Jane Fonda . . . the unliberated (sic) saucy sex symbol,"[13] Barbarella becomes important as a sluttish pariah figure with which they can equate, and thereby disparage, Fonda. The sexualizing wrought by that equation can be seen years later in on-line postings at sites like forum.grunt.com, where Frank calls her a "commie, traitor bitch," OP-gunny posts a simple "(C)harlie (U)niform (N)ovember (T)ango Traitor, and Velcro hopes "the bitch will someday rush to take a vaginal suppository and neglect to read the label . . . Caution: Contains Napalm."[14]

Since *Barbarella* was released just when opposition to the war was peaking, and right on the cusp of Fonda's coming out as an antiwar activist, it is difficult to say just when she began to be sexualized by her critics. What is clear, though, is that those critics have a real stake in the maintenance of the Fonda = Marilyn Monroe = sex star equation because the Hanoi Jane betrayal figure is dependent on it. Moreover, the sexualized content of the Hanoi Jane iconography—Fonda's face on urinal stickers, arm patches with "The Bitch" with a screw between the words, "Boycott Jane Fonda: American Traitor Bitch" bumper stickers—created and distributed by her critics years later underscore its gendered qualities, invoking the long lineage of feminine betrayal figures that encompasses the Athenian Lysistrata, the legendary post-Vietnam hippie chicks who spat on Vietnam veterans, and their successors.

FROM LYSISTRATA
THE CLASSICAL LINEAGE OF FEMALE BETRAYAL STORIES

Had Jane Fonda "merely" betrayed the trust of the POWs and diminished the morale of U.S. troops by cavorting with the North Vietnamese, Hanoi Jane would probably be a footnote in history. Its perseverance as an iconic figure through which Americans continue to know and talk about the war well into the twenty-first century, however, suggests something exceptional about its qualities. There is something enduring about Hanoi Jane, and by turning to classical tales of traitorous women, such as Lysistrata, Malinche, and Tokyo Rose, we see that, in each story, the particularities of national loyalty are transcended by the more universal issues of sex and gender. The real wound threatened, if not inflicted, by each of these mythical femmes fatales is to the warrior cults that defined the masculinity of their day.

Sex (Strike) in the City

From 431 to 404 BC, war raged between Athens and Sparta. Known as the Peloponnesian War, the conflict was driven by Athenian expansionism that drained the city's resources and demoralized its citizens. Women and children on both sides bore the brunt of the home-front deprivations. Distraught by its futility, the playwright Aristophanes wrote *Lysistrata*, a play about the women of Athens who began a sex strike against the men who continued to prosecute the war.

Lysistrata is the play's heroine who calls together the women of Athens and other cities to propose that they abstain from sex to force their husbands to give up war. The idea is met with horror. "Anything, anything but that! Bid me go through the fire, if you will,—but to rob us of the sweetest thing in all the world, Lysistrata darling!" her friend Cleonice pleads.[1]

The women turn their backs on the idea (and on Lysistrata) before Lampito, from the enemy city of Sparta, turns the tide. " 'Tis a hard thing, by the two goddesses it is!" Lampito declares, "for a woman to sleep alone without ever a strong male in her bed. But there, peace must come first." Cleonice remains skeptical, prompting Lysistrata to lay out a strategy of deception by which the men's virility will be used against them: "We need only sit indoors with painted cheeks, and meet our mates lightly clad in transparent gowns of Amorgos silk and perfectly depilated; they will get their tools up and be wild to lie with us. That will be the time to refuse, and they will hasten to make peace, I am convinced of that!"—as are Cleonice and the others.

A consensus seemingly arrived at, Lysistrata administers an oath to which the women pledge allegiance: "I will have naught to do with lover or husband albeit he come to me with an erection," it begins. Following one last objection from Cleonice—"Oh! Lysistrata, I cannot bear it!"—Lysistrata completes the swearing-in ceremony by passing a bowl of wine, from which each of the enlistees sips. She then dispatches Lampito to "organize the plot" in Sparta.

A lengthy comedic scene follows when Cinesias, the husband of Myrrine, approaches. With Cinesias suffering from "obvious and extreme sexual excitement," Lysistrata orders Myrrine into combat: "To work then! Be it your task to inflame and torture and torment him. Seductions, caresses, provocations, refusals, try every means! Grant every favour,—always excepting what is forbidden by our oath on the wine-bowl." Myrrine executes the plan and, failing to secure Cinesias's promise to vote for peace, leaves him "stiff and rigid." A herald arrives from Sparta in the same condition, and with news that "everything is turned upside down at Sparta; and all the allies have erections." We must have peace, he begs. An erected Athenian magistrate now sees the "general conspiracy embracing all Greece." He calls for an assembly of envoys that will negotiate a peace and end the play.

Aristophanes wrote *Lysistrata* in 410 BC, anticipating the centuries ahead in which imaginations would twine the intrigues of sex and war. We see in Lampito's words—that peace must come to the bed before it will come to battlefield—his speculation on war as an extension of unsettled relations between the sexes. His casting of women to play both men's and women's roles suggests that gender identities are interpenetrating and that the presence of "the feminine" in "the masculine" dilutes men's will to war, an observation that will be made time and time again throughout the history of war and peace.

These subtextual qualities of *Lysistrata* are discernable in the myth of Hanoi Jane, but the themes of duplicity and treachery are still more pronounced. Lysistrata's strategy to lure the men into bed on the false promise of sex is duplicitous on its face, and her audacious plotting with the women of the enemy Spartans is just as obviously treasonous. In her turn, Jane Fonda is cast within the Hanoi Jane myth as the seductive actress who casts a spell on the boys to then betray them as a political radical; doing Lysistrata one better, she serves as her own Lampito, journeying into the enemy capital to treat with the enemy. The likeness of Aristophanes' fable to the myth of Hanoi Jane is confirmed by the recognition that Fonda's trip to Hanoi was facilitated by her prior contact with a North Vietnamese group of female cultural workers.

Lysistrata is the best-known story of war and sex in the Greek classics, but it is not the only one to problematize the relationship of women to war. Western culture's most universally recognized symbol for wartime deception is the Trojan Horse—surely a woman-horse, as the bearer of warriors from her innards (and the literary conventions that have neutered her an "it," notwithstanding). Penelope is usually regarded as a paragon of virtue for her fidelity to Odysseus, but he returns from war to find her surrounded by suitors, making his homecoming story a cautionary tale that wends its way into the culture of each military generation.[2]

Samson and Delilah

War and sex twist through Jewish and Christian mythology, as well. The classic story is about Samson and Delilah, told in the Book of Judges, chapters 13–16. Samson was born at a time when the Children of Israel were at war with the Philistines over rights to the Promised Land. An angel told his parents that Samson was special and that if he lived his life according to Nazarite law, he would do great deeds for God and his people; one of the provisions of the law was that he never cut his hair.

As Samson's hair grew, so did his strength, until he had the power of several men. He fought gallantly against the Philistines. In one battle he slew a thousand of the enemy using only the jawbone of a donkey. After the victory, God granted peace to the Children of Israel and Samson became a famous judge who ruled the land for twenty years.

But Samson wasn't perfect; he had a weakness for beautiful women and fell hopelessly in love with Delilah, a Philistine beauty. Unbeknownst to the hero, Delilah was in the hire of enemy leaders to discover the secret of his great strength. When she begged him to reveal the secret, the warrior misled her with false answers. But after several rounds of her pleading and his lies, Delilah's expressions of love and exasperation wore him down: Samson told Delilah the truth, that if his hair were cut, he would be a man of ordinary strength. When he fell asleep, Delilah betrayed Samson, ordering the Philistine soldiers to cut his hair. Shorn of his manhood, Sampson was easily captured by the enemy and put into slavery.

Eventually, Samson's hair grew back. He asked God to forgive him for his sin and give him the power to avenge the suffering he and his people had endured under the Philistines. God heard his prayer and enabled the rehabilitated Samson to pull down the enemy's temple. Samson died that day along with three thousand Philistines, but the Children of Israel were liberated, as was the land that God had given them.

Few anatomical features have more significance for our notions of sex and gender than hair: (long hair) = female, (short hair) = male. One cannot project those equations backward with any certainty that they held and meant the same things in biblical times, but paintings of biblical scenes done during the Middle Ages generally depict men with shorter hair than women. The "Power of Women" scenes from the mural painting of the Distaff House in Konstanz, for example, shows the tousled Delilah (Samson's head cradled in her lap) surrounded by Philistine soldiers whose short helmets suggest the closely cropped hair they cover. The depiction of Delilah's long hair in contrast to the short hair of the male Philistine soldiers looking on suggests some gender blending in the character of Samson, the long-haired warrior. Samson and

Delilah complicates *Lysistrata*'s association of "the masculine" with military prowess but, like *Lysistrata*, the story of Samson and Delilah tells us that "the feminine," represented as long hair, has the power to infiltrate and transform "the masculine."[3]

La Malinche

The theme of female betrayal during wartime carries over from antiquity to modernity, an indication of the primal sensibilities tapped by stories like *Lysistrata* and the centrality of Samson and Delilah to the establishment of something as basic as religious identity. The beginning of European conquest in the fifteenth century strained loyalties to old identities and brought new ones into being. As in times of old, women played leading roles in the stories spawned by those continental encounters and no figure was more enchanting and enduring than La Malinche.

The historical woman, damned in legend as La Malinche, was one of twenty maidens given to the Spanish conquistador Hernán Cortez in 1519 by the chiefs of the defeated Tabasco Indians on the Gulf Coast of what is now the Mexican isthmus. Described by Bernal Diaz del Castillo, who chronicled the conquest, as "handsome, talkative, and self-assured," the girl was christened Doña Marina and later became a mistress to Cortez, to whom she bore a son.

Doña Marina also served Cortez as a translator. As the daughter of an Aztec chief, the girl had learned Nauhautl, the Aztec language. Her mother later gave her away to another Indian group who, in turned, passed her to the Tabascoans, whose Mayan dialect she spoke by the time Cortez arrived. With Cortez was Jeronimo de Aguilar, a Spanish priest who had learned some Mayan language after being shipwrecked. Communicating through de Aguilar and Doña Marina, Cortez was able to fool the Aztec emperor Moctezuma into thinking he had come in peace. Simultaneously, the conqueror used his interpreters to build an alliance with the Campoalans, with whom he then marched on the Aztec capital, Tenochtitlan. Along the way, Doña Marina negotiated with other enemies of Moctezuma, such as the Tlaxcalans, to enlist them in the ranks of Cortez's army. After his triumph over the Indians, Cortez wrote that the success of the mission was attributable to God and Doña Marina.

Mexican popular culture would not remember her so gratefully. Doña Marina's Indian name may have been Malintzin and her allegiance to Cortez as both linguist and lover gained her the pejorative appellation "La Malinche," which was translated as either "the captain's woman" or, referring to Cortez, "Marina's captain," both of which implied disloyalty to her own people and blame for the Spanish conquest of the Aztecs. Roger Bartra points out that "the Malinche is, in Mexican legend, the Grand Whore of paganism . . . the symbol of female treachery."[4]

Like other classical figures of feminine betrayal, La Malinche is a sexualized symbol that represents the betrayal of blood purity and culture, as well as the military mission. Given to the Spanish as a virgin, she stands for the primal innocence of the indigenous people that is violated by the enemy. In the legend, her feminine vulnerability provides the alien Other an opening through which it can enter the *indegina* genetic stream and contaminate its innermost being. But like Lysistrata, who, while penetrable, is capable of penetrating the enemy perimeter, La Malinche is able to use her womanly wiles for an under-the-covers collaboration with Cortez that, her champions say, actually saved thousands of Indians previously subjugated by the Aztecs from slaughter by that imperialist tribe. The story of La Malinche, the offspring of Aztec royalty who, by a torturous course, nevertheless ends her days in the company of Spanish military elites, speaks as much to the universality of class character, and loyalty to privilege, as it does to the fluidity of the pre-Christian libido.

"Rebel Rose," "La Belle ReBelle," and the Hoopskirts of the Civil War

Episode 7 of *The Civil War*, a series produced for public television by Ken Burns in 1989, contains a segment called "The Spies" that begins with the note that Allan Pinkerton provided intelligence services for the North while Confederate spying was led by Major William Norris. At the end of the piece, we are told that Sam Davis was executed in Pulaski, Tennessee, in 1863 for spying on the South. But, other than Davis, who were the sneaks who actually did the dirty work?

Davis gets twenty-five seconds of the three-minute segment on spies, but the rest of the Civil War's history of espionage belongs to women—if we are to believe this influential series that is widely used at all levels of education in the United States today. "Spies were everywhere," the narrator intones, continuing with the words of Mary Chestnut, the South Carolinian whose wartime diary has become a primary source for historians: "Women who come before the public are in a bad box now. All manner of things, they say, come over the border under the huge hoops now worn; so they are ruthlessly torn off. Not legs, but arms are looked for under the hoops and, sad to say, found." We learn about "Rebel" Rose O'Neal Greenhow, a Washington widow, who, the Burn's production tells us, "ran a Confederate spy ring just a few blocks from the White House" and Belle Boyd, known as "La Belle ReBell," who, despite being in prison, managed to coax secrets out of Union officers and pass them in code to Richmond inside rubber balls that she tossed from her cell windows to a "shadow agent" on the outside. One Northern agent, a black servant named Mary Elizabeth Bowser, even worked inside the Confederate White House.

These were, indeed, all fascinating characters, but the fact that Ken Burns would have us know the Civil War's history of undercover operations almost solely through the figures of female spies may say more about the legacy of gender in the construction of wartime betrayal stories than anything about the Civil War. The sexuality implicit in the images generated by the stories is particularly interesting. Mary Chestnut's riddle-like description of hoopskirts concealing arms but not legs is more than a clever piece of writing; the specter of women hiding items of strategic significance in their underwear harkens forward to stories that circulated in interwar Germany about women who hid handguns under their skirts. The Freudian scholar Klaus Theweleit locates the source of those stories in the imaginations of defeated German soldiers, who he says had associated their losses on the battlefield with debased manhood and subsequently attributed their defeat to home-front betrayal. Subconsciously, Theweleit writes, they had conjured that betrayal in gendered images that included women with weapons-bearing genitalia.[5]

Women's bodies, and the clothing that covers them, have conspicuous prominence in the stories of female spies—the Civil War generation not excepted. The arsenal dispensing hoopskirts also deployed Betty Duvall's swirled hair in which "Rebel Rose" embedded the cipher warning Confederate General Toutant Beauregard of the coming Yankee army, enabling him to make the preparations for his victory at Manassas. When her spy ring was uncovered by Pinkerton and she was cornered by detectives in her Washington home, "Rebel Rose," according to the historian Harnett Kane in *Spies for the Blue and Gray*, allegedly swallowed the code she had used for messages and stuffed what remained of her surreptitious correspondence into the stocking of her assistant, Lillie. As the enemy agents closed in, Greenhow ditched her handgun in her "boudoir," foiling the detective who "searched her to her linen."[6]

Not surprisingly, the cloak-and-dagger tales-of-the-times tease us with suggestions that more than coded messages may have been passing between the female spies and their informants. "Belle Boyd," Kane writes, "was above all overwhelmingly feminine; she made good use of her womanly appeal, of which she had an enormous amount." Rose Greenhow's attractiveness, and aptitude for its strategic use, is repeatedly captured in passages such as the following:

> She was now forty-four and her wild, fresh charm had been replaced by a softened loveliness, a great elegance. Rose's figure remained excellent. Her dark hair, parted in the center, was still drawn tightly back . . . uncurled despite the current style of ringlets and whirls; it had a sprinkling of gray that she did not try to hide. And her warm lips smiled more than ever on those from whom she wanted military information.[7]

Describing her as "a woman of almost irresistible seductive powers," Kane recalls that Greenhow "entertained" (the author's quotation marks) Oregon senator Joseph E. Lane, with whom she shared "not only a mutual interest in politics but also a more personal interest," that her "intimacy" with President James Buchanan was the subject of Washington gossip, and that "she had the ability to fascinate younger men." In his PBS series, Burns tells us that she got much of her information from Senator Henry Wilson, an "infatuated suitor" who was chairman of the Senate Military Affairs Committee.[8]

Unlike Lysistrata, who is the figment of a playwright's imagination, and Malinche, who has a place in Mexican culture that is as much legendary as historical, Rose Greenhow and Belle Boyd were real undercover agents who add a degree of materiality to prevailing images of female wartime duplicity. As Confederate loyalists, they also deviate from the Delilah/Malinche model, in which Fonda is later set, which holds the treason of a woman responsible for the loss of the war. That femme fatale role in the Civil War story is filled by Pauline Cushman, surely one of the most interesting characters of the era.

Cushman was an actress in Louisville, Kentucky, a North-South crossover city where sympathizers of both sides intermingled, and political intrigue coursed the streets and clubs. Remembered in the fashion of most female spies, she is described as "a man's woman," a "well-curved brunette" with the "heavy-lidded look of the professional temptress" who was not averse to shedding a few clothes on stage. When some Southern officers offered her money to raise an on-stage toast to the Gray, the all-Blue Cushman turned the tables, informing Northern authorities of what she was about to do. Present for the performance, a federal marshal watched to see who rose to the toast, thereby identifying the secessionists in the audience. Having endeared herself to the South with the public testimony of a toast to the Confederacy, and to the North for her volunteerism as an agent-provocateur, Cushman embarked on a short-lived career in counterespionage.

Trusted by the Rebels, Cushman accepted an assignment to infiltrate their field units and collect information for the Unionists. On the pretense that she was searching for her brother, a Confederate soldier, she charmed her way from one Southern army camp to another, all the while plotting her route to General Braxton Bragg's army, whose fortifications were of particular interest to the Yankees. Along the way Cushman wooed a young quartermaster and lied her way past sentries and pickets too naïve to uncover her ruse. By the time she arrived at Bragg's position in Shelbyville, Tennessee, however, she had been captured and the maps and documents she had collected along the way were peeled out of the shoe soles where she had hidden them. Cushman was given a military trial and convicted and, by one account, sentenced to the firing squad. Soon after the trial, however, the Union army arrived and Bragg's forces abandoned her to them.

Mata Hari

The most eccentric name in the female-spy anthology is Mata Hari, believed by some to have been schooled by the Germans for espionage during World War I, by others to have been a counterspy loyal to the

French. By either account, Mata Hari packaged sex and flamboyance with ambiguous identities and thespian abilities to cut one of the most fascinating figures in the history wartime intelligence.

The spy known as Mata Hari was born Margaretha Zelle on August 7, 1876, in Leeuwarden, Netherlands. Her mother died when she was thirteen and her father abandoned her to relatives. When she turned eighteen, she married Rudolph MacLeod, a military officer, who took her to Java with their newborn son. MacLeod was abusive and unfaithful and met the attraction between Margaretha and Javanese men with physical retribution. When their first child died of suspicious causes, he blamed Margaretha and left her, taking their surviving child with him.[9]

Margaretha sought an independent livelihood and new life by moving to Paris. There she reinvented herself as Mata Hari, the exotic dancer who shimmied around a statue of the Hindu god Siva. Doffing her sarong and shawls as she shook, Mata Hari ended her act on the darkened stage, writhing in faux nakedness before the four-armed Indian deity. By some accounts, she elevated the striptease to an art form and, as her fame as a dancer faded into the shadows of younger and sexier talent, Mata Hari expanded her repertory to pleasuring men in other ways. While plying her trade in Germany in 1914, she was recruited to spy on France and even attended a school to learn the trade—or did she?

Mata Hari did return to France when the war began in August 1914. She fell in love with a Russian half her age, named Vadim, who was soon dispatched to the front, where he was wounded. Mata Hari needed special permission to visit Vadim in the hospital, because she was a civilian and under suspicion for having been in Germany just before the war. To prove her loyalty and make some quick money for her and Vadim, she agreed to carry out an espionage assignment for the French involving the seduction of the German general Moritz Ferdinand von Bission, who headed the occupation of Belgium. Under the covers, so to speak, the stripper turned spook hoped to pry some secrets out of the general.

While taking a circuitous route to Brussels, Mata Hari was arrested in Britain, in what appears to have been a case of mistaken identity. Her French handler, Georges Ladoux, gained her release and passage to Spain, where the story might have ended—except that in Madrid she entered a love affair with a German major, Arnold Kalle. From Kalle, Mata Hari learned about a German plan to transport spies, by submarine, onto the coast of French-occupied Morocco. Thinking she had scored an intelligence coup, she fed the information back to the French, but when she approached Ladoux for her reward, things began to go badly. For one thing, the submarine plot was old information that Kalle used as bait to test Mata Hari. For another, she had traded French secrets to get Kalle talking and when French counterintelligence intercepted coded messages from Kalle to Berlin, she was exposed.

So for whom was Mata Hari really working? Some biographers answer, "no one" besides herself. The jacket-cover endorsement of Russell Warren Howe's *Mata Hari: The True Story*, written by the Vietnam-era director of the CIA, William Colby, calls her "the victim of a monstrous miscarriage of justice as a result of a fraud perpetrated by French intelligence." Other historians speculate that she had been schooled for spying in Germany and was their secret agent known as H-21. When they had finished with her, they intentionally let the French "discover" her duplicity, allowing them to arrest and execute her—which is what happened.

Arrested on February 13, 1917, and held for six months in the degrading conditions of Saint-Lazare prison—she was allowed a small bowl for occasional "bathing"—Mata Hari went on trial in July of that year. The prosecution paraded former lovers, all military men, by the jury in an apparent attempt to suggest that the defendant had used sex as a weapon to loosen the tongues of her targets. She was defended by a former lover and corporate lawyer with no experience with espionage cases. Mata Hari lost her case and died by firing squad on October 15, 1917.

Mata Hari to Hanoi Jane: But First, "Tokyo Rose" and . . . "Seoul City Sue"?

The uncanny resemblance between Mata Hari and Hanoi Jane begins with the likeness of the corporeal characters behind them. Both their mothers died when they were young, leaving them with fathers who shirked their parental responsibilities. Margaretha Zelle and Jane Fonda both traveled abroad as young adults, led adventurous lives, and had identities as entertainers before they were known for their politics. With biographies tangling the wartime intrigue of their times, they met their respective "Vadims" in Paris.[10]

Unlike Zelle's self-consciously constructed Mata Hari, Fonda's Hanoi Jane was an appellation laid on her by detractors. Yet both come down to stories about the power of women to manipulate the will of men at war; stories with their own mythopoeic power to conjure dangers and deceptions through overtones of Asian exoticism. Told by almost anyone, either of the stories has enough empirical reality to it to be compelling—there really was an erotic dancer called Mata Hari who was executed for spying, and Jane Fonda really did oppose the war in Vietnam and go to Hanoi—and yet the telling of either cannot be done without generating such inviting unknowns that the mind does not run to fantasy to answer all the questions: Who was Mata Hari working for? Was she guilty of anything? Who heard Hanoi Jane on Radio Hanoi? Was she guilty of anything?

However similar the stories of Mata Hari and Hanoi Jane, it is doubtful that Fonda would have morphed into the trope that she became had "Tokyo Rose" not appeared out the ashes of post–World War II Japan. Whereas nowadays it works to cast someone like John Kerry as a traitor simply by suggesting, "He's like Jane Fonda," the earlier denigration of Jane Fonda depended on the equation of her with Tokyo Rose. Besides the generational proximity that gave the two considerable resonance, Tokyo Rose also modernized the imagery of wartime duplicity from figures like Pauline Cushman stealing into the enemy's camps and Mata Hari wooing her way into their soldiers' uniforms, to the propagandists who, far removed from their targets, used the electronic media to work the minds and emotions of their foes. The allegation that Tokyo Rose used the radio to tug at the heartstrings of GIs in Asia is what made Fonda's comparison to her so damningly effective. But who was she really and what did she do?[11]

Long after I suspected that Hanoi Jane was more right-wing figment than historical fact, I nevertheless believed that Tokyo Rose was real—in a sense making Hanoi Jane a myth deserving of a good debunking precisely because she was not like Tokyo Rose. So I was taken aback, to say the least, when a friend handed me a posting from History News Network in December 2001 that reads, "There was no Tokyo Rose." The context was the hysteria gripping the nation in the immediate aftermath of the 9/11 attacks in which rumors circulated that the hits were an "inside job." The hard version of the rumors was that traitors within the

American intelligence apparatus actually facilitated the attacks; the softer versions alleged that high-level government officials knew they were coming but did nothing to stop them—"Bush knew" was a popular anti-administration refrain at the time. The capture of John Walker Lindh, a young American who had converted to Islam and joined a Taliban unit in Afghanistan, raised questions among journalists about other Americans who, in the past, had been accused of and prosecuted for treason. News stories in the *New York Times* and other newspapers had revived the story of Tokyo Rose in the course of reporting on "Taliban John" but few of them, as the *History News Network* posting points out, bothered to tell the full story.[12]

The woman known as Tokyo Rose was really Iva Toguri, a Japanese American woman who graduated from UCLA in 1940 and went to Tokyo to care for a sick aunt five months before Pearl Harbor. Like thousands of other Japanese Americans, Iva was unable to return to the United States once the war began and, pressured by the Japanese authorities to renounce her U.S. citizenship (she refused), she took a job with a Japanese news agency. Soon, she was being asked to lend her voice to English-language shortwave-radio broadcasts to the Pacific, some of which targeted American soldiers. The propaganda operation involved the use of allied POWs to read scripts on the air, one of whom was the Australian Major Charles Cousens, who subtlety coached the readers to sabotage the authenticity of the broadcasts.

Cousens recruited Toguri precisely because she did not sound sexy and smooth and would not appeal to the ears of the soldiers and sailors in the U.S. forces—thereby again subverting the intent of his Japanese managers. Using the "stage" name Orphan Ann given her by her superiors, Iva, or Iva's voice, was used for broadcast production during the last two years of the war, although there is no evidence that she or anyone other woman ever used the name Tokyo Rose. In his definitive study of her, the historian Russell Warren Howe quotes an Office of War Information document that reads, "There is no Tokyo Rose; the name is strictly a GI invention. . . . Government monitors listening in twenty-four hours a day have never heard the words Tokyo Rose on a Japanese-controlled Far Eastern radio."[13]

In fact, the evidence that any GIs heard, or even claimed to have heard, Tokyo Rose during the war is sketchy. Nevertheless, reporters in search of a good postwar story heard rumors of the seductive Tokyo Rose and went in search of her. By chance, they "found" Toguri, who fell prey to the myth and for a promised two thousand dollars claimed the Tokyo Rose persona for herself. Within days, the Hearst-owned *Los Angeles Examiner* ran the story of Iva Toguri, the traitor.[14]

It is thus equally possible that Tokyo Rose entered the American memory of the war courtesy of reporters' imaginations as that she entered courtesy of GIs'. But whatever the origin, Tokyo Rose had a vivid existence in the minds of veterans by 1948 when the FBI asked to hear from anyone who had listened to Tokyo Rose during the war. The response, according to Russell Warren Howe was "farcical, . . . the huge pile of interviews with Pacific veterans who had listened to Japanese radio [of interest only] for a sociologist studying how a myth begins." One respondent dated his reception of Tokyo Rose to a period when Toguri was not even at the station, another recalled Rose with a "cosmopolitan accent similar to what is heard in Pennsylvania . . . with no Jap mannerisms." One veteran said his unit was convinced that Tokyo Rose was the pilot Amelia Earhart, who went down in the Pacific in 1937 while attempting to circumnavigate the globe. According to Howe, who obtained the interview documents through the Freedom of Information Act, many of the veterans were sure they had heard a female broadcaster who actually identified herself as Tokyo Rose.[15]

Tokyo Rose, like Mata Hari before her and Hanoi Jane after, lives mainly in public memory as a velvety-voiced Siren who plied the emotional vulnerability of young men far from home and scared of dying in war. In the immediate aftermath of the war, however, the minds of veterans were braiding the image of seductress-Rose with black-ops-Rose, "remembering" not only that she sweet-talked them into despondency but that she walked the counterintelligence beat as well. Accused of terrorizing GIs with promises of air attacks on their units and forecasts of their doomed landing parties, Toguri expressed doubt in postwar interviews that any such broadcasts were ever made and that, if they were, it was only local commanders who used them on very remote islands. "Tokyo Rose," she averred, existed only in the minds of GIs whose "imaginations were working overtime."[16]

Like other figures with mythical standing, the absence of evidence seems to have increased the verity of Tokyo Rose. Toguri was arrested in

1948 and taken to San Francisco, where she was tried for treason. Convicted on one vague count of "speaking into a microphone concerning the loss of ships," she was sentenced to prison and fined ten thousand dollars. Toguri served her time in the federal prison for women in Alderson, West Virginia, and then settled in Chicago to run the family's import business. President Gerald Ford pardoned her in 1977.[17]

What is fascinating is that the imaginations of men—be it the playwright Aristophanes, veterans of World War II, or the wizard of television documentary, Ken Burns—conjure the figures of wartime betrayal in gendered images and either create, in the playwright's case, or foreground, in the historian's case, the sexual themes in the stories they tell. That women are so popularly represented in the anthologies of espionage is remarkable enough but that Malinche is rendered la Chingada, "Rebel Rose" is identified by her "seductive powers," and Mata Hari the traitor is preceded in that legend by Mata Hari the stripper, ad infinitum, suggest a quality in the canon of wartime treachery that begs more attention than it has received.

Thus, it is not Everyday Delilahs or Citizen Janes who ascend as apparitions in the collective conscious but female figures who use their extraordinary sexual power as a weapon against men, their own men, the very men they birthed and bathed. Tokyo Roses and Hanoi Janes are manufactured in the space where mind and emotions meet, the cradle of anxiety that nurtures male fears that their separation from the amniotic existence of fore-life—the separation that is life itself—is incomplete and tenuous and subject to take-back by the same femaleness that gave it.

And "Seoul City Sue"? Well, what better validation could there be than Sue's appearance on the television series M*A*S*H that, by the Vietnam era, the image of a radio demoness broadcasting from the enemy capital had the status of a cultural trope. M*A*S*H was set in the Korean War but universally understood to be an allegory for the war in Vietnam. Her name was an appropriation of the popular 1950s hit "Sioux City Sue," the title song of a film starring the country-western singer Gene Autry. The song had particular resonance for minor-league baseball fans in the Midwest who knew the New York Giants affiliate in the Double-A Western league as the Sioux City Soos.

Sue comes on the air in "38 Across," the double-entendred episode that opens with the M*A*S*H team in the operating room, where they are finishing repairs on an anesthetized Chinese POW with a head injury. As they cut and stitch, they are also helping the doctors Hawkeye Pierce and B.J. Hunnicutt, two of the show's main characters, finish a *New York Times* crossword puzzle for which they need one more word—38 across: the five-letter Yiddish word (first letter *v*) for bedbug.[18]

By the end of the episode, the Chinese patient has been exchanged for an American POW, Klinger has tried to eat a Jeep—literally, in one of his stratagems to get sent home from Korea as unfit for service, to eat the component parts of a Jeep beginning with the lug-nuts from the wheels and working up to the windshield wipers—and the crossword puzzle is complete. With the cast assembled around a mess hall table we hear the camp radio: "This is Seoul City Sue with a special message for the M*A*S*H* 4077. One of the prisoners you have returned has had head surgery for the purpose of inhuman experiment. We brand Colonial Hawkeye Pierce a war criminal." Sue is broadcasting from enemy territory, of course, across the 38th parallel that hardened into a boundary separating North and South Korea—providing the other inspiration for this episode's title.

But was there really a "Sue?" The August 21, 1950, edition of *Time* magazine reported soldiers of the U.S. Army's 1st Cavalry Division tuning in to hear her—but then one of the sources for the story claimed to have heard Tokyo Rose a few years earlier, even comparing their voice qualities (he thought Rose was better). Knowing as we do now that there was no Rose, we have to wonder how dependent the belief in Sue was on belief in Rose.

By the time "38 Across" aired in the mid-1970s, Sue's sister seductress "Hanoi Hannah" was making her way into American popular culture, so it is possible that M*A*S*H writers were using Sue as Hannah's stand-in—that is what M*A*S*H writers did, after all. By that time, though, Hanoi Jane was also in play, making it possible that we were not supposed to think "Hannah" at all.

BETEL NUTS
AND RAZOR BLADES
SEX AND DANGER,
AIRBORNE RANGER

I wanna be an airborne ranger,
I wanna live on sex and danger.
Airborne!
All the Way!
—*Marching cadence, U.S. Army, 1968*

Sex and danger seem to go together in the public imaginings of American military life: the lore of young men
separated from home and family for military duty is
readily associated with the occasions for "first sex";
next to the pawn shops and storage lots abutting military bases, the mind's eye sees peep shows and whore-
houses; beside the image of the man in uniform fur-
loughed home before overseas deployment are the
figures of girls bedazzled by epaulets and chevrons.

Hollywood film has probably done more than any
other medium to wed the two. In the 1949 John Wayne
classic *Sands of Iwo Jima*, Sergeant Stryker's marine
squad is retraining in New Zealand just before its as-
sault on Tarawa. On the eve of their departure, the
unit is given "liberty" in Wellington, where they are
drawn to a servicemen's club for booze and women.
Swept to the dance floor by a pretty New Zealander,
the young and innocent Private Conway falls in love
and within hours is contemplating marriage. Rumi-
nating on the step he is about to take, Conway wonders aloud to a buddy why men get married during

wartime. "It's the worst time," he says, before answering his own question: "I think it's when you get out here you realize deep down inside maybe you want to leave a little bit of yourself behind, it doesn't matter if it's a boy or a girl."

The trend away from post–World War II simplicity began with Brian De Palma's 1968 film *Greetings*, in which a Vietnam veteran schmoozes with some draft-age peers. In this apolitical scene, there are neither girls agog on the soldier's shoulder nor spit on his lapel. In *The Activist* and *Alice's Restaurant*, both 1969 films, we are shown Vietnam veterans with comfortable relationships with female antiwar activists, and in *The Revolutionary* (1970) Jon Voight plays an army deserter who has joined a leftist antiwar organization and met Helen, who shelters him from the authorities in the home of her wealthy parents.

Yet as the war ground toward its end, the modestly political imagery of Vietnam veterans' relationships with women took a turn toward sex and violence that would dominate war films for decades. The powerful first entrée on that list was Chris and Eliza Kazan's *The Visitors* (1972), in which Mike and Tony appear at the doorstep of their erstwhile army buddy Bill and his wife, Martha. Bill's testimony had put Mike and Tony behind bars for their part in a My Lai–type atrocity; having served their time, the culprits have come for revenge. Bill is their principle target, but when they learn that Martha was an activist who had opposed the war they had just fought, they berate war protesters as "long-haired freaks, almost like Indians" and then rape her before bludgeoning Bill. The use of rape by Vietnam veterans for the purpose of redressing their own defeat—personal defeat, for Mike and Tony, but sociopolitical defeat in the contemplations of the nation facing its first lost war—took the filmic interplay of sex, violence, and experience at war to levels it had never been to.

Martin Scorsese followed that trajectory into the cirrostratus with *Taxi Driver* (1978), in which Robert DeNiro plays the crazed Travis Bickle, a demented Vietnam veteran who gets involved with a twelve-year-old prostitute before ending the film in an orgy of guns and blood.[1] Unlike *The Visitors*, in which the script links the rape of Martha to Mike and Tony's gendered images of the home-front betrayal, *Taxi Driver* leaves to our imagination the connection between Bickle's sexual dysfunction and his Vietnam experience. That connection is more explicit in *Coming Home*, also from 1978, which gives us Marine Captain Bob Hyde (Bruce Dern), who returns from Vietnam to find that his wife, Sally (Jane Fonda), has been opposing the war and is in a relationship with Luke (Jon Voight). Bob presents symptoms of sexual impotence before retrieving an automatic weapon from the foot locker he has shipped home from Vietnam and threatening to kill Sally and Luke. In the end, Bob walks into the ocean, taking his own life.[2]

The interconnecting imagery of war-related trauma and sexual violence may have reached its dramatic apex in *Coming Home*. In its wake, there followed a generation of on-screen veterans inadaptable to the civilian world: some, like the drifters in *Ruckus* (1980), *Americana* (1981), and *The Pursuit of D. B. Cooper* (1981), were relatively benign, whereas others were unfit for anything but more war—be it war on the home front as it was for Rambo in *First Blood* (1982) or the continuation of war back in "the 'Nam" as it was for Sergeant Frantz in *Hamburger Hill* (1987). The psychosexual carnage of the war itself is deepened by the women who betray veterans in *Alamo Bay* (1985), *Cease Fire* (1984), and *Betrayed* (1988).

Sex and the Military Inductee

Film is a powerful medium, a point made by the frequency with which Hollywood-made Vietnam War scenes that are not in the historical record appear nonetheless vivid in the memories of veterans.[3] But the sexualized impressions of military experience embedded in popular culture are not entirely fictive. Vietnam-era draftees had to wait only a few hours after induction to learn that they were now "swinging dicks" and within days they knew the difference between a gun and their weapon:

> this (grab your rifle) is a weapon,
> this (grab your crotch) is your gun.
> this (your rifle) is for fighting
> this (your crotch) is for fun.

In chaplain's assistant school at Fort Hamilton, we trainees were awakened one summer morning in 1968 with the first sergeant's melodious

call:

Drop your cocks and
Grab your socks;
It's time to rock.

Many marching songs had sexual themes that repeated juvenile ditties such as:

I know a girl who lives on a hill,
She won't do it but her sister will.

Some of the cadences are remembered as "Jodies" because they referred to Jody, the mythical boy back home who had taken the girlfriend or wife:

Johnny got a letter that drove him crazy
Suzie's pregnant with Jody's baby.

Ain't no use in calling home
Jody's got your girl and gone
Ain't no use in feeling blue
Jody's got your sister too.

The Jody legend does more, of course, than keep recruits in step on the parade grounds. The acculturation of trainees to military life entails their bonding with fellow soldiers and subordination to the authority of officers; it is a passage that is as much about separation from what was—family ties, loyalties to peers, and young loves—as it is attachment to what is new—the dependence on comrades-in-arms for personal survival and success of the mission. The inducement of distrust and suspicion of all things civilian facilitates that transition for the inductee.

Basic training operates as a cultural threshold across which the recruit passes into the disciplined self-denial that defines the life of the warrior. On the warrior side, pursuit of pleasure is a thing of the past; pleasure for the young fighter, if it be had at all, is found in the power of the mind to defer gratification, the satisfaction that the will to control can triumph over the emotions and desires of the flesh. And nothing constitutes a stronger test of the will than the desire for flesh. Warrior culture is a male preserve—no girls allowed—and sex, being the most powerful of all instincts, represents a challenge to the protection of that closed society. Women are dangerous, allowed into the discourse only when represented as the whore-enemy now in Jody's bed—where she belongs.[4]

The sexualizing of military induction also helps it operate as a generational rite of passage. Mothers, sisters, and the girls on the block may have been role players in the arousal of the pubescent male imaginations now in the tutelage of a drill sergeant, but attachment to the opposite sex for nurturance is different from attraction to it as an object eroticized by libidinal cathexis. Attraction *to* presumes a prior separation *from*, a change in the relationship of young men to women that the military experience helps to define, and that, in turn, helps form the consciousness of manhood.

The particular reconfigurations given male-female relations by wartime conditions and military institutions may well be a constant across the ages—from Lysistrata's sex strike in the Peloponnesian War to Mata Hari's turning from stripper to spy in World War I. But the extraordinary length of the Vietnam War and its guerrilla warfare combined to give it, and its postwar representations, a sexual tonality that set it apart from anything that had gone before.

The Girls at the Gate

Before Vietnam, the great American wars were about taking terrain from the enemy and moving on to the next engagement. During World War II, for example, the 25th Infantry Division was dispatched to Guadalcanal in the Solomon Islands in January 1943. By July, the island had been taken from the Japanese, and the division had moved on to other islands in the chain. By the end of the year, the 25th was in New Zealand for rest. In 1944 it retrained on the small Oceania Island of New Caledonia before shipment to the Philippines in January 1945 for a fight-and-move campaign that ran to the end of the war five months later.[5]

Vietnam, by contrast, was a body-count war. A hill on which a hundred enemy Vietnamese were killed today could be abandoned by the Americans only to be retaken a month later with more enemy killed—it was the kills that counted, not the hills. The same U.S. units stayed in the same areas of operation, sometimes taking and retaking the same hills and valleys for years.

In Vietnam, the 25th Infantry Division moved into Cu Chi in January 1966 and stayed until April 1971, establishing a large sprawling complex that, over the years, employed thousands of Vietnamese women and mediated the off-base contact between thousands more GIs and female civilians. The 25th's five years in Cu Chi were twice as long as its entire World War II deployment that spread across three different countries and many islands.

Even though most GIs were in-country for only a year, there was a degree of institutional regularity to American-Vietnamese relations that quickened acquaintanceships between the troops and the local people. By the end of his first day, a replacement soldier arriving at his new unit was likely to have been introduced by the "short-timers," GIs who were nearing the end of their year-long tours of duty and were about to go home, to the "girl-san" who swept the hooch. At guard posts and checkpoints throughout the country, local kids on a first-name basis with the Americans in the sandbag bunkers appeared daily, as if by appointment, looking for handouts or selling whatever they could. Even occasional visitors to those posts, as I was, might be casually introduced, just as if meeting someone's friend or neighbor in a stateside setting.[6] Through body language and the pidgin combinations of English, Vietnamese, and French that the GIs and Vietnamese girls could confect, the exchanges could quickly turn flirtatious.

From the point of view of the U.S. military brass, the danger in those situations was that security could be compromised by the "loose lips" of GIs overly eager to make friends, and the familiarity with the architecture of military sites that kids in-service to the Viet Cong could come away with. From the Vietnamese side, the situation was more complicated. On one hand, the presence of foreigners with deadly firepower in their hands was a danger to the children and others who fraternized with them, and the encampments of the Americans in and near their communities spelled a kind of in-your-face cultural dominance that was probably offensive and dispiriting. On the other hand, the material deprivations wrought by the war made the meager exchanges of cigarettes for gum a welcome stimulus to the economies of some families and villages.[7]

And smokes and sugar were not the only things exchanged. What began as a glance across the sandbags could escalate to a kiss around the gate post and sex in town the next time the trooper could get there. Like most sex, that between GIs and civilian Vietnamese was a complex intermingling of desires, emotions, and needs. The large number of American-Vietnamese marriages that came out of war testifies to the strength of the affection between many of the couples, and the length to which some American veterans went to find former lovers and the children they had fathered speaks volumes about the emotional depth of those relationships.[8] But it wasn't all innocence either. Vietnamese women were quite expressive of their desire to get to the United States. The promise, "I marry you GI," carried the mixed messages of proffered sex as well as emigration to the United States as the soldier's war bride—if and when that could be arranged. Off-base, most GIs heard Vietnamese boys offering their sisters for sex in exchange for money; rumors of virtual sex camps run by the U.S. military for prostitution have circulated for years.[9]

The extent of prostitution in Vietnam remains a disputed subject. Assigned to an artillery unit in 1969, I had more mobility than most Americans and greater access to information, which ranged from rumored to classified. I moved on a weekly rotation from base camps to fire bases and landing zones to the cities of Qui Nhon, Nha Trang, Ban Me Thout, and Phan Thiet. Rumor among the enlisted men at the 41st Artillery Group Headquarters had it that their officers bought sex from the girls who worked in the camp. It was also rumored that the guys who drove the camp workers to and from the village would steal some time for sex along the route. But who knows? And who could, even then, disentangle the trysts from the trades in those encounters. In the fashion of schoolyard romances, we all "knew" that Mai was Kenny's girlfriend—with no more to go on than the smiles that passed between them. What is clearest in my memory is that contact between GIs and civilians—on and off base—was narrowly circumscribed by military regulations, with the opportunities for sex being minimal.[10]

It may well be that the most salient fact in the matter of sex and the GI in Vietnam is that young men are likely to exaggerate the manly impressions they left with Vietnamese women. And, as is the wont of manly impressions, the older they get, the bigger they were. Consider that five men go into an alleged brothel in Nha Trang. One goes behind the curtains and comes out smiling. The other four know nothing about why he is smiling—for all they know, she might have paid him for the Ipana moment that would lure them and their friends behind the curtain. It is not hard to imagine, either, that with five smiles walking out the doorway, it was also the moment when the number of veterans who would some day tell of the night they spent in a whorehouse had increased.[11]

Booby-trapped Boom Boom

David Cline was a Vietnam veteran and leading antiwar activist. In a 2004 interview he recounted his 1967 arrival in Vietnam as a replacement soldier for the 25th Infantry Division. Newly arriving troops were given an orientation session in which sergeants who had been "in-country" for a while emphasized that the Vietnamese could not be trusted. They weren't really people, Cline recalled being told; they were "gooks" and "dinks." The Vietnamese were treacherous; they would sell you Coca Cola with ground glass in it and put razor blades in their vaginas.

By the time I read Cline's interview, the legend of razor-bladed Vietnamese vaginas had been dispelled for me, but there was a time when I believed it to be true. In the summer of 1969, my unit got a one-day R&R at the beach in Qui Nhon. We were trucked to and from the beach, where U.S. Military Police made sure that the Vietnamese stayed on the city side of the street and we on the sandy side. Nevertheless, one of our guys managed to slip into town and missed the ride home. Later that night or the next day, the rumor circulated that he had returned to camp with a sliced penis; seems Vietnamese girls working for the Viet Cong would put razor blades in potatoes and embed the spiked spuds in their vaginas. What, if anything, in the rumor was true I do not know, but in retrospect I understand how it worked as a cautionary tale about Vietnamese duplicity as well as a lesson to be learned about what happens to those who disobey orders. The story is also an interesting counterweight to the widespread belief in later years that the U.S. military condoned and even sponsored easy access to sex with the Vietnamese. Whatever else the military brass intended by telling, rather than quelling such stories, they certainly inhibited GIs' desire for sex with local women.

Coincidentally or not, the legends of lethal female genitalia are deeply rooted in rural Asian culture, where the participation of women in public affairs was traditionally suppressed. According to one theory, these "denied voices" came to be imagined as mouths without teeth—the absence of teeth being suggestive of more general oral incapacitation. According to the theory, men in those cultures were advantaged by the inequalities of gender and came to repress to their unconscious their fears of female retribution. Those repressed fears are what subsequently appear in the male imagination as images of female body parts to which the missing teeth have removed. Those same cultures give rise to legends of the "shrinking penis" and even epidemics of "penis panic," whereupon men express exaggerated fears of losing their genitalia or even that it will recede into their body. The gendered symmetry provided by the legends suggests the centrality of sexual anxiety to their origins.[12]

The idea of anatomical instability has a long standing in mythology and folklore, appearing in beliefs such as "the wandering womb," an understanding of hysteria held by some, well into the nineteenth century, that certain female maladies were due to the migration of the uterus throughout the body—it could be in the wrist one day, the neck the next—causing paralysis or tics wherever it settled down. Freud wrote about the fantasy of teeth in vaginas as *vagina dentata* in *Three Essays on the Theory of Sexuality*. It was a myth, he said, that expressed the male fear of castration, a fear formed at an early age when boys see their first female bodies, sans penis. Fearing that the same could happen to them—after all, if the insertion of the penis into the vagina could result in its shrinkage, why not loss of the whole thing—the imagination conjures vaginal capacities to cut it off. In some Native American cultures, there is even the belief that the vagina can chew and digest the severed units.[13]

As mythology, the *vagina dentata* imagery has proven impervious to modern science, and its utility for the representations of female power and treachery in popular culture is undiminished. In the 1992 film *Basic Instinct*, for example, a Los Angeles police detective, Nick Curran, played by Michael Douglas, is trapped in the machinations of the detective writer Catherine Tramell (Sharon Stone) and the police department's psychiatrist, Beth Garner (Jeanne Tripplehorn). Dr. Garner has leaked Curran's psychiatric profile to the writer. Feeling betrayed, Curran retreats to his apartment for an evening of booze and television reruns.

When Garner drops in to explain and apologize, Curran roughs her up, tells her to leave, and then falls into a drunken stupor. To make sure the audience interprets his pain as gender inflicted, the filmmakers fill his television screen with scenes of a toothed vagina from the 1987 horror film *Hellraiser*.

Women Who Chew and Spit

In the spring of 2005, Jane Fonda was touring the country to promote her new autobiography, *My Life So Far*. At a stop in Kansas City she was approached by Michael Smith, who bought her book and asked for an autograph. After she signed, he spat in her face. Smith was arrested and later told reporters he had done it as payback for the way veterans were greeted by protesters when they returned from Vietnam. A veteran himself, Smith said he returned from Vietnam through Los Angeles airport where, "people were lined up to spit on us." "Most veterans were spat on," he said.

Stories of spat-upon Vietnam veterans began appearing around 1980. For my book *The Spitting Image* I looked back on the time when the spit was supposedly flying, the late 1960s and early 1970s, and found very little. There was one news report of a spitting incident and a few second-hand claims of someone being spat on. Characteristic of urban legends, the point of origin of the stories in time and place was obscure, even though the details in the stories were often similar. Like Smith's, many of the stories lack credibility. GIs landed at military bases, not civilian airports, and protesters could not have gotten anywhere near deplaning GIs. And it is not true that most veterans were spat on—or even felt that way. A 1971 Harris poll conducted for the Veterans Administration found over 90 percent of Vietnam veterans reporting a friendly homecoming. The truth is that the antiwar movement reached out to recruit veterans and tens of thousands of them joined in opposition to the war.[14]

The image of the spat-upon veteran persists as an icon through which many people remember the loss of the war, the centerpiece of a betrayal narrative that understands the war to have been lost because of treason at home. Many tellers of the spitting tales identify the culprits as girls, a curious quality to the stories that gives away their gendered subtext. Moreover, the spitting images that emerged a decade after the troops had come home from Vietnam are similar enough to the legends of defeated German soldiers defiled by women on their return from World War I to suggest something universal and troubling at work in their making. Klaus Theweleit examined those stories for his book *Male Fantasies* and concluded they helped construct an alibi for Germany's defeat: the military mission had been subverted by disloyal fifth-columnists. The war's loss was perceived by some men to be a loss of manhood, a blow to their masculinity inflicted by their gendered opposite, "the feminine" in the culture. Thus, according to Theweleit, veterans' reports of women spitting on them were fantasies, conjured emanations of unconscious male insecurities that had been heightened by wartime defeat.

Locating the source of betrayal imagery in the subconscious does not, however, rule out the role that real-life experiences may have played in arousing something deeply repressed, and vivifying it for projection through storytelling. In the 1960s, and especially in rural areas, many Vietnamese women chewed a psychoactive nut from the betel palm tree, producing red-colored sputum that had to be regularly expectorated—spat, as it were. The sputum also turned the teeth black and rotted the gums, accelerating dental deterioration. Whether so many partially toothed women prompted Americans to wonder where the teeth had gone, and pried to consciousness the images of migrant teeth, we cannot know. We do know that spitting in most of the United States is viewed so universally as a male behavior that the saying "Girls can't spit" has the status of a cultural trope. With the possible exception of soldiers who grew up in the rural south, few GIs would ever have seen women spit, and on seeing such, may well have taken it to be masculine behavior.[15]

The American war in Vietnam formed the bridge across which the cultural practices of both countries passed from one to another. For some soldiers, the encounter with chewing women was a formative experience, an initiation rite of sorts into the "otherness" of Vietnamese culture. The sight of women chewing and spitting was so remarkable that the 1967 Marine Corps "Unit Leaders Personal Response Handbook" reportedly included a seven-hundred-word explanation of the practice that thoughtfully called it a "blending of the past, the present, and the future with an infusion of religious, cultural, and economic overtones."[16] The impressions left by betel-nut-chewing women were carried home by GIs and suffused through their stories into the American awareness of the practice. Excerpts from an Internet posting in 2006 suggest the indelibility of those impressions on veterans' memories:

My first experience with betel nut was in Vietnam. With only a few days in country, I tagged along with a Vietnamese reconnaissance platoon and one U.S. Sergeant for an ambush. . . . As I approached a house with half a squad of Vietnamese, I looked down and saw a large splotch of red colored liquid which I took to be fresh blood. Motioning for the squad to stand fast, I excitedly called up the sergeant, reporting that I had found a blood trail. The Vietnamese troopers looked at me and grinned. When a passing peasant woman let loose a long stream of liquid that splashed an identical red splotch on the pathway, the Vietnamese troopers laughed hysterically and quickly spread the news throughout the platoon.[17]

But not all the memories are so benign—or even as plausible. In *Marine Sniper*, his "true story" written in 1988, Charles Henderson describes the attack on a marine squad near Chu Lai. The Viet Cong platoon is led by a woman the marines called Apache. Three marines are wounded and one is captured. Later, in the dark of the night, the captured marine is heard screaming in pain. The marines' gunnery sergeant, Hathcock, exclaims, "That bitch! That filthy-assed Communist whore!" after which the author describes what was happening to the captured American.

The Viet Cong woman had pried off each of his fingernails and was in the process of bending his fingers backward, snapping them at their middle joints. . . . The woman chewed betel nut, spitting the juice between her feet as she squatted with her arms resting across the tops of her knees. She looked at the youthful Marine. "You cherry boy? I think maybe so. You get plenty pussy back stateside, yeah. You get Vietnamese pussy too? I think you do. You go China Beach swimming, fuck plenty. . . .

She shouted in Vietnamese at the men squatted by her, and they glared at the Marine. The woman walked to where the boy hung limp on the bamboo rack and spit a mouthful of betel nut into his eyes. "You goddamn-fucking GI!" she said.[18]

This scene is fictional, of course: Henderson's creation of what Hathcock is imagining, or Henderson's imagining what Hathcock could have been imagining. What is interesting about this all-male imagining is that its coup d'image is an enemy woman spitting betel nut juice at a helpless marine.

The War on Duplicity

The yearlong proximity to toothless spitting women with dangerous genitalia may well have aroused some apprehensions about the opposite sex that young GIs did not know they had. But there were other aspects of the war that were probably more salient in priming their receptivity to the betrayal narrative they would consider years later as veterans.

In its aftermath, many Americans came to understand the war in Vietnam as an act of aggression that the United States had pursued for its own economic and political interests. Vietnam was rich with natural resources that included the climate and soil for intensive agricultural production, while the conditions of its underdevelopment promised cheap labor to manufactures and, in the long term, a lucrative sales market. To take advantage of those opportunities, the United States would have to stabilize the political situation by putting in place a governmental regime that would be friendly to outside interests.

At the time, though, U.S. public opinion was driven by cold war preoccupations, and the war was sold to voters as a war to defend a nation called South Vietnam against the aggression of a communist North Vietnam. In turn, North Vietnam was itself understood by most people to be a hostage of Soviet and Chinese communism. The war, in short, was about communism and the need to defend against its spread. Americans coming of age during the 1950s and early 1960s, furthermore, had little sense of communism as a socioeconomic system with a base of popular support among workers and peasants. Rather, they thought of it as pernicious belief system, a set of vile and corrupting ideas that were spread by deception. Like the biblical Antichrist that presented himself as "good" in order to trick God's people into following him, communism was an incarnation of evil that deceived good people into doing bad things. Communism was duplicitous and communists were dupes.

Framed by the presumption that the conflict was about ideas, the American war in Vietnam came to be known as a war for hearts and minds. Although it was fought with the material trappings characteristic of all wars, the objectives of the military operations were always the political and ideological sentiments of the people. One pillar of the early strategy in the South, for example, was the so-called strategic hamlet program, which removed people from their farms and villages and congregated them in guarded compounds—thereby quarantining them from the lure of communist propaganda. Meanwhile, elements of the U.S. military were mustered for good works among the people—MEDCAP missions that took medicines, food, building supplies, and educational programs to the Vietnamese.[19]

Spies and Counterspies

The war against the North, exposed years later in declassified documents, was also premised on the understanding that its communist leaders maintained their control and command of the people for their war of expansionism through a system of lies and deceptions. If the people could see and hear the truth, American planners reasoned, they would abandon the war effort and turn on their leaders. The two-pronged U.S. strategy against the North followed that presumption: impose enough hardship through the bombing campaign that the leadership in Hanoi would be discredited for its inability to protect the people, while simultaneously bringing the truth to the people through clandestine informational campaigns. The most ingenious tactics involved "black operations" designed to induce paranoia in the communist leadership, causing it to act more repressively against the populous and thereby foment discontent that would eventually lead to open rebellion. One of those tactics was to parachute ice blocks into remote areas of the North. The empty parachute, found long after the ice had melted, would raise the suspicion that a spy had landed and was now secretly operating in the area. The hunt for the spy would pit village leaders against residents, divisions that the Americans hoped would erode the social solidarity of the North and weaken its war effort.[20]

Not all U.S. efforts against the North were as evanescent as ice blocks. Suspecting that the North infiltrated secret agents into the South to stir up the peasants, the CIA adopted the maxim "If they can do it, so can we" and began infiltrating teams of friendly Vietnamese agents into the North, where they were supposed to gather intelligence and carry out psychological operations against the civilian population. Contact with many of those teams was soon lost, however, leading to speculation that they had defected to the North and maybe reinfiltrated into the South as counterspies. In short, the U.S. war for hearts and minds, based as it was on the notion that communism was first and foremost a social system of lies and deceptions, grew into a classic case of what is known in the espionage business as "blowback"—the very paranoia that the United States hoped to induce in the North came home to haunt the Americans, infecting everything about their conduct of the war.[21]

Postmortems on the United States' lost cause in Vietnam revealed that high levels of the South Vietnamese military and government had been infiltrated by the communists; but that was only the tip of iceberg. Communists had played a leading role in defeating the Japanese occupation during World War II and then expunging the French after the war, accomplishments that gave them widespread credibility; many if not most Vietnamese viewed the Americans as the latest in that long line of foreign occupiers who needed to be expelled. Far from cooperating with the U.S. military and the government it propped up in Saigon, the Vietnamese in the rural South were waging an armed struggle against the Americans. The hardships wrought by the war caused people to move from one side to another and back again in search of security and daily sustenance, a fluidity to the situation that made it difficult to stabilize the loyalty of large numbers of people. American combat units sometimes complained about the reliability of their South Vietnamese allies, reporting that they would flee rather than fight when the going got tough. In cities and base camps, GIs were routinely warned by officers and NCOs to watch what they said around the Vietnamese civilians lest some of the friendly camp workers turn out to be imposters spying for the Viet Cong.

In retrospect, it is clear that the Vietnamese were doing what occupied people had done since the "Swamp Fox," General Francis Marion, helped drive the Redcoats out of South Carolina during the American Revolution: use their popularity with the people and familiarity with the terrain to wage a hit-and-hide war of attrition against a better-provisioned foe. It was guerrilla warfare for which deception is a defining characteristic and the blurring of identities is a fundamental tactic: the lines of identity separating combatants and noncombatants, leaders and followers, home front and battle front, all become subject to strategic considerations. As those dichotomies soften, the sex-gender boundaries that are both exploited by, and constructed through, the production of conventional-war culture also fade: the merging identities of civilians and warriors, planting fields and killing fields, also break down the distinctiveness of gender identities. Indeed, guerrilla warfare plies the gender boundaries for tactical advantage, turning the conventional perception of women as homebound dependents into a vulnerability that can be exploited.[22]

Paranoia strikes deep | Into your life it will creep

Those lines from Buffalo Springfield's "For What It's Worth," popular in 1966, became the representative lyrics of the Vietnam-war years. By the late 1960s, the war against communist duplicity had become for many U.S. soldiers a war against the war—or at least a war against the authority figures responsible for the war's conduct. Rank-and-file resistance to military authority spread as U.S. losses mounted and the numbers of draftees in Vietnam with prior exposure to the antiwar movement at home increased. First briefed on the treachery of the communist enemy by the brass, replacement troops were then briefed on the treachery of the brass by their lower-ranking peers. Fearing the harassment of rear echelon officers and NCOs that many GIs saw as provocations setting them up for military discipline, some men choose to stay in the field, where the exposure to combat was greater and the pettiness of "lifers" more restrained.

The drug culture that permeated the later years of the war added to the paranoid atmosphere enveloping the experience of young Americans in Vietnam. Reputationally at least, lifers were known to be heavy drinkers, an image with a sort of generational stigma that the younger conscripts defined themselves against. By the late sixties, moreover, the popularity of marijuana among the newer troops added a degree of separation between those who were there by choice and those who but for chance of life or lottery would have been somewhere else. The convergence of rank and habits, in turn, meant that drinkers had authority over smokers. With no private space, smokers were subject to a regime of search and surveillance and everyone became suspect as a "narc," an undercover stoolpigeon of the brass. Rumors about the next surprise "inspection" were rife in base camps and staying "straight" meant isolation from the "heads" who distrusted all but their own.[23]

By the fall of 1969 some troops in Vietnam were refusing to carry out orders, while others carried out "fraggings," violent attacks on their officers and NCOs. Fearing for their safety, officers amped up their tactics, sometimes locking away weapons and ammunition from their own troops. On occasion, perimeter guards were as alert to who might be sneaking up behind them as to who was in the dark bushes in front of them. The hyper-vigilance that many men returned with from Vietnam—usually attributed to combat experience and associated with post-traumatic stress disorder—could, for some, have been a normal response to the edginess of life in a paranoid military environment.[24]

If Vietnam had primed veterans to be receptive to betrayal stories about who did what to whom over the course of the war, the home-front culture to which they returned was hardly an antidote. The anti-communist hysteria of the 1950s had left many Americans jumpy, but government prosecutions of liberal film makers, militant trade unionists, and political college professors made those who would later lead the opposition to the war in Vietnam particularly sensitive to who was saying what about whom. The assassination of President John F. Kennedy in 1963 created a wake of rumors about the involvement of the CIA in the shooting that merged with those implicating the FBI in the killing of Malcolm X two years later. And "the sixties" were just getting started.[25]

By the time large numbers of troops began returning from Vietnam in 1970, the involvement of the FBI and Chicago Police in the assassination of the Black Panther leader Fred Hampton fueled internecine fighting over who was or was not a police informant that had torn the organization apart. Government documents later released through the Freedom of Information Act revealed that New Left antiwar organizations, such as Students for a Democratic Society, had been infiltrated by government agents who planted false stories in the press to discredit leaders. The Watergate affair that eventually brought down the presidential administration of Richard Nixon revealed a regime of spying and political chicanery that included the planting of William Lemmer as an agent provocateur in Vietnam Veterans Against the War (VVAW). In the month leading to the 1972 Republican National Convention in Miami Beach,

Lemmer encouraged VVAW members to commit acts of violence at the convention that would then lead to a police crackdown. Instead, the conspiracy to destroy VVAW added to length of the indictment against the Nixon administration.[26]

The centrality of drugs to the counterculture of the late 1960s and early 1970s added to the climate of suspicion and distrust that the politics of the times were breeding. Reaching levels of unprecedented popularity in the populations of middle-class, college-aged people, marijuana and hallucinogenic drugs heightened the paranoiac sensitivities of users who were already on guard against parental figures and political authorities. It was a social scene all too receptive to the many Vietnam veterans who had smoked their first joint on guard duty and were still looking over their shoulder for the first sergeant.[27]

Even the Women Must Fight

The thought of Vietnam being America's first lost war was enough to evoke feelings of having been betrayed from those committed to its cause. The anguish of that unprecedented outcome increased in the postwar years with the growing perception that Vietnamese women had played central roles in the defeat of the Americans. This sense—that America's only lost war had been lost to an army of women—helped gender the war's remembrance for which Hanoi Jane became symbolic.

The Trung Sisters

Soon after seeing his first spitting woman and hearing his first story of sexual sabotage, the newly arrived GI probably heard that Vietnam's George Washington was a woman. For me, it was at a roadside stop near Qui Nhon where the chaplain I was assigned to interpreted for me a sculpted relief portraying the history of Vietnam. "See here," he said, pointing to the beginning of the story, "these are the Trung sisters who led the war of independence against the Chinese." He went on to explain that that formative moment begat a society in which women are considered differently than in our own, one in which women as fighters is not so strange.

The chaplain was a career man, an army major, and the fact that he knew this important facet of Vietnamese history and culture, and thought it important enough to convey to me, is indicative of some level of consciousness within the officer ranks that the war had gendered dimensions to it. The legend of the Trung sisters has a basis in the historical record: the aristocratic sisters Trung Trac and Trung Nhi led a first-century rebellion against the Chinese Han Dynasty. Following the retreat of the Chinese commander, Lien Lau, the sisters proclaimed themselves queens of an independent state of the northern region of what is now known as Vietnam. About three years later, the Chinese retook the area and by some accounts the sisters committed suicide by drowning near the present city of Son Tay.

Karen Gottschang Turner, in her book *Even the Women Must Fight*, a study of the North Vietnamese women who worked on the Ho Chi Minh trail, fills in the centuries between the Trung sisters and the American war in Vietnam with figures such as the nine-foot Lady Trieu, who tossed her three-foot-long breasts over her shoulder and mounted an elephant for battle against the Chinese in the third century. In the eighteenth century Bui Thi Xuan trained in martial arts and became a general in the peasant army that fought the Chinese-influenced Nguyen Dynasty. In the twentieth century the peasant girl Nguyen Thi Hung joined the Communist Party and became a leader in the resistance to French colonialism and the Japanese occupation during World War II.[28]

Turner notes that "very few women joined the regular armies against the French" but recounts the extraordinary contribution they made as military laborers in the fight for independence. Quoting the Vietnamese historian Nguyen Quoc Dung, she writes:

> From North to South, from the plains to the mountain regions, from the enemy-occupied zones to the free zones, as soon as night fell, line upon line of *dan cong* resumed their long march, which they interrupted during the day, following a labyrinth of invisible roads leading to the front. For nine years, goods and munitions were transported continuously to the front, to the hot spots of the resistance. [They] brought the wounded back to the rear, and removed the war booty.[29]

The American war produced "a new crop of heroines." In July 1966, six months after the United States began bombing the supply routes

running from North Vietnam to the South, Ho Chi Minh asked for the commitment of Vietnamese young people to help fortify the Northern home front and rebuild the bomb-ravaged transportation network. According to one official account: "The youth kept open 2,195 kilometers of strategic roads and guarded over 2,500 key points that were bombed day and night. They built 6 airstrips, neutralized tens of thousands of bombs, shot down 15 planes and transported tens of thousands of kilograms of cargo, weapons, and food by any means, including pack bicycle." Turner adds that over 70 percent of this work was carried out by women.[30]

Blossom and Lissom

It is more difficult to confirm the level at which women participated in combat units in the South where Americans would have encountered them. War photographs, however, are a source of primary documentation and the shots taken by photographers assigned to cover the war from the Vietnamese side are particularly valuable for that purpose. What we have of that record is, unfortunately, not very conclusive. For his 2002 volume *Another Vietnam: Pictures of the War from the Other Side*, the U.S. combat photographer Tim Page scoured Vietnamese archives and interviewed the now-elderly Vietnamese men who photo-documented the war from their side. His 240-page collection has many dramatic shots of North Vietnamese Army and National Liberation Front (Viet Cong) soldiers in combat and noncombat situations, but only seven of them capture images of women. Of the seven, four show North Vietnamese women in home-front, militia defense roles; two of the four have vintage carbines slung over their shoulders, while the others appear to be functioning in noncombat roles. American flyers shot down over the North may have encountered these armed militia-women but there are few, if any, accounts of shots being exchanged in those situations, making it unlikely that American perceptions of being defeated by an army of women could realistically have come from those occasions.

There are three photographs in the Page volume indexed as women "guerrilla" fighters, women in the South that U.S. combat troops could plausibly have crossed paths with. One of the three shows ten unarmed and masked women identified in the caption as "activists" who are assembling for a 1972 meeting on the Ca Mau Peninsula; another, dated 1973, after U.S. ground troops had left, appears to be a staged photo of a woman carrying a U.S.-issued M-16 rifle; the third shows a Viet Cong woman taking a South Vietnamese Army soldier prisoner in 1972.

Wilfred Burchett, an Australian journalist who was sympathetic to the communist side of the war and traveled through the bush and tunnels with the Viet Cong, has left us another primary record, but that too suggests that the combat roles of women were minimal. In his 1965 book *Vietnam: Inside Story of the Guerilla War*, he notes the presence of a few women in the situations he experienced, but he most often identifies them as a housewife, a member of the "Soldiers' Mothers" organization, "skilled women propagandists," and the like. He credits a few, such as Chi Kinh of the Bahnar minority tribe, who was president of her provincial Liberation Women's Association, as heroines for being outstanding organizers. The notable exceptions to that pattern of women noncombatants are "Blossom" and "Lissom," two young women who had engaged enemy forces in small-arms combat to heroically defend their village. From Burchett's account, it is unclear whether the enemy in this instance was U.S. ground troops or units of the South Vietnamese government.[31]

One of the most detailed and often-quoted English-language histories of Vietnamese women in the war is Arlene Eisen's *Women and Revolution in Viet Nam*, published in 1984. Like the accounts already mentioned, Eisen's highlights the importance of women's contributions to noncombat activities, such as coordinating political demonstrations with military operations to divert enemy troops away from guerrilla placements. Women also infiltrated top levels of the Saigon army as servants and secretaries and from those positions collected intelligence and sometimes acted as saboteurs. According to Eisen, 40 percent of the regional commanders of National Liberation Front's military wing, the People's Liberation Armed Forces, were women but most women served in local, militia units that kept the villages fortified with trenches and booby traps. "Few women," Eisen concludes, "joined the Viet Nam People's Army—the mobile, full-time soldiers who usually travel far from home."[32]

Apache: The Cong-girl Sniper

When I asked a twenty-one-year-old friend whether it was his sense that

many women fought in the Vietnamese military, his response was a quick and unequivocal yes. Asked where he had gotten that impression, he replied, "Well, from what I've seen . . . or heard." Pressed further, he recalled seeing something—he wasn't sure what—on television, maybe a History Channel documentary, and in movies he had seen Vietnamese women portrayed in military roles. Later he told me that he owned *Full Metal Jacket*, a 1987 film that features U.S. Marines pinned down in Hue by a sniper who turns out to be a girl.

The first half of *Full Metal Jacket*, a film by Stanley Kubrick, portrays the brutality of marine boot camp, with graphic emphasis on the sexualized socialization trainees receive on entering the corp. "Sound off like you gotta pair!" the drill instructor, Hartman, yells at the trainees on their first day in uniform. When one of the recruits makes a wisecrack, Hartman responds with a stream of "fuck"-laced invective:

Who the fuck said that? Who's the slimy cocksucker who said that?
(*No response from the trainees.*)
    The fairy-fucking godmother said that, huh?
(*Still no response.*)
    Who the fuck said that?
(*A trainee takes credit for the remark.*)
    Well, what have we here, a fucking comedian? Private Joker?
(*sarcastically*) Hell, I like you. . . . You can come over to my house
      and fuck my sister.

It is 1968 and the story follows the young marines to Vietnam, where they join the battle for the city of Hue. In the climactic scenes, the sniper picks off the squad leader, Cowboy (Arliss Howard), leaving Joker (Matthew Modine), the unit journalist, in charge. With only a couple of men left, Joker closes in on the shelled-out building where the sniper is nested. One of the marines disables the sharpshooter and then, identifying her, stands over the girl in an undulating motion and says, "No more boom boom for this baby san." (*Boom boom* is the common expression for sex with Vietnamese women and *baby-san* the term used by GIs for young girls.) "Okay, let's get the fuck out of here," Rafter Man (Kevin Major Howard), the photographer assigned to Joker, says. When Joker asks, "What about her?" Rafter Man answers, "Fuck her, let her rot." With the girl gasping for breath, Joker takes out his handgun and fires a round into her head.

Full Metal Jacket, as much as anything else, embedded the girl-Cong image in the American memory of the war. And, given the centrality of duplicity and deception in the betrayal narrative for the loss of the war that was washing over the nation at the time of the film's release, it is significant that the girl is a sniper—hidden, silent, and stealthy. But the popularization of that image by Hollywood is a separate matter from its origin: who invented the idea of an enemy girl sniper as a way to represent American military impotence? In a nod to the power of filmmakers to shape our culture, some students of the subject would probably say Stanley Kubrick. And they could be right, except that the fantasy predated the film by several years.

Gustav Hasford co-wrote the screenplay for *Full Metal Jacket*, and he had a girl sniper in *The Short Timers*, a 1977 book on which the film was based. Elsewhere in the book he has the marines waiting for orders to move on the Citadel at Hue. They are eating C-rations when one of them begins bragging about his pursuit of Vietnamese girls. "Cowboy," he asks, "you remember when we was set up in that L-shaped ambush up by Khe Sanh, and blew away that NVA [North Vietnamese Army] rifle squad? You remember that little gook bitch that was guiding them? She was a lot younger than the one I saw today. I didn't get to fuck that one either."

Hasford is writing fiction, and yet he was a marine in Vietnam and he is credited with capturing "the truth" about the war in his writing. But the only truth being told through the inclusion of female enemy combatants in his story would seem to be that the Apache legend recounted earlier appeared in various guises and was given currency that holds to this day.[33] Consider the request a student named Nicole posted on the Internet in 2005, thirty years after the war ended. Looking for a Vietnam veteran to interview, she wrote:

Hello.

My name is Nicole and i need some on to interview. I am in 8th grade right now, going on to 9th grade. This interview is needed becuase it is an expectancy from my English teacher. We are doing a report about any of the wars: World War 2, Vietnam War, and the Korean War, obviously I have chosen the Vietnam War.[34]

Nicole asked several questions, including: "What jobs were there for women, if can explain?" In response, Nicole received the following from a Vietnam veteran:

> In the NVA [North Vietnam Army] and the VC the women did a lot of digging of tunnels and trenches, and a number of them were in combat units, sometimes in leadership positions. There were a couple of units in I Corps (the Northern provinces) that were all female. There was one female leader nicknamed the Apache who used to skin captive Americans alive in the night and you had to lay there and listen to them scream. (She was finally killed by a Marine Corps sniper.) In North Vietnam the women led a lot of militia anti-aircraft units, and worked a lot on repairing roads, bridges, and dikes. The Deputy Commander of the PLA (the VC) was a woman.

In the first instance, a story like this distorts the historical record of how the Vietnamese treated U.S. POWs and dehumanizes the Vietnamese by exaggerating their capacity for cruelty. The story also shows how deeply the lore of the Vietnamese girl-warrior is embedded in postwar American culture and the extent to which the feminization of the enemy Other is a central component in how the war's loss is remembered. Vietnamese women did, as we know, play combat-support roles in the armies of North Vietnam and the National Liberation Front, but Henderson's Apache and Hasford's NVA squad leader are characters more likely found in the comic books than history books.

The Rising of the Women

Unlike the almost purely imaginative girl spitting at deplaning GIs in San Francisco, the idea that the United States fought against women warriors in Vietnam is a more complex mix of fact and fiction. It is likely that veterans' "memories" of an image like Apache are distillations of their experiences with Vietnamese women, combined with rumors they heard in Vietnam, and the powers of their own imaginations to represent the anxieties and discomforts they felt as veterans of America's first lost war.

What would otherwise have stayed in the cultural realm of folklore (like the spitting stories), however, was given cultural and even political cachet by the American antiwar movement. The women's wing of the movement, in particular, added to the militarized image of Vietnamese women through its use of photos and interview material that emphasized their roles in combat. A story in the radical women's newspaper *Goodbye to All That* on the 1969 Canadian conference attended by North Americans and a delegation of South Vietnamese women uses photographs showing Vietnamese women in combat positions and attributes to them the claim that they were "crack shots, much better than the men."[35]

The early 1970s also spawned a generation of radical movements within American professional and academic organizations, including economics, history, social work, and sociology. Most of those groups had newsletters or journals, one of which was the *Insurgent Sociologist*, begun at Columbia University and later edited at the University of Oregon. The summer 1975 issue of the journal celebrates "the end of U.S. imperialism" with a dedication to "the victory of the Cambodian and Vietnamese people." The issue features drawings of Vietnamese fighters, several of which portray women in combat positions: one is camouflaged with a rifle, another is sighting an artillery or anti-aircraft piece, and a couple more are depicted carrying small arms. Although the books from which the graphics were drawn appraised their artistic quality, readers of the journal would have gotten the impression from their use there that the demise of imperialism was due in no small measure to the rising of the women.[36]

The celebration of women's independence and power through the lenses of America's defeat in Vietnam and the dissolution of Western colonialism was an easy addition to the many other sociopolitical realignments taking place in the late twentieth century. But even more than gains of, say, national sovereignty in Asia and Africa or voting rights for African Americans, the gains made by the American women's liberation movement during the 1960s and early 1970s were perceived by many men to have come at the expense of their own social and economic standing. Coming as they did during the war years and integrally linked as they were to gender relations within the antiwar movement, it was no surprise that those hurt feelings would combine with resentments stemming from the lost war with their own sexual and gender connotations specific to the war and the way each side fought it.

The status loss felt by many men was heightened by the one-two punch of war-front, home-front indignities, a combination that helped write a cultural narrative spelled "class." With class and gender at play in a social environment already wooed by betrayal imagery, it was a certainty that Hanoi Jane would get a casting call.

7

WORKOUT JANE

THE COMPLICATIONS OF

CLASS IN HANOI JANE

In the fall of 1987 I had a faculty fellowship from Lawrence University to work in Chicago mayor Harold Washington's administration. I lived with student interns near the Belmont El stop on the city's gentrifying northside. On an afternoon walk one day, my housemates and I passed a set of low-income flats that were being converted to condominiums. "Yuppies," one of the students sneered, referring to the newcomers who would soon be occupying the condos, "they're taking over the neighborhood."

Yuppies. I may have heard the acronym before but I asked anyway: "What's a yuppie?" The answer—young urban professional—spawned further conversation about that disdainful demographic and its representations. For one of the students, yuppies were those ultra-fit thirty-something types darting through traffic to the lakefront running paths when real people were trying to get to work. Her mother was one, caught up in the fitness craze of 1980s, addicted to Jane Fonda's exercise tapes.

Once again behind the cultural curve, I had to be briefed—not on Jane Fonda, of course, but on "Workout Jane," the Jane Fonda who produced the best-selling home video *Workout* in 1982. Popular with stay-at-home mothers and wives, the video smacked of the leisure-class self-indulgence that Thorstein Veblen would have written about a hundred years earlier. Coming at a time when thousands of men were being laid off in the automobile and steel industries, the idea that some people and their wives had the money to buy VCRs and videos, and the free time to buff their otherwise underused bodies, stiffened some blue-collar collars. By then, moreover, at the time I first heard "yuppie" and Jane Fonda in the same breath, it is possible that emanations of Hanoi Jane from more political quarters were amplifying the class sensibilities aroused by Fonda's commercial success.

Class and the War in Vietnam

The idea that poor kids fight rich men's wars may have rooted itself in American consciousness during the Civil War. Twenty-four year-old J. P. Morgan bought rifles from the government one day and sold them back at a higher price the next. Under the terms of the draft law of the time, he also paid for another young man to go to war in his stead, freeing himself to stay home and manage his ill-gained fortune into a financial empire. In *Labor's Untold Story*, Richard Boyer and Herbert Morais recount how John D. Rockefeller, James Hill, and Andrew Carnegie, similarly, paid for others to fight on their behalf while they exploited wartime economic opportunities to make themselves into barons of oil, railroading, and steel.[1]

During World War I, the only son of a landowner could be deferred from the draft to stay home and take care of the farm. Farm boys may not have been fortunate sons in the same sense the Morgans and Rockefellers were, but plowing the homestead was undeniably preferable to the military duty on the Western Front that the thousands of young men who owned nothing but their labor power faced. Because of the widespread support for World War II, the government was able to abolish the only-son exemptions, and the postwar depopulation of rural America all but ensured that they were gone forever.[2]

By the 1960s, the basis for privileged draft status shifted from the ownership of land and capital to the possession of cultural assets, when Lewis B. Hershey, director of the Selective Service, became convinced that academic skills were important for the national defense. To induce young men into fields such as engineering and teaching, Hershey permitted them to defer their availability for the draft while in school and then granted postgraduation deferments to those who entered certain occupations. In his book *Working-Class War*, Christian Appy makes the case that this system favored middle- and upper-class boys over those from the working class, because they were better able to meet the standard of full-time college enrollment necessary to stave off military induction; they were also more likely to face draft-broad members from their own racial and socioeconomic backgrounds and had better access to professional counselors who could inform them of their rights. Perhaps because their sons were disproportionately "channeled" into the draft, compared with other groups of Americans, a greater proportion of the working class opposed the war.[3]

One of the great paradoxes of those years is that many Americans opposed the war while simultaneously opposing those who opposed the war—and there was no segment of the population where that discrepancy was more evident than in the working class. While war protesters consistently expressed empathetic support for draftees and worked vigorously to end the draft, working-class conscripts and their families were often disdainful of the peace activists. Appy points out that the nub of the irony lay in class-based sentiments and the ability of pro-war demagogues like George Wallace to manipulate the insecurities and anger of lower-, middle-, and working-class voters for political gain. Running as a third-party candidate in the 1968 and 1972 elections, Wallace was able to parlay the resentment felt by workers of the draft-privileged upper and upper-middle classes into hostility for the antiwar movement by ridiculing its leaders as parasitic intellectuals.[4]

Wallace lambasted protesters as "pointy-headed liberals," an expression honed into the signature phrase of the Nixon administration when Vice President Spiro Agnew derided the moratorium protesters in October 1969 as "an effete corps of impudent snobs who characterize themselves as intellectuals." The use of *effete* in that context was an appeal to populist values that extol hard work and deferred gratification as virtuous; referred to in the context of that ideology of "producerism," *effete* was a code word with pejorative connotations for both the cause of welfare rights associated with political liberalism and the presence of unearned wealth associated with the coupon-clipping capitalist class. Agnew's combination of "snobs" with "intellectuals" touched the nerve of anti-intellectualism harkening back to centuries-old fears that a cabal of knowledgeable elites knew things that others did not and used that knowledge to exploit and control the masses; going forward, it was the kind of suspicion that animated the ultra-rightist militia movements of the 1980s.[5]

By the late twentieth century, the suspicion of intellectuals had grown beyond the distrust of a narrow band of philosophers and free-thinking pamphleteers, as they were once imagined, to encompass a wide range of social scientists and media and cultural workers. The evolution of communication technology from the printing press to the array of electronic media that in some ways became the hallmark of mid-century socioeconomic development also increased the occupational diversity of knowledge producers and the means at hand for the distribution of ideas. If "intellectual elites" once conjured images of bearded eccentrics holed up in dank clock towers, it now included sweatered college professors, button-downed journalists, radio and television personalities, and playwrights and screenwriters, some with accompanying teams of research assistants, make-up artists, agents, and publicists. By the 1960s, the power to influence how people thought about something as important as war was a power shared by Manhattan publishers with the photojournalist in Saigon and the balladeer from the Iron Range; Americans feeling powerless in a world of ideas and images produced far from their hometown print shop were more likely to envision Jane Fonda huddled with conspirators around a movie script in Hollywood than a shadowy conclave of rabbis in a Prague cemetery.[6]

For people harboring resentments rooted in either their sense of what the antiwar movement was or the unsettledness left by the loss of the war, Fonda was not an inappropriate target. She had been a vocal opponent of the war and an effective catalyst for organizing opposition to it. The resistance movement within the military was emboldened by her endorsement, and her support for Vietnam Veterans against the War helped propel the organization to national visibility. In the memories of friends and foes alike, Fonda's importance to the antiwar movement and the loss of the war was growing by the time the neoliberal movement for renewed expansionism set out to banish the legacy of Vietnam from the national consciousness in the closing years of the century. But legacy is as much about the present as the past and Fonda's image in those memories virtually ensured that it would be a force for peace and diplomacy in the coming decades, a certainty requiring its reconfiguring by the political Right as Hanoi Jane.

The lexicon of "class" also comes with subtle gender connotations. Work in the modern world carried forward the sexual division of labor typical of rural life in the pre-industrial era—women at home, men in the fields. The rise of manufacturing, however, led to the commodification of nearly everything: foods once grown in the garden and canned for winter were bought at the grocery store; clothes once sewn at home could be ordered from a catalogue. Slowly, the economic role of women was reduced from coproducer of family economic life to designated household consumer. At the same time, however, the Protestant-infused culture of modernism was valorizing work—the more joyless and deprecating its forms, the more virtue and status it was assigned. The twist on that equation was that the assignment of class privilege (which was not a Protestant virtue) then went to those relegated to the margins of production—and no one was more marginal to production than non-producing consumers. Those who lived off the production of others—be they the usurious rich or the welfare-dependent poor—had an exploitative relationship to those who worked; and no characteristic was more common to the population of parasites-on-production than gender—real men produced, all women consumed. To be in an upper class, relative to those in production, was to be effeminate.

The central role played by upper-class women in the antiwar movement added to the "us" versus "them" polarization of the United States that the draft-vulnerable working class sensed. The prominence of women in the movement continued a tradition that went back to ancient times and was extended into the modern era by women such as Julia Ward Howe, who was moved to pacifism by the suffering she witnessed during the Civil War. The daughter of a banker and wife of Samuel Gridley Howe, director of the Perkins School for the Blind in Boston, Ward Howe was an abolitionist who initially supported the Union cause in its fight against the slave South, writing the "Battle Hymn of the Republic" as a morale-lifter for the troops. But her work for sanitation reform on behalf of soldiers on both sides convinced her that it was war itself that was the problem, and when the Franco-Prussian War erupted in Europe, she issued a Lysistratian call for women everywhere to join hands across national borders in unity for peace. Her subsequent efforts to found a Mother's Day for Peace caught on in the last years of the nineteenth century and led to President Woodrow Wilson's declaring the first national Mother's Day in 1914.

By that time, the nation was on the brink of yet another war and the appearance of a new generation of female peace activists. Ward Howe died in 1910 just as the social reformer Jane Addams was coming onto the scene. Addams was the daughter of a well-to-do Illinois business-man, state senator, and friend of Abraham Lincoln's. She graduated from Rockford College for Women and studied for a career in medicine before opening a center for the improvement of life for immigrants in Chicago that became famous as Hull House.

Addams followed Ward Howe's prescription for internationalism, lecturing against U.S. entry into World War I and turning Hull House into a center for draft counseling. When the war began in 1915, she be-came chair of the Women's Peace Party and went to The Hague for an international women's conference at the newly formed Peace Palace, where she headed a commission that met with world leaders to find a path to peace. In 1919, Addams was elected the first president of the Women's International League for Peace and Freedom, an organization that advocated negotiation over confrontation as the way to national security. For her opposition to the war and rearmament, Addams was regularly derided in the press as a traitor, and in the anticommunist hysteria that swept America after the 1917 Russian Revolution, her internationalism invited coloration with the hue of the day—called a Red, a Bolshevik, and an anarchist, she was expelled from the Daughters of the American Revolution. Addams's response was to join forces with other dissenters to form the American Civil Liberties Union in 1920.[7]

Opposition to U.S. entry to World War II became an unpopular cause after Pearl Harbor, but Jeanette Rankin, who had voted against World War I as a Republican member of the House in 1918, kept the seed grain of women for peace alive, casting the only vote against Franklin Roose-velt's declaration of war on December 8, 1941. After the war, the tradi-tion of border-crossing women of privilege fraternizing with would-be foreign enemies was picked up by Women's Strike for Peace, founded in 1961 to mobilize women in opposition to nuclear testing. One of the organization's co-founders was Cora Weiss, daughter of women's cosmetics magnate, Samuel Rubin. By the mid-1960s, Women's Strike for Peace was a leading force in the antiwar movement. With other women, Weiss led the effort to maintain contact with U.S. POWs in Hanoi by transporting letters between them and their families—against the wishes of the U.S. government. Some critics labeled her a communist for her work, and David Horowitz's *FrontPage Magazine* would later skewer her "dilettantism," citing her as proof that some people "have more money than sense."[8]

Homecoming Parades—But Not for Me

With military service a rite of passage for men, and class the gender-tinted identity that valorizes production over consumption, the political culture surrounding a controversial war like that in Vietnam was almost certain to metastasize in a symbol like Hanoi Jane. But those dynamics played out in complicated ways. On one hand, Fonda had some following among lower-ranking draftees and enlisted men through her association with FTA (Free the Army), the antiwar variety show that toured military bases in 1971. The content of FTA was directed less at the war itself than the country's political and military leadership. Jokes that pilloried military officers were particularly popular. In one skit, an officer played by Michael Alaimo needs coins to place a long-distance phone call. Holding the telephone receiver in one hand, he turns to a private played by Jane Fonda.

> OFFICER: Excuse me Private, do you have change for a quarter?
> PRIVATE: Oh, yeah.
> OFFICER: Yeah?! You don't say "yeah" to an Officer! An Officer is addressed as "Sir." Now I learned that in basic training, Private, and so did you. You always address an Officer as "Sir!" Now, Private, I'll give you one more chance and I want to hear that "Sir" loud and clear!
> OFFICER (giving the Private another chance): Private, do you have change for a quarter?
> PRIVATE (loud and clear): No Sir!

In the skit that followed, Alaimo played President Richard Nixon with Fonda cast as First Lady, Pat.

PAT: Richard, there's a terrible demonstration going on outside. You have to do something.

NIXON: Oh, there's always a demonstration going on outside, Pat.

PAT: But this one is completely out of control.

NIXON: What are they asking for this time?

PAT: Free Angela Davis and all political prisoners, out of Vietnam now, and draft all government officials.

NIXON: Well, we have people to take care of that—they'll do their job, you do your job, and I'll do my job.

PAT: But Richard, you don't understand. They're storming the White House.

NIXON: Oh, in that case I better call out the 3rd Marines!

PAT: You can't, Richard.

NIXON: Why not?

PAT: Richard, it is the 3rd Marines!

The appeals FTA made to class instincts were never more passionate and explicit than in Donald Sutherland's recitation of lines from Dalton Trumbo's *Johnny Got His Gun*, a story written in the aftermath of World War I that brought down the curtain at some FTA shows. War injuries had left Trumbo's character, Johnny, with no limbs and no face; he could not hear, see, or speak. But Johnny could think and he learned to communicate with enough body motion to tap out Morse code and receive back taps on his body. In this manner he spelled out his warning to the war makers of the future, a warning that Sutherland repeated from the FTA stage:

> If you make a war, if there are guns to be aimed, if there are bullets to be fired, if there are men to be killed—they will not be us. They will not be us, the guys who grow wheat and turn it into food, the guys who make clothes and paper and houses and tiles, the guys who build dams and power plants and string the long moaning high tension wires, the guys who crack crude oil down into a dozen different parts, who make light globes and sewing machines and shovels and automobiles and airplanes and tanks and guns; oh no it will not be us who die. It will be you.
>
> It will be you—you who urge us on to battle; you who incite us against ourselves; you who would have one cobbler kill another

cobbler; you who would have one man who works kill another man who works; you who would have one human being who wants only to live kill another human being who wants only to live. Remember this. Remember this well, you people who plan for war. . . . If you tell us to make the world safe for democracy we will take you seriously and by god and by Christ we will make it so. We will use the guns you force upon us we will use them to defend our very lives. . . .

Put the guns into our hands and we will use them. Give us the slogans and we will turn them into realities. Sing the battle hymns and we will take them up where you left off. Make no mistake of it we will live. We will be alive and we will walk and talk and eat and sing and laugh and feel and love and bear our children in tranquility in security in decency in peace. You plan the wars you masters of men, plan the wars and point the way and we will point the gun.[9]

The year after FTA toured, Fonda went to Hanoi, whereupon her standing with GIs and veterans gained nuance. Like most Americans, veterans of the war empathized with the POWs held in North Vietnam and supported the efforts of peace activists to maintain contact with them and work for their early release. Many veterans openly rejected the claims of the Nixon administration that the war had to continue until all the POWs were returned, sensing in that position a thinly veiled excuse that exploited POWs in order to lengthen a war that Nixon's people wanted for other reasons. The antiwar frame of reference on the POW issue effectively reversed the administration's logic, arguing that the ending of the war would bring the POWs home—being antiwar and supportive of activists like Jane Fonda, in other words, was to be pro-POW.

When the POWs returned home in spring 1973, however, some of them claimed they had been mistreated by the North Vietnamese, tortured even, claims that Fonda initially said were not true. Years later, her disavowal of the POWs' charges would be remembered as an outrage, near religious heresy, but at the time skepticism of the POWs' stories abounded. The February 26 issue of *Newsweek* magazine, for example, quoted Dr. John Ord, hospital commander at Clark Air Base in the Philippians, where the POWs made their first stop after release, as saying, "Their care must have been quite good." In particular, Ord "praised the diets and especially the dental hygiene that the men had in North Vietnamese prisons." On March 5, Time magazine expressed doubt about the claims of mistreatment, averring, "The health and high spirits of the prisoners themselves seem to suggest relatively humane treatment."

While the press and public sorted through the claims and counter-claims over the POWs' treatment, the returned prisoners were being feted as heroes. Time magazine kicked off the hoopla with a February 19 cover-page photograph of Air Force Major Joseph Abbot's children holding a banner that reads, "Welcome Home Daddy." Under the page 13 headline "A Celebration of Men Redeemed," the story continues with personal features on the men and their families and a six-point how-to prescription for welcoming the returnees: Rule 4. Don't treat the POW as mentally ill. Newsweek's cover story came a week later with the observation: "The homecoming touched off a surge of national pride and a burst of uninhibited emotion. The prisoners return and their courageous bearing seemed to give America a new sense of hope—hope that these impressive men who had become symbols of American sacrifice in Indochina might help the country heal the lingering wounds of war." Under the subhead "A Surge of Admiration," Newsweek assigned the former POWs the "old fashioned qualities of discipline, mutual loyalty, and unyielding determination."[10]

Offering it as an example of the country's euphoria, Newsweek described the homecoming planned for Lieutenant Commander Larry Spencer at the Des Moines airport by his hometown, Earlham, Iowa:

> A caravan of farm trucks, old buses and every other available set of wheels will honk Spencer's way home . . . where Iowa Gov. Robert Ray and the Earlham High School marching band will be waiting. . . . A vice president of the local bank is even trying to arrange a flyover of four Phantom jets, the plane Spencer was flying when he was downed.

But not everyone was cheering. The March 5 Newsweek carried a sidebar, "The Permanent War Prisoners," with a portrait of the men left disabled by the war. One of them, Max Inglett, wounded during a mortar attack a year earlier, says he cried when he saw the returning POWs, "cried out of self-pity," with memories of getting off the plane when he returned with nobody there to meet him. In the same column, Marine Lance Corporal Terry Holder, wounded in 1969, is quoted as saying he hopes the POWs "take everything they can get from the government and American people," adding, "though I haven't exactly had a Rear Admiral hug me."

A week later, *Time* printed a letter from Sam Bunge: "Sir: As an exgrunt I feel a certain churlish resentment about the solicitous attention the returning POWs are receiving. It seems to me the draftees who faced the war 24 hours every day are deserving of somewhat more than . . . a dismal employment rate."[11]

The class resentments brought to the surface by the ceremony heaped on the POWs were sharpened when the senior ranking officers among them threatened to bring legal charges against some of their underlings for aiding the enemy and being disrespectful to officers while confined in Hanoi. While some air force and navy pilots who were officers had also made antiwar statements as prisoners, only lower-ranking army members and marines were singled out for reprisals. The newspaper of Vietnam Veterans Against the War, *Winter Soldier*, points out that the ground troops "fought a dirty war," "slept on the ground," and "ate out of cans," whereas "the pilots [were] airmen who ran milk-runs, [and] who killed from thousands of feet up." At night the pilots "went back to their bases to eat steak and sleep between sheets." The article argues that it was "easier to place the blame on lower ranks, the ones who carry out the dirty work, whether it is ground fighting in Indochina or car-polishing and grass-cutting here in the U.S."[12]

The memories that Vietnam veterans were met with overt hostility on their return home are mythical, but the nation's exuberant embrace of the POWs may have been a bit of compensatory behavior, make-up for the apathy that had overtaken its response to regular returnees. What could have been an iconic affair to bookend America's longest war—a four-hour parade for Vietnam veterans through Manhattan on March 31, 1973—turned out to be a sterile event that, the *New York Times* notes, "lacked the blizzard of confetti that had greeted returning servicemen in the great military parades of the past." With all the aura of an afterthought, the parade from Times Square to 72nd Street on Central Park West said to many veterans that, were it not for the return of the "real" heroes having stirred the emotive juices of the country in the preceding weeks, there would not have been this parade either. In reality, soldiers and sailors and marines had been returning home from Southeast Asia to the greetings of friends and family for ten years and the nation was tired of the war.[13]

From Communist to Capitalist,
Hanoi Jane to Workout Jane

Two decades after the return of a few hundred POWs overshadowed the place in public consciousness where three million grunts, mechanics, clerk-typists, and cooks would otherwise be remembered, Fonda's role in the emerging American betrayal narrative was being rescripted from that of devious ideologue to behind-the-scenes wielder of financial power with the wherewithal to buy the hearts and minds of students, GIs, and the press.

Ted Sampley, editor of the on-line *Veteran Dispatch*," wrote that Fonda used her wealth and influence to garner support for communism from college campuses. Titled "Hanoi Jane: Yesterday's Communist Revolutionary, Today's Rich Capitalist," Sampley's essay said she "concocted" a series of coffeehouses near military bases where "special employees would attract off-duty servicemen, get them relaxed," and then use "promises of jobs and money" to get them to desert. Fonda, he says, "was the major financial support to one of the most damaging pro-Hanoi groups called Vietnam Veterans Against the War (VVAW)," which, he claims, was later led by John Kerry. In 2004, Sampley would step from cyberspace with a phony photo showing then-presidential candidate Kerry on stage with Jane Fonda. Released to the press, the photo became part of the so-called Swift Boat campaign to discredit Kerry's military record.[14]

Sampley's crediting of the coffeehouse idea to Fonda is almost certainly wrong. In the 2006 documentary film *Sir! No Sir!* Fonda says Howard Levy, an army captain court-martialed for in-service resistance to the war, came up with the idea. David Zeiger a civilian antiwar activist who ran the Oleo Strut coffeehouse for GIs near Fort Hood in Killeen, Texas, agrees that Fonda had nothing to do with founding the coffeehouses and says it was policy throughout the network that linked several of them across the country to discourage desertion. Rather, Zeiger says today, dissidents were encouraged to stay in the military and organize the opposition to the war from within.[15]

129

In his essay, Sampley reminded readers of other misdoings attributed to Fonda, such as the aid and comfort she lent to communists on her trip to Hanoi, revising that long-standing indictment to emphasize the importance of her wealth and class position. While Fonda enjoyed the blessings of wealth, he wrote, the POWs she betrayed rotted in North Vietnamese gulags; the communists she befriended now befriend Western bankers and capitalist businessmen, hoping to "bring more big business and money back to Vietnam, so like Hanoi Jane, they too can be rich."

Doing Jane

The specter of purse strings pulled by duplicitous figures has sustained conspiracist themes in populist culture for centuries. And, as in other historical instances, one can find in Hanoi Jane a certain amount of grist for the belief that her money factored importantly at times in the antiwar movement. But while the benefits of family wealth undoubtedly trickled down to her—in her autobiography, My Life So Far, she tells of borrowing forty thousand dollars from her father to buy a house in 1972—and may have made her activism look like the exercise of privilege to someone harnessed to a work-a-day grind, Fonda's contribution of herself to the cause of peace, inclusive of her celebrity cachet, likely outweighed the dollar value of any checks she signed.

Fonda's Workout studio, founded in 1979, for example, was begun as a fund-raising venture to support the Campaign for Economic Democracy (CED), a pro-union, antipoverty, and political-reform organization that had grown out of Tom Hayden's campaign for the U.S. Senate three years earlier. Her acquired or accumulated assets may have made it possible for her to buy the studio property on Robertson Boulevard in Beverly Hills, but, if so, they were deployed as part of an anticapitalist strategy, not capitalist, and her motivation for doing it was more political and altruistic than self-interested. The CED owned the Workout business, not Fonda.[16]

In her autobiography, Fonda says she never imagined the Workout business would be as successful as it became and never thought of it as a big moneymaker and that, at the time, she did not even own a VCR or know anyone who had bought a video. That it did make money—

seventeen million dollars for CED by the 1980s—despite Fonda's lack of business acumen or vision of next-generation home entertainment technology is due more to the socioeconomic contingencies of post-Vietnam America than the avarices attributed to her by Sampley. The VCR arrived at the same time that the post–World War II population bulge was hitting its income-earning years; their goal-oriented ethic fueled by the optimism that an expanding economy would reward hard work, the go-getters growing up in the 1950s hit the late 1970s more interested in lower running times than after-work downtime. The pace of their involvements in civil rights and antiwar activism, moreover, had left deficits to be filled by health foods and exercise regimens in the years that followed; the emotional rushes once felt on the picket lines were replaced with the endorphins of runner's highs, and the social spaces once filled by planning meetings and long rides to protests and demonstrations were filling with the camaraderie of running clubs and workout groups.

The arrival of the VCR also coincided with the Boomer-generation marriages that had been put off by the higher priorities of draft resistance, fulfilling military service, and ten years of movements to end the war in Vietnam. The first marriages that might have been celebrated by twenty-somethings fresh out of college in the late 1960s and early 1970s were instead on the calendars of the early 1980s—with a modest boom of kids to follow. The relative confinement to home that child bearing and caring meant to a generation of working women growing to adulthood in the heady atmosphere of political protests and second-wave feminism was what primed their receptivity to the Workout. Recalling her own regrets of having to give up exercise during pregnancies, Fonda started pregnancy, birth, and recovery workout classes and produced videos that used pregnant women and new mothers to demonstrate the techniques.

Fonda eventually separated the workout business from CED, but not before her book became a New York Times #1 bestseller and her first video produced in 1982 reached the status of the all-time best-selling home video that it retained twenty-five years later. By that time, Fonda recalls receiving basketsful of letters from women "doing Jane" all over the world, women pouring their hearts out "about the weight they had lost and self-esteem they had gained."[17]

Making Myth with Sex and Class

There is plenty of irony in the fact that Fonda's workout venture, begun to support the anticapitalist work of CED, grew into a moneymaker that got her reviled as a capitalist. In the 1980s though, when that irony played out, populist sentiments against big government, big business, and big labor were resonant with middle-class anxieties, so the attack on Fonda-the-capitalist from the libertarian Right found open ears.

Still, the class issues alone may not have given Hanoi Jane the staying power it would have—but the class issues were not alone. If "doing Tom" had been in Hayden's future, it is unlikely that he would have achieved the bête-noire status that awaited Fonda. But through the same gendered logic that explains why we do not remember the loss of the war through a male figure like Ramsey Clark, we can understand that the personal and social accoutrements of wealth come with gender-specific connotations in a patriarchal society. Wealth brings independence, but the same independence considered a virtue for men can quickly be recast as vice when it is exercised by women in a male-dominated group. A daughter privileged by family inheritance who can get money from her father by asking is one matter; a woman with her own money is quite another.[18]

In her 2006 study of post-9/11 American life, Susan Faludi found that the attacks were being used in the news media and popular culture to reestablish conservative images of women as the protected gender, the gendered Other without whom the male warrior-protector has no place in the national imagination. In the aftermath of those deadly days, policemen and firemen were raised to heroic standing through a dialectical interplay with women reportedly lusting for the manliness under the uniforms.[19]

Faludi recalls the founding mythology of the American woman needing the protection of their frontiersmen, pointing out that when Puritan women like Hannah Duston defended themselves, because male safeguards had broken down, they were condemned for moral failure. Likewise, she writes, the widows of 9/11 who rejected the victim role assigned them by the dominant culture by criticizing the conduct of political authorities, and reestablishing their personal lives through new social relationships and even remarriage, were accused of perusing lavish lifestyles, taking exotic vacations, and romancing the buddies of their dead husbands.

Scorned by the conservative commentator Ann Coulter as self-obsessed witches and harpies who were enjoying life without their spouses, 9/11 widows, like the so-called Jersey Girls, were ticketed for "driving female while independent," the same charges made against Hannah Duston and, centuries later Jane Fonda, whose political voice and free-spirited love life coupled with her economic independence to scare the pants off the mythical American male.

MAKING TROPE

BIRCHERS, LAROUCHEIES, AND AYN RANDIANS

The authorship of myths is typically as obscure as the times and places of their origins. The *Iliad* and *Odyssey*, for example, are said to have come from Greece in roughly 700 to 800 BC and they were written by Homer. But who was Homer? Or, who were Homer?—since some researchers suggest that those stories began as folk tales heard by many different writers who eventually recorded them.

The same is true of stories now described as "urban legends." The "Hookman in Lovers' Lane," for example, tells of a young couple trysting in a parked automobile. Startled by a mysterious sound, they quickly vacate their secluded location and hurriedly drive home, whereupon they open the car door to find a prosthetic device, the "Hookman's hook," dangling from the door handle. Looking into the origins of the story, scholars can trace it to the early post–World War II years and say that it was commonly told in Southern California and Long Island, New York, suggesting that the newness of the automobile and the suburbanization it spawned may have provided fertile ground for the story's popularity. It could also have been the increased visibility of prosthetics on veterans who had lost limbs in the then-recent war which piqued some imaginations. But the authorship of the legend's first telling, or even first writing, remains unknown. And so it is with Hanoi Jane.

The Elusive Coinage of "Hanoi Jane"

Newspaper stories will occasionally credit "Vietnam veterans" for dubbing Fonda "Hanoi Jane," but "Vietnam veterans" is far too vague and, whatever its merit, overly generalized, since we also know that many veterans have always thought well of Fonda for opposing the war. More commonly, it is said that it is the POWs who hate her, because they had to listen to her criticisms of the war through the Radio Hanoi broadcasts piped into Hao Lo prison. For the reasons given in Chapter 2, though, it's not clear how many POWs would have heard those broadcasts, and so it is no surprise that of the several POW memoirs published by 1988, only two mention Fonda and one of those is a positive mention. The phrase "Hanoi Jane" was not used in the POW memoirs until after the moniker was already in popular use.[1]

Searches for the first iterations of "Hanoi Jane" lead to third-person claims such as that made by Fonda's biographer Thomas Kiernan, who wrote in 1973 that on her return to New York from Hanoi she was greeted at the airport with epithets such as "Hanoi Jane," Red Pinko," and "Commie Slut." But Kiernan provides no footnote to his claim and my own search of the New York press coverage of her arrival turned up reports of other slurs being hurled at her but not "Hanoi Jane."[2] The May 1973 edition of the John Birch Society's monthly news and information bulletin *American Opinion* used "Hanoi Jane," but even then, it does not appear in mainstream journalism until 1978 when Richard Blue dropped it rather benignly into his *Los Angeles Times* story about that year's Academy Awards. A year later, Jack Schuller used it pejoratively in a *Chicago Tribune* story when he reflected back on Fonda's award for her role in *Klute*: "Tokyo Rose got 20 years, Hanoi Jane gets an Oscar." Interestingly, these early appearances of the name have a tropelike character even before Hanoi Jane has a life off the margins of the nation's political culture—almost as if an ethereal force is pressing the phrase into the people's vocabulary.[3]

The first mainstream news report of Fonda being called "Hanoi Jane" came later in 1979 when she and Tom Hayden toured the country on behalf of their Campaign for Economic Democracy. In some cities they were met by protesters carrying signs reminding the public that Fonda had gone to Hanoi during the war. "Go Home, 'Hanoi Jane'" one placard in Washington read, according to the *Post* reporter Myra MacPherson. MacPherson identified the protesters as members the Nazi Party and Ku Klux Klan, while noting that those ultra-rightists were joined by members of the American Legion and Veterans of Foreign Wars.[4]

I'm not Fond'a Fonda

Whether or not Kiernan coined "Hanoi Jane," the phrase's passage into more popular forms was abetted by the John Birch Society. This more political beginning for the trope was suggested to me in an interview with Guy Russo in Waterbury, Connecticut. Russo, a retired general, had led the effort to stop the filming of *Stanley and Iris* because of Fonda's Vietnam-era activism; I wanted to know why he had felt so strongly about the issue and how he was able to mount such an effective opposition.[5]

Russo graciously invited me to his home in Waterbury for the interview in November 2002. Mrs. Russo came to the door and welcomed me into the family room, whereupon I exchanged greetings of the day with the general. Briefly, I reminded him that I had come to hear about his involvement with the Fonda affair. "Well," he said, "she's a communist, you know."

The comment caught me off guard. I knew Fonda was not and had never been a communist; besides, the charge struck me as odd because I was not used to hearing sixties-era leftists described as communists. The collective identity of the activists of the day was New Left, a term intended to separate them from the "old," Communist Left of their parents' generation. Vietnam-vintage radicals like Angela Davis, who had been members of the Communist Party, had long since acquired new public personas and were seldom any longer referred to as communists. Of all the ways I could think that a Fonda critic might color her, "communist" was not expected; her FBI files sometimes labeled her "subversive" or "anarchist" but not "communist." An undated page from those files reports, "Fonda denied being a Communist," and a Bureau memo from around 1972 classifies her as "not dangerous."[6]

Russo's tone in making the remark had been conversational, not adversarial, leaving me to wonder whether his intent was nothing more than putting something on the table for us to talk about. But as he went on for several minutes, linking Fonda and communism, there was no mistaking that, for him, the Fonda issue went beyond her alleged endangerment of the POWs or even the charge that she had sold out the military mission in Vietnam—it was about communism. I listened as though hearing a voice from another time; at the moment, the thought must have crossed my mind that it all sounded a little Birchesque, but I don't recall putting that word to it.

Russo seemed somewhat proud of having made "Hanoi Jane" the household phrase it is—and well he should be, because the Waterbury movement shined national light on the anti-Fonda cause. Waterbury put names and faces to an otherwise amorphous set of veterans with grievances that critics and the media could have dismissed as fictitious. Russo and the people gathered around him were real, and ready for the press; they did not invent Hanoi Jane but they do take credit for crafting the "I'm not Fond'a Fonda" bumper stickers that were still being driven around the city twenty years after they were printed.

That Waterbury should have cradled Hanoi Jane puzzled me nevertheless. Why Waterbury? Fonda's previous film, *On Golden Pond* (1981), had been shot in the even more conservative state of New Hampshire, where there had been some objections to the use of Squam Lake for the production site, but nothing like the brouhaha in Waterbury. The social and economic conditions that created a receptive audience for her vilifying in 1988 were no different than those in 1981. So why was Waterbury such a caldron?

Things became clearer on my next trip to Waterbury when I talked to Jim Noonan, a life-long resident of the city with a record of social activism going back to the 1960s. Noonan recalled that, during the war in Vietnam, there was a local group connected to the Minutemen, a national paramilitary organization formed by Robert DePugh in 1960. DePugh had been inspired by the John Birch Society, and the Minutemen recruited from the Birch organization. The Waterbury branch, named the Defense Survival Force, was a militia-type organization that was training to stop the communists, should they come up the Naugatuck River valley from Long Island Sound. According to Noonan, Guy Russo had belonged to the Defense Survival Force.[7]

Noonan also recalled that Russo had been a leading figure in the reaction to the peace movement. On one occasion, the general came with war supporters to an antiwar meeting at the First Congregational Church.

The guest speaker was the Reverend William Sloane Coffin, a national spokesman for the antiwar cause. Noonan was sitting at a literature table that evening when Russo approached and began shouting that the American flag was displayed incorrectly on the table. When Noonan tried to reply, Russo, according to Noonan, "lunged across the table, saying 'I'm going to kill you.'" Russo was pulled off the table and the meeting went on as planned. Reportedly, Coffin later remembered the Waterbury demonstration against him as "the worst I ever faced."[8]

After talking with Noonan, I met with Veterans of Foreign Wars (VFW) members who had participated in the 1988 protests against Fonda. The meeting at the VFW hall had been arranged by John Rinaldi, whom Guy Russo had referred me to as his "right-hand man" in the anti-Fonda effort. I entered the downstairs barroom, and before the bartender could respond to my question about where I might find John Rinaldi, a patron on the stool next to me muttered, "Communist bitch," signaling that my research interests had arrived ahead of me and that tempers there had not cooled in the years since the filming. The angry man turned away as the barkeep sent me to the meeting room upstairs where five men awaited my visit. All of them were wearing some veteran-identified clothing or insignia; the exception was Rinaldi, whose civilian dress distinguished him as the liaison to me, the visitor. After some cordial introductions and what I took to be a turf-staking statement—"There are still POWs in Southeast Asia, you know"—we spent a rather pleasant hour together talking about their role in the protests against Fonda fourteen years earlier.[9]

Near the end of the time, Yillidi "Whitey" Zyko, one of the men arrested while protesting Fonda, offered a set of printed materials he had saved from 1988. Included in the collection was a dossier-like document labeled "Evidence File for Case Against: Jane Fonda/Tom Hayden." The "file" consisted of a long letter written by retired Brigadier General Curtis J. Irwin, detailing the case for treason charges against Fonda and Hayden. The faux dossier was distributed by the National Security Center, a private Washington, DC, group.[10] The existence of the document in the hands of the anti-Fonda veterans suggested that there had been more than local involvement in the Waterbury movement—and a background check on the National Security Center pointed, again, to associations with the John Birch Society.[11]

The Viet Cong Front in the United States

The attribution of Fonda's late-1980s disparagement to rightist political organizations fits with what else is known about the origins of the attacks on her. Whereas her time in Hanoi had been reported fairly, if critically, by the press, and the Justice Department rejected the motions of the State Department and Nixon White House to prosecute Fonda for treason on her return, the John Birch Society kept hold of the anti-Fonda baton and ran with it into the annals of postwar myth and legend.

The point man for that effort was Fletcher Thompson, a Republican representative from Georgia running for the Senate against Democrat Sam Nunn in 1972. Thompson had co-authored an article with John G. Schmitz titled, "The Second Front of the Vietnam War: Communist Subversion in the Peace Movement," which was printed in the April 21, 1971, issue of the *Congressional Record*. The article was an alarm bell that had gone off on October 24, 1969, when North Vietnamese prime minister Pham Van Dong cabled a message to the New Mobilization Committee to End the War in Vietnam calling the organization's Moratorium Days a "Fall Offensive" against the war and wishing those efforts "a brilliant success." Attending the Stockholm Conference on Vietnam five months later, the Vietnamese delegation reportedly referred to the United States' peace movement as "the 'Second Front' of the Vietnam War," the appellation taken by Schmitz and Thompson for the title of their article.[12]

Schmitz would be the John Birch Society's presidential candidate in 1972 and was a frequent contributor to the organization's publications. The lengthy article he and Thompson wrote, later published as *The Viet Cong Front in the United States* by Western Islands, the publishing arm of the Birch Society, contains long lists of names of leaders of the peace movement, including Sidney Peck, David Dellinger, Cora Weiss, Sidney Lens, and Dagmar Wilson, and then associates those individuals with organizations such as the Communist Party and the Socialist Workers Party.

Describing what they refer to as the 1970 "spring offensive" against the war, the authors write that planning for the May 8–10 demonstration took place at the "home of pro-Hanoi WSP [Women Strike for Peace] leader and New Mobe co-chairman Cora Weiss." The demonstration at the Ellipse south of the White House, they say, drew between eighty thousand and one hundred thousand protesters to hear speeches from Dr. Benjamin Spock, Coretta King, Dellinger, and Robert Scheer from the California Peace and Freedom Party.[13] Another speaker was Jane Fonda, whom Schmitz and Thompson identify as "a well-known actress who has recently emerged as a supporter of communist causes, including the Wilfred Burchett 60th Birthday Committee, a communist front established to aid the work of *Guardian* writer Wilfred Burchett, Australian communist and KGB agent."

In the late summer and fall of 1972, Thompson had tried to parlay the Fonda issue into campaign currency for his run for the Senate. Referring to her as "Hanoi Hannah," he urged his colleagues on the House Internal Security Committee to subpoena her to answer his charge that she had committed treason by "giving aid and comfort to the enemy" and encouraging soldiers in Vietnam to desert and defect. The committee did not get Fonda, but they did get Assistant U.S. Attorney General A. William Olson, who made it clear that the Justice Department found no basis for a prosecution of her for either treason or violation of the Logan Act, which makes it illegal to travel abroad to meet with foreign leaders about U.S. security issues.[14]

Stage Left

The interest of the John Birch Society in Fonda, however, went beyond even the garden-variety anti-Communism of the day and her usefulness as a campaign prop in Thompson's run for office. The Birch Society was a mid-twentieth-century American incarnation of fears and suspicions dating to the post-Enlightenment reaction to the secular thought and presumed importance of intellectuals associated with the French Revolution. The immateriality of ideas lent them an elusiveness that, combined with their power to move people and turn order into chaos, made suspect those who work in and with the world of ideas. The difficulty of associating dangerous ideas with particular people—the ideas held by someone are, after all, known only to him or her—was unnerving to those favoring social stability, leading them to fear what they could not see. The intangibility of ideas conjured fears of an intelligentsia, a class of people with interests that conflicted with those of others, a class disparaged by some as the enlightened ones—the illuminati.

As with the Continental expressions of anti-intellectualism, the American strain had anti-Semitic overtones and made periodic reappearances during times of rapid social change and apprehension about the future. The historian Richard Hofstadter describes it as a "paranoid style" in American politics that emerged in nineteenth-century New England with beliefs that certain secular intellectual movements were actually manifestations of Antichrist.[15] After the Civil War, those anxieties reemerged as fears that the faraway seat of centralized government in Washington, DC, could nurture alien and subversive influences, fueling post-Reconstruction reaction to the federal occupation of Confederate territory in the 1870s. Those same fears reached into the twentieth century when the contagion of Russian Bolshevism was blamed for the Rooseveltian collectivism masking as the New Deal for America, and the Potsdam settlement of World War II for a train of toppling dominos in Eastern Europe, creating widespread panic in the United States that the Red Tide of Communism would soon wash over Long Island—and then up the Naugatuck valley into Waterbury.

The May 1973 edition of the Birch Society's *American Opinion* carries a lengthy piece by Frank A. Capell, "Entertainment: There Is a Movement Stage Left," purporting to expose the subversive role Hollywood was playing. Identified for the article as a "professional intelligence specialist," Capell writes that "the masters of the [Soviet] Kremlin have long been aware that mass entertainment is an ideal means of communicating their propaganda" and goes on to claim that Moscow had "funneled millions of dollars into the American screen industry."[16]

Capell continues with a review of cold war allegations of communist infiltration of Hollywood, citing the investigations carried out by the House Committee on Un-American Activities in the early 1950s. Hundreds of authors, scriptwriters, producers, and directors, he writes, were under communist influence, many of them having been duped by the Reds. Capell indicts Marlon Brando for his role in the "pornographic" *Last Tango in Paris* and support of Leftist causes, including "Marxist terrorists," and then rails against Pete Seeger and other entertainers for their communist associations. Turning to Fonda, he recites her résumé of activism and collaboration with the enemy North Vietnamese but concentrates on her effectiveness as a campus lecturer and a link

141

connecting Hollywood and world Communism. Comparing her to "La Pasionaria," a leader in the Spanish antifascist movement of 1930s, Capell rewrites her work with the GI movement to read "distributing Communist propaganda at military posts."[17]

The Overdetermination of Hanoi Jane

Situated as Fonda was in the lost-war culture of the United States, her credentials as having been an opponent of the war in Vietnam and an attractive, wealthy woman with enormous public visibility presenting ambiguous gender identities made her a lighting rod waiting to be struck by public anger rising in a period of postimperial economic contraction. The OPEC oil crisis and predatory lending practices of banks combined to throw millions of small family farmers off their land and thrust millions more into states of insecurity from which they would never recover. By the end of the decade, the steel and auto industries were grinding to a halt, turning the crown jewels of American enterprise in the Great Lakes states into a rust belt. By adding *elite*—culturally and intellectually elite—to her dossier, the John Birch Society supercharged the ionic imbalance between themselves and the economically stressed middle- and working-class people they claimed affinity with, at one pole, and its Birch-constructed opposite pole around which they imagined a gathering of privileged and self-identified literati.

The hard times of the 1980s animated reactionary political tendencies lying dormant since the Great Depression. Figures marginal to mainstream politics, such as H. Ross Perot, trumpeted the promises of economic nationalism, using the specter of abandoned POWs and MIAs as a metaphor for the many Middle Americans left behind by Big Government. Beyond the political margins but always in the public's face were demagogic characters, such as Lyndon LaRouche, whose amalgam of Left-Right fantasies and brown-shirt thuggery confused and disrupted efforts to deepen and broaden progressive coalitions that had been forged in the antiwar movement.

LaRouche's political trajectory, too, traversed from Left to Right, exploiting as it moved the insecurities of activists adrift in the dissolution of the antiwar movement, farm families displaced from the land, and workers left behind by runaway shops. Dennis King likens LaRouche to Benito Mussolini, pointing out that LaRouche's "new American Fascism" wooed labor and small-business groups with propaganda campaigns against the Tri-lateral Commission and Rockefeller interests, while attacking mainstream liberal politicians such as Jimmy Carter and Ted Kennedy. His National Caucus of Labor Committees (NCLC) fashioned Jane Fonda into an all-purpose stickpin, appealing to misogynist, pro-war, and anti-environmentalist sentiments with bumper stickers reading, "Feed Jane Fonda to the Whales"—and a slogan specially designed for the nuclear industry, "Don't Let Jane Fonda Pull Down Your Plants."[18]

Trope-ing to the Present

In April 1999, Barbara Walters featured Fonda on an ABC special, highlighting her recognition by *Ladies' Home Journal* as one of the most important women of the twentieth century. Reaction to the show grew when a story began to circulate on the Internet claiming that POWs had given Fonda tiny pieces of paper with the names and serial numbers when she visited them in Hanoi. They hoped she would use the information to contact their relatives when she returned to the United States but, instead, she betrayed them and gave the information to their guards. According to the Internet story, some of the prisoners were beaten and three of them died.

Nothing in the story is true, however. In a three-part column at UrbanLegends.com, David Emery wrote on November 3, 1999, that the "tiny pieces of paper" story became popular when Jon E. Dougherty, a columnist for the Internet journal *WorldNetDaily*, posted a version of it entitled, "Not Saluting Jane Fonda." Dougherty's article was actually a clumsy compilation of three stories, the first of which was Colonel Jerry Driscoll's. The story attributed to Driscoll was that he had been forced to meet with Fonda while a prisoner in Hanoi. When he spat at her, he was beaten and dragged away. The second story was Colonel Larry Carrigan's, supposedly the only one of the POWs who had slipped Fonda a serial number and survived the beatings to tell the story. The third story, and the only one told in a first-person voice, was Michael Benge's. Benge had been taken captive as a civilian working for the U.S. government's Agency for International Development. He said he had been beaten and tortured after he told his captors that if he was forced to meet with Fonda he would tell her the prison camp conditions were horrid.[19]

143

Dougherty ends his article the way he begins it, with a renunciation of the *Ladies' Home Journal* for having chosen Fonda one of its "best"; seven days later, however, he published a correction, acknowledging that parts of the text were false. Carrigan reported he had no idea how the "tiny pieces of paper" story came to be attributed to him. "I never met Jane Fonda," he later told About.com's Emery. Driscoll also disavowed the account of his spitting at Fonda, saying it was "the product of a very vivid imagination." Benge stood by his story, according to Emery, but the provenance of his claim turns out to be suspect as well. Indeed, Benge might well be the source of this particular vein of Fonda lore.

Benge was an early responder to the Barbara Walters show, writing an April 28 piece entitled "Shame on Jane" for the Internet site Advocacy and Intelligence Index. Benge's story is that he was a "civilian economic advisor" when he was captured by the North Vietnamese. He says that after being held for a year in a cage in Cambodia, he was moved to Hanoi, where his captors asked him to meet with Jane Fonda. When he told them he would tell her about the terrible conditions in which he was held—far different from the conditions "parroted by Jane Fonda as 'humane and lenient,' " he writes—he was tortured. Benge ends the article with a claim that the North Vietnamese murdered eighty thousand political prisoners at the end of the war and laments that those souls rested on Jane Fonda's head. He cc'd his piece to "Mr. Eisner, Walt Disney Co."

From what we know, it seems as though the core parts of Benge's story of capture and imprisonment might be true, but the parts about Jane Fonda and his torture for not talking to her are post–Barbara Walters add-ons. Benge's story had previously circulated on-line in a June 1990 version based on the version that appears in *We Came Home*, Barbara Wyatt's edited collection of first-person POW stories; neither of those two earlier versions of his story contains references to Jane Fonda or beatings for refusing to talk to her.[20] Seemingly a mixture of fact and imagination that Benge concocted to get an audience for his anti-communist and anti-Fonda views, the 1999 version of his story was well suited for further myth-making, which is the use to which it was inadvertently (perhaps) put when Dougherty fitted it with the ersatz stories about Driscoll and Carrigan to create the most vile of all the Hanoi Jane tales.

Aid and Comfort

The attention Barbara Walters gave to Fonda's place on the *Ladies' Home Journal* list was clearly the match that lit the fuse, and another of the rockets that went off was Henry Mark Holzer. Holzer is a retired attorney with a long résumé of legal work for right-wing causes. Among his clients was Ayn Rand, author of *Fountainhead* and *Atlas Shrugged* and leader of the libertarian "objectivist" movement.

Holzer put aside work on his own memoirs and began a personal crusade to publicly expose Fonda as a traitor whose 1972 activities in Vietnam should have been legally prosecuted. His case against Fonda, published in 2002, in collaboration with his wife, as *"Aid and Comfort": Jane Fonda in North Vietnam*, was as much an attack on what he considered to be the weak-kneed liberalism of the Nixon administration's Department of Justice. The department, headed by Attorney General Richard Kleindienst, feared losing a treason case against Fonda, Holzer argues, because of the power of the left-wing movement in the country. The government, he concludes, had capitulated to the Left.[21]

Of the dozens of books and articles written about Fonda, this was the most straightforward effort to treat her as a political figure and condemn her as such. Coming thirty years after the war, the book probably would have been ignored as the product of one man's obsession, but the timing of its appearance gave it an unexpected resonance. Within weeks of the September 11, 2001, attacks, rumors were flying about President George W. Bush's foreknowledge of the events and the CIA's complicity in the attacks themselves. "Bush knew" became the bumper-sticker suggestion that the attacks were an "inside job" by enemies hidden in the Washington woodwork. The lexicon of conspiratorial betrayal was soon in play, its images enlivened with references to past instances of treason. In this context, it was not entirely surprising that pundits would put Hanoi Jane in play and Henry Holzer's book would find a market.

The disparaging of Bush administration critics as Hanoi Jane cutouts began soon after the attacks when Georgia congresswoman Cynthia McKinney criticized New York mayor Rudy Giuliani for refusing a ten-million-dollar check from the king of Saudi Arabia as compensation for the damage done by his countrymen who flew the planes into the twin towers. In response, the Internet columnist Debbie Schlussel 145 lampooned McKinney with the headline: "Cynthia McKinney: Today's Hanoi Jane." Schlussel went on to attack the congresswoman as "an American Villainess," beginning a trail of political events that ended with her unseating in the November 2002 elections.

Little did we know at the time that developments in Afghanistan were about to give Hanoi Jane a playmate, Taliban John. The new kid on the block was John Walker Lindh, captured in Afghanistan in late November. Lindh was an American convert to Islam who had gone to Pakistan for religious training and then Afghanistan for military training from the Islamist fighters known as the Taliban. At the time of his capture by the anti-Taliban and American-backed Northern Alliance, Lindh was going by a Muslim name. Subsequently, Lindh was held in Kala Jangi prison near Mazar-e Sharif, where he was interrogated by U.S. intelligence agents, among whom was the CIA's Mike Spann. Lindh was uncooperative, and shortly after he was questioned, there began a prison uprising in which Spann was killed. U.S. Special Forces then took custody of Lindh and his true identity as an American citizen became known to the world.

The unveiling of Lindh as the "American Taliban" dominated the news throughout December. Interest in him was driven by Lindh's identity as a possible traitor, an American who apparently had chosen to fight for an enemy who had dealt the country its largest-ever loss of life, property, and pride on its own soil. The possibility that Lindh had also collaborated in the death of Spann intensified the emotion around his case, as did speculation that he might be the link to so-called sleeper cells, units of Islamic terrorist organizations operating underground in the United States. From the moment of his arrest by U.S. officials then, press coverage of Lindh drew parallels between him and other traitors of the American cause, such as Benedict Arnold.

It was also clear that newsmakers were going to interpret the John Walker Lindh affair through the lens of "the sixties." Stories about Lindh's background featured reports that his parents' permissive child-rearing practices were influenced by Dr. Benjamin Spock, the psychologist often held responsible for the rebelliousness of the flower-child generation of student activists and antiwar protesters. Lindh had grown up in what one reporter called "a Birkenstock family" who had named him for the Beatle singer John Lennon. Lindh was inspired by the movie

Malcolm X to become a Muslim and his home was Marin County, California, the San Francisco suburb where many Americans remember something happening—something like a jailhouse riot having to do with the sixties. With cues like these telling Americans bewildered by September 11 to "think betrayal, think sixties," it was only a matter of time before the personages of Lindh and Fonda were aligned.

Six months after the attacks, Hanoi Jane and Taliban John were paired on the tool bar of Henry Holzer's Web site. Mostly, the alignment appeared to be a promotional gambit to parlay Lindh's infamy into attention for the author's book. Internet surfers looking for material on Lindh were inevitably led to the TalibanJohn.info address, which was essentially Holzer's home page. Clicking on TalibanJohn.info yielded a list of short commentaries by Holzer in which he discussed the details of Lindh's involvement with the Taliban and the legal liabilities he faced. Several of the first pieces, written shortly after Walker's capture, mentioned Fonda, along with other historical cases of treason. Anyone not acquainted with Hanoi Jane, which would be a large number of the twenty-first-century cyber searchers who happened onto Holzer's home page, could go back to the tool bar and click on TalibanJohn's neighbor, hanoijane.net.

Clicking on hanoijane.net led to "The Official Site for Information about Jane Fonda's 1972 Trip to Wartime North Vietnam." This "official" page was actually an advertisement for *Aid and Comfort*, with links to reviews of the book. The reviews by the former leftists Ronald Radosh and David Horowitz (his from his own *FrontPageMag*, a portal preoccupied with immigration issues and communist plots to take over American universities) are interesting guides pointing to the larger set of conservative concerns from which the anti-Fonda campaign emanates. A click on "endorsements" is similarly revealing. Horowitz and former POWs Colonel "Bud" Day and Captain Mike McGrath endorse the book, as does Fred Kiley, author of *Honor Bound*, about the POW experience. The most interesting endorsement, however, is from Nelson DeMille, avowed libertarian and best-selling author of several novels, including *Charm School*, a cold-war fantasy about the U.S. government's betrayal of Vietnam-war POWs.

Holzer made the Lindh-Fonda link work in two directions: read one way, it said we should recognize the evil in John Walker Lindh because he is like Jane Fonda; read another way, it reminded us who Fonda was by saying, in effect, she is like John Lindh. Few people probably needed the association with Fonda to understand the treasonous implications of Lindh's involvements, so Holzer's more lasting contribution will probably be his re-demonizing of Fonda. When he appeared on the March 6, 2002, television talk show *The O'Reilly Factor*, for example, the host introduced Holzer, saying American resentment of Jane Fonda was "inflamed by the indictment of John Walker," implying that if Lindh was indictable, the Fonda case should be given a second look.

John Kerry: He's Like "Hanoi Jane"

The media attention to the Lindh case and Holzer's self-promotion pushed *"Aid and Comfort"* into respectable sales numbers and broadened the popularity of the Hanoi Jane image beyond what it had ever been. A Google search in December 2002 for "Hanoi Jane" yielded 11,800 entries, a large proportion of which were related to either Fonda's selection as one of the *Ladies' Home Journal* "best" or, in some way or other, to Holzer's book. Five years later, that number had grown to 113,000.[22] In its largest role ever, Hanoi Jane played what may have been the deciding character in the 2004 presidential campaign. Honing their electioneering rhetoric and hoping to neutralize John Kerry's record as a decorated war veteran, conservatives released photos supposedly connecting him with Jane Fonda, the antiwar activist, and thereby brushing him with the hues of anti-Americanism that many voters associated with Hanoi Jane.

Most commentary around the Kerry-Fonda alliance focused on Kerry and the complexity of his identity as a veteran and antiwar activist, public roles that helped launch his political career. Some Americans were given pause that his activism may have endangered troops still fighting in Vietnam, and that his leading role in settling with the Vietnamese on the issue of unaccounted for POWs in 1996 may have been naïve; but, as suggested by his successful three-term career in the Senate, the electorate seemed able to abide his record on war-related issues—until 2004, that is.

Within weeks of announcing his run, Kerry met opposition from a group of Republicans known as the "Swift Boat" veterans, named for the small, speedy craft in which they had patrolled the inland waters of Vietnam during the war years. Kerry had commanded one of the boats as a young navy lieutenant in 1968 and won medals for valor. But the Swift Boaters questioned his record, even contending that he may have falsified an after-battle report to embellish his role in saving a fellow sailor and killing a Viet Cong soldier. Those charges detracted from the image of a combat-tested veteran that was important to Kerry's credentialing for the commander-in-chief position he would be filling as President, but it was hardly a fatal blow to the campaign.[23]

Kerry's military record, however, would not be the sticking point in the campaign; even his claim of having been upriver on a covert raid into Cambodia on Christmas Eve 1968—a story that sounded suspiciously like the 1978 film *Apocalypse Now*—added little traction to Swift Boaters' efforts against him. What did stick, though, was the characterization of him as a "flip-flopper," a politician whose changeable policy positions went beyond the usual opportunism of the campaign season to issues of character and personal stability. As drawn by his critics, Kerry's portrait conveyed uncertainty, lack of commitment, perhaps even insecurity about his sexuality—features that stood out from the canvas for the eye preconditioned to seeing them in another character: "You know John Kerry, he's like Jane Fonda."

The use of Hanoi Jane as a stand-in for issues unrelated to the war in Vietnam may have signaled its passage into simulacrum, a trope with independence from the person and events of its origin, a symbol that became a referent able to transfer its own meaning onto other persons and events. It was a trope with multiply determinants brought together by history. But history, too, has a structure and that structure makes the story of Hanoi Jane more than a war-postwar story, more than a place in the lineage of female betrayal figures, and more, even, than the responses of people and groups to economic crises.

Hanoi Jane works the way it does not just because of its place amid those other elements but because it is a linguistic form that also has a biography, a form that laid down tracks in which future uses of it would travel. Hanoi Jane satisfies the mind's patterned need for "oneness," the mind's preference for a single figure that enables us to forget all the other candidates for remembrance—in this instance, the three hundred other peace travelers to Hanoi and certainly the "whole," the social movement that the group comprised.

The three-syllabic structure of Hanoi Jane has an auditory familiarity—resonance with Tokyo Rose—an attribute that Barry Schwartz says comes with repeated reuses of prior forms.[24] It connects the mind with places—Tokyo and Hanoi—that have specific time- and war-related connotations and gender-specific names. It is that "prior coinage" that constitutes the historical-linguistic structure in Hanoi Jane that eases the mind into an association of Fonda with treason.

9

JANE FONDA

HANOI JANE'S

EVIL TWIN

Like the sounds of Huey helicopters and the picture of little Kim Phuc's napalmed body, Jane Fonda is an iconic character through which Americans remember the war in Vietnam, the image of a peace activist who traveled to the enemy capital, Hanoi, where she collaborated with the communists, perhaps even compromising the welfare of the U.S. prisoners they held. Critics call her Hanoi Jane, evoking the treasonous figures from World Wars I and II, Mata Hari and Tokyo Rose. As with its mnemonic models, Hanoi Jane is a structure with many dimensions, one of which is the textured life of its namesake, Jane Fonda.

The Politics of Personal Assassination

Biographies of Jane Fonda are almost always teleological, pulled through a chronology of vignettes and images by Hanoi Jane, the troubled end point where writers feel the journey has to arrive. The format is formulaic: her mother's suicide; her father's emotional absence; her anxious teen and college years; her French period, first marriage, and sexualizing as Barbarella; her radical years and second marriage to Tom Hayden; her film career; and her (re)christening as Hanoi Jane in Waterbury, Connecticut. Editions with the epilogue have her born still again as a Christian fundamentalist, the wifely Mrs. Ted Turner, and then a third-time divorcee as Ted's ex.

Left at that, though, the Fonda biography has no political and cultural legs. It is what it is, a kind of cautionary tale that family dysfunction reproduces itself, infecting its victims' personal and professional lives before spreading through political and cultural institutions and becoming a hazard to national security. On that level the Jane Fonda story might have been useful in the neoconservatives' post-Vietnam campaign to begin rebuilding the American empire with its own shored-up sense of traditional family values but it would never have worked for the construction of Hanoi Jane, qualities for which what real-life Jane did are less important than who and what she is, qualities that are, for the political Right, hard to discern and harder still to name.

It is not uncommon, then, that the political transformation of Jane Fonda into Hanoi Jane is explained through "the personal." Referring to her life as "convoluted," Thomas Kiernan writes on the last page of his 1973 *Intimate Biography of Jane Fonda* that her turn to the political came with her marriage to Tom Hayden, wherein she found "the magical family ties that had slipped from grasp during her first thirty-five years." In a 1979 *Washington Post* article, Myra MacPherson points out a path of instability that began with Fonda's sublimation to her father's needs and ran through "the Hollywood makeovers and falsies of the 1950s," to "exile" in Paris and return to the United States for involvement in the civil rights and antiwar movements. The London *Observer*'s Paul Harris says that Fonda's life was "marked by yearning for a father who was never there." Fonda's childhood was "traumatizing," he writes, leading her to a life of "twists and turns." Her search for a lovable father-figure, Harris thinks, led her to Tom Hayden "with whom she transformed into an anti-war campaigner."[1]

Critics are wont to find, as well, a checkerboard pattern in her film career, a bothersome trait they then attribute to her unsettled sense of self. George Haddad-Garcia, for example, sees an odyssey in her filmography, beginning with what he calls a "cotton-candy star, half-child in the frothy American comedy" *Walk on the Wildside* (1962) and running from there to "soft-core European romps" in her work with Roger Vadim for *Barbarella* (1968). According to Haddad-Garcia, she then grew into feminism for *They Shoot Horses, Don't They?* (1969) before returning to the parental hearth playing opposite her real-life father, Henry, in *On Golden Pond* (1981). But not everyone saw that change as "development" in Fonda's personal character, or if they did, they saw it as irreversible. Feminists, Herman and Downing remind readers, saw Fonda's Oscar-winning "Bree" in *Klute* (1971) as having choices limited to the whore-housewife range of options, her "Sally" in *Coming Home* (1978) seemed stuck with choosing between the men in her life, and the parallaxan story line of *On Golden Pond* about her strained off-screen relationship to her father, Henry, just made the discontinuities in her life all the more visible to the public.[2]

The search for flawed character in their enemies that could then be used for personal smear campaigns was a hallmark of conservative political strategy during the Nixon years, raising its head most prominently in the events leading to Watergate. The release of the classified documents later known as the "Pentagon Papers" induced a paranoia in Nixon circles about the "enemies within" that focused on Daniel Ellsberg, who had photocopied the papers and turned them over to the *New York Times* for publication. In retaliation, the administration broke into the office of Lewis Fielding, Ellsberg's psychiatrist, hoping to find records on his mental condition that could be used to embarrass him publicly. The Right's affinity for the tactics of character assassination continued beyond the 1970s with innuendos about Gary Hart's character and personal life to hang the "flack" label on him and derail his "new ideas" campaign for the 1984 Democratic Party nomination; mounting the counterslogan "Where's the beef?" they turned his diploma as an Oxford University graduate with a Ph.D. in philosophy into a sign of effeteness and a political deficit.[3]

By the 1990s, "character" was the litmus test of political qualification and Republicans tied up two terms of the Clinton presidency with scrutiny of his family business affairs and sexual dalliances with the intern Monica Lewinski. In 2004, Republican supporters of George W. Bush charged Democrat John Kerry with falsifying his military record, an accusation that went to heart of his character. Attacks on Kerry's personal tastes, like that for French wine—an attack the *New York Times* columnist Frank Rich observed was code for "faggot"—and caricatures of his policy changes all bespoke, for enough voters, personal instability and unresolved identity issues that could surface in a time of crisis as a weak link in national security. Thinking there might be something political in "the personal," Americans reelected George W. Bush.

The Micropolitics of Power

Attacks on a person's character can lead to her being isolated, disparaged, or even rejected by family and friends on whom her sense of self-worth depends. Social psychologists call that effect "status deprivation" and the power of it can lead victims to make adjustments in their behavior in order to recover their social standing. Those adjustments, however, can then be interpreted as signs of instability, a character flaw, setting off another cycle of status deprivation and response to it. The historical trajectory of American political culture and Fonda's biography coincided closely enough to ensure that that pattern would evince itself in her life.[4]

In an April 1974 *Playboy* interview with her and Hayden, for example, Fonda speculated that the rising hostility to her was due to her having violated feminine norms by speaking her mind in public places, punctuating the point by saying she "would no longer accept the image of a mindless Barbarella floating through space." Intending to strike a pose of mindfulness through those words, she inadvertently and unnecessarily—in the light of later interpretations of *Barbarella*—fed the perception of discontinuity in her career that critics would soon throw back at her. Ten years later she was still putting distance between herself and the galactic warrior-woman, telling Erica Jong for a *Ladies' Home Journal* interview that that film and her role as an activist were contradictory.[5]

The crumbling of the antiwar Left after 1975 eliminated any chance that Fonda could turn there for the ego support she may have sought. A liberal faction of the movement followed the lead of the balladeer Joan Baez, who, like Fonda, had gone to Hanoi in 1972 to help end the war but then, in 1979, upbraided the communist regime for its repressive practices. Fonda said publicly that she did not see a basis for Baez's charges, but other stalwart peace activists now wondered, too, whether their opposition to the war had been naïve. The years of activism took a toll on personal lives, and needing to realign their priorities as they moved into middle age and new commitments to family and community, some radicals probably took Baez's rethinking of the war's politics as license to step away from the movement; even more of them may have willfully heard Fonda to be recanting her radical period when she appeared on Barbara Walters's 20/20 show in 1989 and said she was sorry for the way she had spoken about the POW issue in 1973. Twenty years later, it was common to be told, as a "matter of fact" by people who simultaneously professed to like her, that Fonda had denounced her political past and was no longer active.[6]

Pinning the (Devil's) Tail on Jane

The real-world Jane Fonda is not easily reduced to disposable essences, a quality that confounds political rightists and adds to the danger she represents to them. To begin with, her "convoluted" personal life that supposedly indicates some deeper and troubling psychoanalytic trait is too nuanced to be captured by pop psychology.

Fonda's father, Henry, whom some conservatives hold up as the pillar of the staid Americanism from which they say Jane Fonda strayed, was actually a "populist liberal" with values not so incompatible with those of the daughter he raised. In his 1991 book *The Fondas: A Hollywood Dynasty*, Peter Collier recalls how the young Henry had resisted his father's entreaties to stay in Omaha, Nebraska's small-business world, opting instead for theater and the East Coast. In New York City, twenty-five-year-old Henry's imagination was seized by *Gods of the Lightning*, a play by Maxwell Anderson and Harold Hickerson about Sacco and Vanzetti, the Italian immigrants who were executed in Massachusetts for robbery and the murder of two payroll clerks. The case gained political prominence because Sacco and Vanzetti were anarchists, followers of the "direct action" workers movement. According to Collier, Henry left the theater "scowling like a syndicalist at the beat cop on the street."[7]

Henry Fonda was headed for the stage and movie set, not the picket line, but the political values rooted and nurtured in New York City's Greenwich Village of the 1920s went with him. By the time the House Un-American Activities Committee began ferreting out communists in the film industry during the 1950s, his political persona was established through the public's association of him with the roles he played on stage and screen. The largest of those was that of Tom Joad, the union organizer in *Grapes of Wrath*, an image from which some Americans would never be able to distinguish him—an image his conservative fans would like to forget. There was also Doug Roberts, the anti-authoritarian navy officer in *Mr. Roberts*; and there was his one-man portrayal of Clarence Darrow, the lawyer who defended the left-wing union leaders

Eugene Debs and "Big Bill" Haywood and John Scopes, the Tennessee teacher prosecuted for teaching evolution. Lost in the glare of those acclaimed performances was his role in the 1942 film *The Male Animal*, in which he played Tommy Turner, a college professor who plans to read to his English class a letter written by the martyred anarchist Bartolomeo Vanzetti. The college's trustees, who have already fired some of his colleagues for being "reds," do not want the letter read and threaten to deny Turner a promotion to full professor.[8]

In their zeal to write a Jane Fonda biography that casts the shadow of her radicalism across their memory of her father, Fonda critics may in fact imagine a Henry who is as mythical as their image of her.[9] The celluloid Henry that filmgoers knew was the real deal, an actor who played the historical figures he admired, Jane explains in her memoir. Against the tide of cold war McCarthyism, he joined Gregory Peck and Katharine Hepburn in objecting to the witch hunt for subversion in Hollywood, taking off-screen the lessons about life and values that Jane remembered years later as having been taught by the roles he played on screen.[10]

Jane and the Impresarios

Just as much as the longer look at her father's career, highlighted by her own recognition that he delivered his parental values through his art—and she got them—works for dispelling real-world Jane's biography as a basis for Hanoi Jane, so too does a second look at the other men in her life. The quick and dirty take on her first husband, the filmmaker Roger Vadim, is that he was a womanizer who pimped out beautiful actresses for his own fame and fortune. If that is an accurate portrait, it means her association with him, through marriage, is evidence for a young-adult Jane whose values were already incompatible with those of her father, Henry—and with the political Tom Hayden, whom she married next. But that is not the only read on Vadim.

Roger Vadim

Collier says the Vadim that Jane knew "was not really a reckless sexual adventurer but actually a good deal like her father—reserved and dignified, even somewhat passive; bourgeois in his belief in marriage and children." In his memoir *Reunion*, Hayden remembers Vadim as "a loving and caring parent."[11] Vadim's relationship with Fonda lacked the signs of possessiveness and male dominance that we would expect to see if he sought and found in her the kind of personal emptiness he allegedly preyed on.[12] As remembered by the Fonda biographer Sean French, Vadim "had a genius for finding and nurturing women [and was] utterly lacking in machismo or in any need to compete with his lovers." Referring to Vadim's "sweet passivity," French writes that the director's actresses always got more from him than he from them.[13]

Most important was the role Vadim played in Fonda's political maturation. Although she was preordained, perhaps, by family background and primed by her early 1960s exposure to Parisian Leftism, Vadim nevertheless jarred her to consciousness. Vadim was born in France but his father was Russian and he made his first trip to the ancestral home in 1964, taking Fonda with him. While they watched the Soviet May Day parade in Red Square together, Vadim used some of her naïve remarks about Communism to point out the insularity of American political culture; when the Tonkin Gulf resolution was passed a few months later, he drew on his familiarity with the French experience in Indochina for a first lesson on Vietnam, declaring to her that the United States would also face defeat there. Vadim, though, was headed for union leadership in the film industry and the events of May 1968, while Fonda, pregnant with Vanessa, was drawn by a U.S. Army resister stationed in Germany named Dick Perrin to the American antiwar movement and the rapidly growing dissent within the military.[14]

By its overassociation of Fonda with her Barbarella image, the American political Right is able to becloud the French period of her biography, making her appearance a few years later as an activist in the company of Tom Hayden seem stark and abrupt, an unforeseeable "coming out" with no or little continuity with her years in France—the kind of incongruity essential to their construction of Hanoi Jane. With the details of those years restored to view, however, that stage of her life looks more seamless. Her relationship with Perrin, meanwhile, dispels the rightist fantasy that Fonda was some kind of subversive force to whom the radicalizing of U.S. soldiers and veterans could be attributed. In fact, Perrin was an activist in RITA (Resisters Inside the Army), an organization that preceded by a couple of years her own involvement in the GI movement against the war.[15]

Tom Hayden

Fonda has written about her vulnerability to strong men but, like her self-criticism for *Barbarella*, the actual record might be more forgiving. She returned from France with Vadim and their newborn daughter in early 1969 and got involved first with the American Indian Movement and Black Panthers and then the GI antiwar movement. It was a chronology that belied, again, popularly held notions that she went from a brainless sex kitten in Vadim's enthrall to a New Left groupie in Hayden's sway.[16]

By the time she and Hayden first met in 1971, Fonda had deepened her identification with the emergent feminism of the time, having been part of a French political circle that included Simone de Beauvoir and then studying for her role as the prostitute Bree Daniels in *Klute*: "I turned a corner," Fonda later wrote about working on the part of Bree, by seeing "hooking" as a performance of power through the control of sex acts.[17] She was likewise an established figure in the antiwar movement before meeting Hayden, having already assisted the Winter Soldier war-crimes hearings in Detroit and then produced and toured military towns with the antiwar variety show FTA (Free the Army), a chronology that discredits claims like that of Paul Harris that Hayden led her into the peace movement. The provenance of FTA, meanwhile, inspired as it was by Howard Levy, an army captain who did jail time for refusal to train Special Forces headed for Vietnam, is more evidence that the GI movement itself moved Fonda, rather than the other way around.[18]

Far from having led Fonda into a political life, Hayden, as he recalled years later in his memoir, *Reunion*, was instead drawn to her at a 1972 antiwar event in Los Angeles. At the time, Hayden writes, "she was an accomplished speaker [with] a persuasive presentation [that was] more political than mine." It was "important," he continues, "that Jane was a woman who could not be eclipsed or diminished in my shadow, and I was a man who was not threatened by her greater fame and power."[19] When Fonda was invited to Hanoi a few months later, Hayden insisted she go alone even though his previous travel there would probably have opened some doors for her (in both logistical and political ways).

Hayden wrote about the years of their marriage in the first-person plural "we," as did Fonda writing about the workout business she co-founded with Hayden to raise money for the Campaign for Economic

Democracy—not the literary form expected from divorcees remembering a marriage wherein one spouse subordinated the other. The irony that rightists can denigrate Fonda for her submissiveness to strong men and in the same breathe belittle Hayden as "Mr. Jane Fonda" for his flaccid dependence on her support for his political career is evidence in itself that attempts to simplify Jane Fonda, like many efforts in stereotyping, tend toward contradiction.[20]

Ted Turner

Right-wing critics would have us believe that Fonda's attraction to Turner was jump-started by her own business success, a kind of premonition that she was ready to leave her radical past and return to the mainstream. But just as the political gap between Vadim and Hayden was narrower than it is made to appear by those painting the checkerboard portrait of Hanoi Jane's biography, so too can a look back find seldom-recognized likenesses between Hayden and Turner.

Not surprisingly, Turner's life story is contested terrain. Reese Schonfeld, an early associate of his at CNN, gives us a manipulative and power-hungry manic-depressive Ted sandwiched between two blonds with a bottle of booze in front of him. Schonfeld says the college-aged Turner admired Hitler and wanted to use the family fortune to make more money on televised entertainment. He hated the news, Schonfeld claims. Some or all of that may be true—or Schonfeld and other biographers may have missed something, or Turner may have reformed himself in the years before meeting Fonda. Whatever the truth may be, Fonda recalled meeting a "funny, quick, complicated, and smart" Ted with "social values that didn't put money first," a Ted with "grand dreams of changing the world for the better."[21]

Turner was imbued with Horatio Alger ethics, the belief that people could pull themselves up by their own bootstraps. He socialized comfortably with businessmen who were responsible for the favelas in Brazil and dollar-a-day maquiladoras in Mexico and was unwilling to engage the realities of structural inequality around the world. These traits bothered Fonda, but she recognized in CNN a revolutionary vision that could "transform the planet into Marshall McLuhan's global village" and make the news a "democratic and empowering medium." His philanthropy, in any case seemed to speak louder than his words. The significance of the billion dollars he gave to counter female genital mutilation was matched by his boldness in choosing the beneficiary: the United Nations, Antichrist to the world of private foundations and businesses that customarily mediate first world–third world charitable exchanges. Subsequently, that gift endowed the United Nations Foundation, an innovative attempt to leverage large-scale private-public financial support for a global governmental institution. Fonda's involvement with Turner's giving increased her exposure to world poverty and the widespread sexual exploitation of young women, experiences to which she attributed her "calling" to the campaign for lower levels of teen pregnancy.[22]

The obvious differences in the public images of Vadim, Hayden, and Turner invites the denigration of Fonda as the vacillating Hanoi Jane. But appearances can obscure other qualities, making it possible that the trope makers might be missing or leaving out biographical details that complicate their work. All of Fonda's men were dynamic and creative individuals who, like her, made their own selves by making the world around them; none of their lives was a constant, all were trajectories of personal growth and development. Vadim, for example, was notably avant-garde, often on the cutting edge of film-making technology and ahead of the images and narratives popular with other artists. Which Vadim do we use for the dramatic contrast with Hayden that supposedly evinces the inconsistency of Hanoi Jane's love life? And which Hayden do we use? If we compare the iconoclastic director of *Barbarella* with the political-realist Tom Hayden who freed American POWs in 1967, the point goes to Fonda's critics. But if we use the Vadim who made up bedtime fantasies for his daughter Vanessa and went on to direct "Beauty and the Beast" for the *Faerie Tale Theatre* television series in the 1980s for comparison with the Little League coach Hayden, the gap narrows. And is Hayden, the political entrepreneur who combined an eighteen-year career as a California assemblyman with campaigns for economic democracy, all that different from Turner, the media mogul who deigned to bring news and information to the world before putting a billion-dollar speed bump in the road to neoliberalism?

From Ted to Thomas

Taken at face value, Fonda's marriage to Ted Turner could have endeared her to conservatives as the prodigal daughter returned to the fold—the fold, that is, of upper-echelon media and entertainment circles into which she had been born. But the Right read the marriage as further evidence of her social and emotional instability and, with a preternatural suspicion that media elites like Turner are modernity's incarnation of the Beast, they were not tempted to cast her in that biblical role. Nor did her turn to Christianity in the last years of the marriage temper their dislike. Indeed, if distrust of appearances weighed on their assessment of her conversion, their hesitation was prudent—her Christianity was not theirs.

On the Left, meanwhile, the "rumor" that she had become "a born-again" suggested to her shrinking circle of radical friends that her slide to the Right was unabated and heading for alignment with the Christian millennialism being fed by end-of-time anxieties and the uncertainties accompanying the United States' declining position in the world. Her fellow travelers on the secular Left who understood religion to be an expression of alienation were dismayed by any reading of her turn, while those practicing their own versions of liberation theology struggled to reconcile their more interpretive approach to scripture with the fundamentalism they supposed she was drawn to. As it turned out, the inclination of foes to put air quotes on Fonda's conversion was no stronger than those of her friends who wanted to see some sign that this was still another yet-to-be explained development in her life.

With the publication of Fonda's memoir *My Life So Far* in 2005 it was clear that the conversion had followed a sincere spiritual search, a desire to integrate her embodied self with the soul self she felt she had externalized, the spiritual self she felt separated from. In a 2006 interview with Robin Morgan for *Ms.* magazine, Fonda recalled being beckoned by *progressive* (her italics) Christians, such as Jimmy Carter and Andrew Young, and then being confirmed in what she was feeling by reading Elaine Pagels's research on the Gnostic gospels, a radical interpretation of Christianity that was consistent with her feminism and provided grounding for a woman-centered spiritualism. Reading the Gospel of Thomas, a text discarded for centuries by the religious movements leading to Christianity, Fonda was able to deconstruct the male-female dichotomy essential to the modern Church and challenge what she called its God-as-male idolatry—all heresy in the eyes of Christian conservatives but entirely consistent with the image of Hanoi Jane they had constructed.

Chickens or Eggs or . . . *Jane Fonda?*

Hanoi Jane is mythical, not so much because its components are not true or never happened: Jane Fonda did play sexually complex characters in films; she did help found an antiwar entertainment troupe with the evocative and double-entendre name of "Free/Fuck the Army"; she was married (and divorced) three times to high-profile men, each carrying his own baggage of fidelity issues; she did trek to an enemy capital, though during a war that was notably unpopular in her own country; and she did speak carelessly about the welfare and integrity of POWs at the very time the country's masculinity, battered by the loss of the war, sought refurbishing through identification with their heroism.

The truth in Jane Fonda's life becomes grist for her mythologizing as Hanoi Jane, however, only by a selective use of its parts. Like those of many others who grew to adulthood in the late 1950s and 1960s, her differences with her father did not constitute a rejection of his values so much as a disappointment that he didn't always live up to them as courageously as she would have liked. Nor was she out of tune with the tenor of the times. While her thirty-something years looked different than her twenty-somethings—new loves, new places, and new commitments—differences allowing critics to cry "inconsistency!" "instability!"—her life, were it to be written as a storyboard and placed alongside the events and changes in which it was lived, would look remarkably in sync with those times, even representative of them.

What is less obvious is whether the world her detractors say she was out of step with ever existed outside their own minds. Myths, after all, are as much about the people who make them as the people and events about whom the stories speak. Thus, the myth that Hanoi Jane betrayed the POWs held in Hanoi is really about Americans needing to believe that the men held there were loyal to the storytellers' idealized notion of masculinity and own sense of Americanism. Without Hanoi Jane, the so-called official story of the POWs' heroic sacrifice loses some of its luster and, with that, the reality that the dissatisfaction and dissent of the Vietnam War years was the hallmark of that period becomes harder to deny; most poignantly, the very emotional and political needs that called forth Hanoi Jane remind us that that discontent also reached into the ranks of the military, into, even, the prison culture of Hao Lo, a truth that is especially hard for some to accept.

The former POW Kevin McManus and his wife, Mary Jane, appeared on the May 2, 2005, edition of the Comcast Network's news show *It's Your Call with Lynn Doyle*. Mary Jane McManus was an activist in the POW/MIA movement during the years of her husband's imprisonment. Together, the McManuses continue their activism through the Veteran's Legacy Project with the belief that the United States had won the war by 1969 but that forces at home conspired to turn that victory into defeat. Asked by the moderator whom she blamed for the defeat, McManus responded, "I don't know on whom to place the blame first, the media or the politicians. I haven't discovered the chicken or the egg but they were definitely working together and Jane Fonda in particular [*sic*]."[23]

Coming near the end of an hour-long program during which there was no mention of Fonda (or Hanoi Jane), the dropping-in of Fonda's name in such an awkward fashion was a kind of shorthand, an attempt to enlist audience participation in forwarding a durable myth into a new century: "You know what I mean? The war was lost because liberal Washington insiders and media elites conspired to sell-out the military. You know, Jane Fonda . . . like Hanoi Jane."

It's like, well, you know—Jane Fonda as coda.

NOTES

Chapter 1. From Hanoi Jane to Osama bin Fonda

1. In his poem "Forever Green," Russ Vaughn states, "Hanoi Jane helped them win," referring to communist North Vietnam. In the poem Vaughn repeatedly calls Fonda a whore and bitch. See http://iwvpa.net/vaughnr/forever_.php.

2. Lembcke, *Spitting Image*, debunks the myth of spat-upon Vietnam veterans, and chap. 1 presents a detailed analysis of how the image was exploited for propaganda purposes during the Gulf War. In many ways, the Gulf War was about Vietnam. When it was over, President George W. Bush said the war had been necessary to shake the nation out of its "Vietnam syndrome," a reference to the supposed collective malaise that the loss in Vietnam had put the country in.

3. MacArthur, *Second Front* has a helpful discussion of Arnett's reputation as a Vietnam War reporter. The author recalls that, during the war, President Lyndon Johnson's assistant, Jack Valenti, once said that Arnett's reporting was "more damaging to the U.S. cause than a whole division of Vietcong" (125).

4. In a fictional essay, "The War over Jane Fonda," Robert Patrick set himself in a living room with his sister and brother-in-law (B.I.L.) as the Persian Gulf War began. They're listening to talk radio:

WOMAN CALLER (to the radio show): No wonder Ted Turner on CNN is showing all of Sadaam Hussein's propaganda. Turner is going out with the Jane Fonda, and she's poisoned his mind against America!

B.I.L.: Shit, she's probably screwing Sadamm Hussein.

ROBERT PATRICK: Who, that lady caller?

B.I.L.: No, Hanoi Jane.

ROBERT: You can't mean Jane Fonda. The woman is adamantly against tyranny everywhere.

B.I.L. (growling): Don't talk to me about that whore. She betrayed her country.

ROBERT: Good God. How?

B.I.L.: She sided with the enemy, swallowed them lies that we was bombing [Vietnamese] civilian targets.

5. Hackworth has written several popular books about his Vietnam War experiences. The most recent is *Steel My Soldiers' Hearts*.

6. The selection panel was Jane DeHart, Anne Fausto-Sterling, Evelyn Brooks Higginbotham, Linda Kerber, Mary Beth Norton, Vicki Ruiz, and Anne Firor Scott. The November 1999 edition of the *Ladies' Home Journal* presents the winners again with brief text and some pictures.

7. In a posting on May 2, 2000, Jack Shafer, the editor of the online magazine *Slate*, upbraided the *New York Times* and *U.S. News and World Report* for their uncritical references to Vietnam veterans' having been spat on during the 1960s and 1970s. In three days, *Slate* received nearly three hundred postings in response. Most of the writers attacked Shafer, and some laid the loss of the war on the home front. "Viet Vet," for example, wrote on May 2, "The media killed us and thousands of Vietnamese and lost the war." On May 4, "Kevin R" wrote that opponents of the war had helped the wrong side win.

8. Ward Churchill, a Colorado University professor, was fired after writing about the attacks as "chickens coming home to roost." Subsequently, David Horowitz used Churchill to headline *The Professors*, his book on the most dangerous professors in America.

9. McDermott and Bonior had appeared on ABC's *This Week*, reposted to the Worldnetdaily blog October 19, 2001; George Will's column ran in the *Worcester (MA) Telegram and Gazette* on October 2, 2002; the *New York Post* letters were in the October 6 edition; the references to Ritter are in Barry Bearak's very interesting article, "Scott Ritter's Iraq Complex," *New York Times Sunday Magazine*, November 24, 2002.

10. "Man Spits Tobacco Juice in Jane Fonda's Face at Book Signing," *Houston Chronicle*, April 21, 2005.

Chapter 2. "This Is Jane Fonda . . . Speaking to You from Hanoi"

1. The itinerary of Staughton Lynd, Herbert Aptheker, and Tom Hayden in 1965 was typical: leaving New York City on December 19, 1965, they made stops in London, Prague, Moscow, and Beijing, before arriving in Hanoi on December 28. In a 1990 interview, Ramsey Clark recalled his 1972 itinerary: Western Europe, Moscow, Tashkent, Calcutta, Burma, Laos, Hanoi (Clinton, *Loyal Opposition*, 253).

2. According to Hershberger, *Traveling to Vietnam*, the State Department had seized the passports of twenty-seven travelers by late 1967, and others had been denied passports for travel. For Ethel Taylor, see Clinton, *Loyal Opposition*, 148.

3. Young, *Vietnam Wars*, 197–202.

4. Ten American women went to Jakarta, where they signed a joint agreement with their Vietnamese counterparts, reasserting the provisions of the 1954 Geneva Accords that had ended hostilities stemming from the war against the French.

5. The Geneva Agreement reached in July 1954 designated the 17th parallel as a military demarcation line. Forces aligned with the nationalist movement of Ho Chi Minh were allowed to group north of the line, whereas those aligned with the pro–U.S. government in Saigon collected in the South.

6. Peace activists were not the only Americans going to Hanoi—or trying. In early September 1972, Teamster Union president Jimmy Hoffa requested permission from the U.S. government to travel there to negotiate for prisoner releases. Permission was initially granted, inspiring the syndicated humorist Art Buchwald to quip that President Richard Nixon wanted him to organize the truck drivers on the Ho Chi Minh trail so they would strike, thereby stopping the flow of supplies to the South. (See *Pacific Stars and Strips*, September 9, 1972, 1, and September 25, 1972, 10.)

7. Holzer and Holzer, "*Aid and Comfort*," 138.

8. It is significant that "Hanoi Rose" was applied to Fonda, because it means that, at the time, her image was being filtered through the lens of the World War II–era figure Tokyo Rose, rather than having its own standing, yet to be established, as Hanoi Jane. (For further discussion of Tokyo Rose and its connection to Hanoi Jane, see chapter 8.)

9. *Parades* was based on the rebellion at the U.S. Army's Presidio Stockade that began when one of the prisoners was shot and killed while trying to escape. The Presidio rebellion is recalled in the 2006 documentary film, *Sir! No Sir!* The other film, better know as *Deep Throat* but advertised in this edition of the *Daily News* as *Throat*, was the first porn-chic film about the sexually frustrated Linda Lovelace. With the help of Dr. Young, she discovers that her clitoris is embedded in her throat, a condition the doctor is willingly able to treat. The juxtaposition of the Fonda news story between *Parades* and *Throat* also merged the symbols of political and cultural decay that conservatives would hold her responsible for years later.

10. My thanks to Mary Hershberger, who gave me copies of the televised newscasts, which she obtained from the Television News Archive at Vanderbilt University.

11. Karnow, *Vietnam, a History*, 490, recalls the controversy surrounding Salisbury's trip. Salisbury's dispatches were published as *Behind the Lines—Hanoi*   167

in 1967. I bought the book in 1968 while stationed at Fort Hamilton in Brooklyn. The book was my introduction to both the war and the practice of political dissent.

12. Carmichael was one of the more well-known figures to have traveled to Vietnam. For 1967, the year he went, the New York Times index records over a hundred entries, more than three times what Fonda had in 1972. Just days before he went to Hanoi, Carmichael was in Cuba, where he used Radio Havana to urge U.S. Negroes to take up arms for total revolution. The number of forty-two for 1972 comes from Clinton, Loyal Opposition. No one is certain about how many peace activists went to Hanoi during the war.

13. As a measure of just how unobjectionable trips like Fonda's and Clark's were at the time, the Times editorial was followed by a letter to the editor on August 25 from Abraham L. Pomerantz, former deputy chief counsel at the Nuremberg trials, in which he took the Times to task for questioning Clark's judgment. In Nixonland, 706–7, Perlstein's findings suggest that the Nixon administration was more interested in Fonda's trip than the press was.

14. The crew's passports were confiscated upon their return. The Phoenix made a second trip to the North in January 1968. For a much fuller account of the first Phoenix voyage, see Hershberger, Traveling to Vietnam.

15. With Hayden in Hanoi were Carol McEldowney, Vivian Rothstein, Norman Fruchter, Robert Brown, John Brown, and Rennie Davis. There had been three previous POW releases by the NLF according to the New York Times, November 12, 1967. For more details, see Hayden, Reunion, 220–41.

16. The Times profile treated Hayden as a bit of a phenomenon but did not demonize him. It is possible that until the Tet Offensive made clearer that the war would be lost by the United States, there was no perceived need to publicly disparage him.

17. Control of the freed prisoners' itinerary was always a source of contention between the Hanoi leadership, peace activists who won their release, and U.S. authorities. Hanoi did not want the former prisoners prepped by U.S. military or political handlers to give anti-Vietnamese accounts of their captivity, and activists were afraid that the emotionally vulnerable among them might curry favor from the military brass by bad mouthing the Hanoi regime and thereby inhibit further releases. U.S. leaders did not want the POWs used in early press conferences to make statements that would legitimate the peace movement and the Vietnamese side of the war. In the New York Times, February 17–20, Zinn and Berrigan traded charges with U.S. government authorities

over what the activists called Sullivan's "violation of the spirit of the terms of release." From the available accounts, it seems that the activists usually let the prisoners decide how they wanted to go home. In a July 1968 incident, Hanoi held up the release of three prisoners for two weeks because Sullivan again promised to take charge of them when they reached Vientiane.

18. Kahin's account is told in detail in Clinton, *Loyal Opposition*, 220–35.

19. This bill-of-particulars comes from Holzer and Holzer, "Aid and Comfort."

20. See Clinton, *Loyal Opposition*, 118, on Weills; and Hershberger, *Traveling to Vietnam*, 119, on the *Phoenix* crew.

21. Hunter's analysis can be found in Holzer and Holzer, "Aid and Comfort," 86. Later in their book, the authors cite a United Press International story of July 18, 1972, in which Georgia congressman Fletcher Thompson is quoted saying Fonda urged U.S. troops in Vietnam to "desert and turn themselves in to the North Vietnamese." Fonda's press conference was covered by all three major television news networks. The NBC News anchor John Chancellor reported Fonda's clarification of what she had said in Hanoi.

22. The transcript of Fonda's "Address to GI's in South Vietnam" is reproduced in Holzer and Holzer, "Aid and Comfort," 193–95. The accuracy of the transcripts is a legitimate concern, so I have used the Holzers' versions because they are among Fonda's most bitter antagonists; if there is a bias in the copies they (and now I) quote from, it favors their case against Fonda and does not reflect my point of view.

23. The exact number of broadcasts attributed to Americans is hard to determine. Some of them are likely to have been tapes of press conferences that were then aired as parts of newscasts. Others are identified as "taped for later broadcast." And according to the Holzers, some broadcasts were actually tapes made by antiwar groups in the United States. The Thach memo is reproduced in Holzer and Holzer, "Aid and Comfort," 23–28.

24. For claims that GIs were demoralized by her broadcasts, see French, *Jane Fonda*, 107; and Anderson, *Citizen Jane*, 278–79.

25. Jim Dawson's story of hearing Fonda during Tet is passed along by Michael Pierce in a November 2004 message. The woman responding to my advertisement promised to send copies of the photographs. It is possible that her father saw another starlet, maybe Ann-Margret or Joey Heatherton, touring with a USO show but that the dominance of the character Hanoi Jane in America's post–Vietnam War culture has distorted the memory. The word *Ho* conjoined to Fonda's name is street slang for "whore" that may have come into

usage years after the war. Its misogynist overtones are characteristic of other attacks on Fonda.

26. Soley and Nichols, *Clandestine Radio Broadcasting*, 264–65.

27. The October 16 edition of *Stars and Stripes* also reported on in-country GIs who were critical of the moratorium, and the October 17 edition reported on an October 15 antiwar demonstration of American civilians at the U.S. Embassy in Saigon.

28. Hoffer and Lichty, "Republic of Vietnam (South Vietnam)," 102, says 60 percent of Radio Hanoi was audible in Saigon, leaving it unclear whether troops in the field could have received it at all. McGrath responded to my inquiry in *Vietnam* magazine in an e-mail to me on January 18, 2005. All quotations by McGrath hereafter are from that message.

29. The same September 15 story continued, reporting that senior U.S. officials in Saigon believed the quickest was to get all the POWs out was to intensify the bombing. A senior air force official in Saigon said, "My judgment is that the fastest way to get these prisoners back is to compel a settlement. . . . Just keep pouring it on."

30. Byrns appeared in the film with Edward Elias and another POW. Byrns said he agreed with what Clark had said on the radio that the war is "a tragedy." It is perhaps notable that Byrns mentioned Clark's broadcast but not Fonda's. Perhaps he did not hear her or, at the time, Clark seemed more important to him than Fonda.

31. Captain Floyd Kushner was a U.S. Army doctor captured in 1968 near Da Nang. Part of a group of captives that came to be known as the "Kushner camp," he survived terrible conditions in the South before arriving at Hoa Lo in 1971. Many other captives of that group perished.

32. Anecdotes in Guarino, *P.O.W.'s Story* (324, 326), are suggestive of the point. In Hoa Lo, Larry Guarino was joined in July 1972 by the recently captured Kevin Chaney, a fraternity brother of his son Allan's at the University of Florida. Ralph Galati, shot down in February 1972, had been active on POW/MIA issues as a high school and college student. See "Physician Tells of Time as POW," *New York Times*, April 14, 1973, for the Kushner story.

33. See Guarino, *P.O.W.'s Story*, 129, 157; and Daly and Bergman, *Black Prisoner of War*, 211.

34. Rochester and Kiley, *Honor Bound*, 180–81.

35. Laura Palmer's photograph with the Vietnamese soldiers is in Emerson, *War Torn*, 261.

36. See Emerson, *War Torn*, 261.

37. Karnow, *Vietnam, a History* (17) cites a personal interview with Colonel Harry G. Summers Jr. in which the colonel said "he would have driven through [the DMZ] and pushed into Neighboring Laos" and that the "basic mistake" not to was made by "U.S. military planners." Summers was less critical of the press and politicians, according to Karnow.

Chapter 3. Prisoners at War

1. The King James Version of the Bible cross-references the prophecy (Isaiah 50:6) with the prophecy fulfilled (Matthew 27:67). For a nineteenth-century interpretation of the links from the Old to the New Testament, see C. H. Spurgeon's *The Shame and Spitting* at www.biblebb.com/files/spurgeon/1486.htm.

2. Boyer, *When Time Shall Be No More*, 68–69. In 1629 John Winthrop implored his fellow colonists to support the venture in New England as "a bulwark against the Kingdom of Antichrist" and the preacher Cotton Mather interpreted the colonists' war against the Indians (King Philip's War of 1675–76) as a manifestation of the red horse of the Apocalypse foretold in the book of Revelation. A century later, with the colonies nearing their final struggle for independence, the Christian prophets reviled their British oppressors as Antichrist and warned that the Stamp Act could be the mark of the Beast in disguise.

3. The following paragraphs on the captivity narratives are indebted to Strong, *Captive Selves*. The preceding quotation appears on p. 1.

4. Strong, *Captive Selves*, 48–51.

5. The absence of any corroborative testimony for Smith's reprieve adds to the question about its accuracy.

6. Strong, *Captive Selves*, 118.

7. Strong, *Captive Selves*, 131.

8. Strong, *Captive Selves*, 2; 294. The captivity narrative spawned a secondary fictional literature, such as James Fenimore Cooper's *Last of the Mohicans*, that expanded eventually into drama, public sculpture, children's games, dime novels, Wild West shows, and film and television. In March 2005, a new production of Laura Ingalls Wilder's *Little House on the Prairie* aired on national television. Soon after arriving in Kansas, the seven-year-old Laura wanders into the woods, where she encounters an Indian child. The audio and visual cues provided by the show's writers evoke in the viewer the exact tension between Self and Other introduced three hundred years earlier by the captivity classics. In

the scene, little Laura suppresses her attraction for her Indian counterpart and returns to the campsite.

9. The relevance of the captivity narrative for America's present is wonderfully developed by Susan Faludi in her 2007 book *Terror Dream* about uses made by the media and popular culture of the September 11, 2001, attacks to restore the image of men as the protectors of women.

10. The idea of "brainwashing" has virtually no standing in mental health studies, but it was made all but indelible in American popular culture by the 1962 film *The Manchurian Candidate*, which was remade in 2004. The former POW James Stockdale, in his memoir, *In Love and War*, recalls the influence that Korean War studies of brainwashing had on him while he was held in Hao Lo.

11. Cumings, *North Korea*, 13. Cumings acknowledges Anderson, *Imagined Communities* for his phrasing. Another defacing and widely used term was "the 'V,'" a one-letter abbreviation for Vietnamese. Jensen, *Six Years in Hell* uses that expression almost exclusively. Writing about the food, for example, the author says, "The 'V' told us not to worry about the worms" (124).

12. McDaniel, *Before Honor*, 50; Guarino, *P.O.W.'s Story*, 139; Gaither, *With God in a P.O.W. Camp*, 132.

13. Gaither, *With God in a P.O.W. Camp*, 128. Howes concludes that the captured pilots were "virtually ignorant about the enemy" because they had flown off bases or carriers and had never seen a Vietnamese face-to-face until they were captured. The POW memoirs, he says, "could serve as textbooks for Western racial stereotypes" (*Voices of the Vietnam POWs*, 126).

14. A helicopter carrying me near Ban Me Thout in 1969 diverted from its planned route and made some passes at clearings in the jungle. An officer told me later that the chopper crew had been hunting elephants. Franklin, in *Vietnam and Other American Fantasies*, writes about the treatment of prisoners by U.S. and Saigon forces (178–79). On the danger of extrapolating from prison culture to national character, one might ask whether the abuse of prisoners by U.S. soldiers at Abu Graib prison in Iraq in 2003 and 2004 was representative of Americans as a group.

15. Alvarez and Pitch, *Chained Eagle* provides one of the more graphic descriptions of prison conditions: "soup smelling of drain water [with] hoof of a cow or pig with the hair still attached, . . . prawns in dirty, brackish liquid, . . . a blackbird feet up on the plate, its head and feathers intact and the eyes open . . . fits of vomiting . . . splattered with my own vomit . . . sick with

diarrhea and dysentery, passing blood in my vomit and stool . . . crap splashed all over my feet . . . the stench lingered pervasively in my cell and on myself" (68). Turner, *Even the Women Must Fight*, reports that, years after the end of the war, residents of Hanoi complained that prisoners got "the best."

16. The biographic details in this paragraph are drawn from published autobiographies and biographical sketches available on the Internet. The measure of relative deprivation suffered by the elites among the POWs is underscored by Army Major William Hardy, an African American, who wrote, "I was able to survive on some food that killed others; I had had it very hard growing up, so some of the foods didn't bother me" (Wyatt, *We Came Home*, n.p.).

17. Jensen, *Six Years in Hell*, 11. Conditions at Korat may not have been as exceptional as Jensen thought. I was stationed at a small army camp just off the perimeter of Phu Cat airbase near Qui Nhon, South Vietnam, in 1969. To get to the camp, we had to pass through the airbase, something my duty as chaplain's assistant required me to do frequently. The airbase had a swimming pool, a bowling ally, a large PX, and a library.

18. Air Force Captain Myron Lee Donald says that he left his dirty clothes lying in his cell for several days while "waiting for the maid or camp laundry to wash my clothes" (Wyatt, *We Came Home*, n.p.).

19. Used in this way, "official story" does not mean official in the sense of government or Pentagon authorized. It means, rather, official in a euphemistic sense that it has become the widely known and accepted account of the POW experience given by hard-line senior officers among the Hanoi prisoners. That version of history was published by John G. Hubbell as *P.O.W.* in 1976. Rochester and Kiley, in *Honor Bound*, temper Hubbell's paean to the POWs and burnish it with additional documentation. Franklin (*M.I.A. or Mythmaking in America*), Gruner (*Prisoners of Culture*), and Howes (*Voices of the Vietnam POWs*), however, have produced the most credible scholarship on the subject. Because it was the earliest and most influential with the public, however, Hubbell's contribution to the Hanoi Jane mythology is the most important.

20. Leo Lewis, " 'John McCain Was Never Tortured in My Jail' Says Tran Trong Duyet," *Times* (London), October 25, 2008. Veterans' memories, as I and other writers have pointed out elsewhere, is an unreliable source for writing the history of the war in Vietnam. Nevertheless, Amnesty International's 1975 *Report on Torture* relies solely on the reports of POWs to say that "torture was systematic in the [Vietnamese] prisons until 1969." The issue of independent confirmation for the POWs' torture claims has dogged their charges from the

beginning. In "U.S. Anger Over P.O.W.s Imperils Aid, Brooke Says," *New York Times*, April 6, 1973, Republican senator Edward Brooke is quoted as saying, "I have no independent knowledge that the American prisoners of war were tortured." On the question of Vietnamese corroboration for torture, I consulted scholars who read Vietnamese or work with colleagues who do. Among them, with dates of our correspondence, are Karen Turner 6/27/05, H. Bruce Franklin 7/4/05, Robert Bingham c.7/05, none of whom knows of any documentation.

21. The number seventy-five is gleaned from the list in Hubbell, *P.O.W.*, 606–18. Howes, *Voices of the Vietnam POWs*, 205–10, provides a useful summary of the book. According to Howes, the *Washington Post* and the *Los Angeles Times* quoted Jim Mulligan, a former POW, as saying that 95 percent of the prisoners were tortured (70–71). The repeated use of an exaggerated statistic in this way is characteristic of myth making.

22. McEldowney died in 1973. Her journal was edited by Suzanne Kelly Mc-Cormack and Elizabeth R. Mock and published in 2007 under the title *Hanoi Journal 1967*. Her remarks on the POWs' condition are on p. 100.

23. Amnesty International, *Report on Torture*, 161. According to the report in "POWs Prove Healthier," *Los Angeles Times*, August 6, 1978, the U.S. Navy's Center for Prisoners of War studies paired pilots who had been captured with those who had not and Vietnam-era POWs with predecessors from other wars. Rochester and Kiley write in the vein of the "official story" and yet conclude, "However primitive enemy medical care was by American standards . . . [it] did in some instances save lives." "On balance," they continue, "Hanoi may not have received enough credit for its medical care record" (*Honor Bound*, 37).

24. Even though the U.S. raid of the Son Tay prison camp in November 1970 was a failure, it was what prompted the Vietnamese to reorganize the camp system. Hubbell's *P.O.W.* was written with the assistance of Kenneth Y. Tomlinson who, twenty-nine years later, would become President George W. Bush's controversial appointee to the Corporation of Public Broadcasting with a mandate to move it to the right. Within the Pentagon, according to Hubbell's preface, Hubbell received "enthusiastic" support and guidance from Admiral Thomas H. Moorer, chairman of the Joint Chiefs of Staff, whose own ultra-right-wing proclivities I profile in CNN's *Tailwind Tale*, chap. 7.

25. See memoirs by Chesley (*Seven Years in Hanoi*, 109) and Jensen (*Six Years in Hell*, 104) on the letter campaign. The letter campaign is central to the "official story" (Hubbell, *P.O.W.*, 519). Howes (*Voices of the Vietnam POWs*, 106) mentions the Amnesty International claim. McCain (*Faith of My Fathers*, 290) gives cre-

dence to the post-Ho logic for the change, as does former POW Phillip Butler in a June 16, 2008, message circulated on the VVAW list-serve.

26. Mary Jane McManus, a POW activist whose husband was a POW, espouses this revisionist view on the May 2, 2005, edition of *It's Your Call with Lynn Doyle*. More commonly, the outcome of the Tet Offensive is understood to have been indecisive in its own right, but because the United States had thought it had control of the South beforehand, the ability of the communists to mount a major offensive was interpreted as a defeat, if only relative, of U.S. policy. The stalemate thesis can be found in Karnow *Vietnam, a History*, 543–47.

27. Alvarez and Pitch, *Chained Eagle*, 62–63.

28. Guy's story is in Wyatt, *We Came Home*. Risner was featured in *Time* April 23, 1965. In his memoir, Risner notes, "In addition to *Time*, the Vietnamese were regular subscribers to *Newsweek*, *U.S. News and World Report*, plus many others. They also received the *Air Force Times* and *Stars and Stripes*. Their favorite seemed to be *The Christian Science Monitor*" (*Passing of the Night*, 70). He does not say how he knew this, although, according to McCain, *Faith of My Fathers*, 319, the interrogator had a copy of *Time* in his hand while questioning Risner.

29. Leopold's story appears in Wyatt, *We Came Home*.

30. The punishment of "burning shit" is portrayed in the 2005 film *Jarhead*, which is set in the Persian Gulf War of 1991.

31. Curiously, though most readers of the memoirs agree that they were written to dramatize the brutality of confinement in Hao Lo, McDaniel, like some other memoirists, uses "rooms," rather than cells, as nomenclature for his quarters. Risner describes Hao Lo as being full of Vietnamese civilian prisoners when he arrived in September 1965 (*Passing of the Night*, 63).

32. Risner, *Passing of the Night*, 72–73, 77–82.

33. There was another twist in the cycle, wherein the confession to the SRO that the prisoner had given the interrogators something came to represent proof of having been tortured, a twist that compelled the subordinate POWs to degrade themselves as "failures" before their own officers. The discussion of this practice in Howes, *Voices of the Vietnam POWs*, chap. 3, is excellent. Denton had a reputation for putting himself and others at risk, even as a flyer. So much so, Howes writes, that his need to have a level-headed copilot was recognized by fellow pilots (*Voices of the Vietnam POWs*, 174).

34. Howes draws on Scarry, *Body in Pain*, to make a social-psychological point that, just as the warrior gives consent for the infliction of bodily pain on him when he joins the battle, prisoners at war give consent for torture.

NOTES TO PAGES 53–55

35. Stockdale and Stockdale, *In Love and War*, 332–38.

36. Risner, *Passing of the Night*, 117–21.

37. Stockdale and Stockdale, *In Love and War*, 336. "Insisting on torture," Howes writes, "was thus the POWs' way of fighting the Vietnam War and of guaranteeing they would return home proudly as victors in 'the battle of Hanoi'" (*Voices of the Vietnam POWs*, 70).

38. There is no doubt that the hardcore SROs thought that signs of physical damage to their bodies could be later translated into propaganda statements about the cruelty of the communists. But their recognition that the same bodily damage could be presented to the world as a statement about them is an even more important insight into the prisoner-at-war mentality.

39. Risner, *Passing of the Night*, 143. What Risner dismisses as "propaganda" can be read today to say more about his misunderstandings of the war than for anything about the North Vietnamese. He writes, for example, "They kept preaching to us [over the radio] that North Vietnam had been tricked [by the Geneva agreement that had ended the French occupation of Vietnam]. To hear them tell it, the Vietnamese people had been guaranteed that they would be reunited, and that all they really wanted were free elections. We knew that was a lie. The story of the Communist takeover in North Vietnam was a three-day blood bath in which they murdered five hundred of the top men in the country to pave the way for Communism. Their 'freedom-loving people' jazz did not pull the wool over our eyes'" (143).

40. One of Salisbury's reports was carried on page 1 of the December 25, 1966, edition of the *Times* under the headline, "A Visitor to Hanoi Inspects Damage Laid to U.S. Raids." In the report, Salisbury describes Hanoi and uses a map issued by the U.S. State Department to juxtapose its listed military targets with the civilian sites said by Vietnamese to have been hit in recent raids. Salisbury's report appears to have the standard journalistic qualifiers—"the North Vietnamese say"; "four persons were reported killed"; "Hanoi residents certainly believe they were bombed"—in all the right places. On a personal note, I acquired Salisbury's book *Behind the Lines: Hanoi*, published in 1967, just before going to Vietnam in early 1969. As Stockdale may have feared, the book was, for me, an eye-opener that raised serious questions about the truth of U.S. government accounts of the bombing and what the war was all about.

41. Stockdale and Stockdale, *In Love and War*, 245–49.

42. Howes, *Voices of the Vietnam POWs*, 95.

43. Howes captures the spirit of jungle POWs (219–20). He also provides details on John Young, an enlisted army man and a member of the so-called Peace Committee that openly opposed SRO authority (101–2, 108–9).

44. Jensen, *Six Years in Hell*, 32; Young is quoted in Howes, *Voices of the Vietnam POWs* (218), which cites Grant, *Survivors*, 283.

45. Daly and Bergman, *Black Prisoner of War*, 211.

46. Howes, *Voices of the Vietnam POWs*, 205.

47. At the headquarters battery of the 41st Artillery Group in 1969, the hooches were cleaned by Vietnamese, haircuts were given by a Vietnamese barber who came into the camp, and Vietnamese did the "shit burning." Daily, a couple of enlisted men made the "gook run" to pick up the work crew. Within days of my assignment to the battery, I knew the names of several Vietnamese; one in particular, a young teenager named Lon, shared his apprehension about his forthcoming decision to join either the Viet Cong or the ARVN, the army of the anticommunist government of South Vietnam. Lon once came to work with a photograph of him and his brother, who he said was "VC." Anton describes mixing with Vietnamese civilians during his first days in-country in Grant, *Survivors*, 47–49. Anton also remembers that a fellow POW named Weatherman had had a "mistress/wife" in Chu Lai before he was captured (91). Weatherman died in captivity before reaching the North.

48. Anton, *Why Didn't You Get Me Out?* 32.

49. Daly and Bergman, *Black Prisoner of War*, chaps. 16 and 17, provides a lot of detail about Daly's interactions with civilian (and military) Vietnamese during his captivity in the South and eventual move by foot, truck, and train to Hanoi. He recounts, for example, meeting the young volunteers from the North (including women) who were working on the Ho Chi Minh trail (162). Recalling the experience, he writes, "I'd seen or talked with [a good number of Vietnamese] in the villages of the South, traveling the Ho Chi Minh trail, as a POW. . . . They'd been peasants, Viet Cong, NVA soldiers, workers, professors, Montagnards. And the more Vietnamese I came in contact with, the more I knew in my gut . . . that the war was wrong and we had no right to be there tearing the country to pieces" (190).

50. Howes, *Voices of the Vietnam POWs*, 220–21.

51. Plumb's story is told in Howes, *Voices of the Vietnam POWs*, 147; Gaither, *With God in a P.O.W. Camp*, 128; Tony Allen-Mills, "Right Rallies to Halt McCain," *Times* (London), February 3, 2008. Larry Chesley reports in his memoir, "As to the revolting sin of homosexuality among the prisoners, it simply did not exist" (*Seven Years in Hanoi*, 93).

52. Howes, *Voices of the Vietnam POWs*, 56–61, has the best discussion of the POW torture issue. The author also acknowledges that prison guards may have sought revenge for the death of loved ones in bombing raids by mistreating their prisoners. Although Rochester and Kiley generally support the "official story" claim of widespread torture, they recognize that tighter control of the prison population after October 1965 may have been a response to Risner's effort to make trouble (*Honor Bound*, 141–43).

53. Howes's analysis draws on Scarry, *Body in Pain*; Ruthven, *Torture*; and Peters, *Torture*.

54. Rochester and Kiley acknowledge the variation in treatment received by prisoners but nevertheless give credence to the unlikely claim that 95 percent of the men were tortured (*Honor Bound*, xii, 146).

55. Dunn's recollection is in Wyatt, *We Came Home*. Air Force Captain Joseph Crecca, who had a B.S. degree in mechanical engineering, wrote, in the same volume, that while a prisoner, he "had the opportunity to study Russian as well as to teach mathematics, physics, classical music, and automobile theory and mechanics."

Chapter 4. Barbarella as Prologue

1. Sut Jhally explores the relationship between male fantasy, music, and film in his 1995 video *Dreamworlds: Desire, Sex, and Power*. George Haddad-Garcia, writing at the time Hanoi Jane was morphing from the real life of Jane Fonda, observes, "After *Barbarella*'s box-office thunder, unplain Jane was referred to as 'the most fantasized-about woman in the world.' . . . Barbarella 'reeked with sex'" (*Films of Jane Fonda*, 142).

2. The gendering of the betrayal narrative for the lost war in Vietnam has been explored in Gibson, *Warrior Dreams*; Jeffords, *Remasculinization of America*; and Lembcke, *Spitting Image*.

3. Lillian S. Robinson discusses the incongruity between gender conventions and female warriors. She writes: "The lesbian connotations of 'Amazon' no longer have to be buried in a hyperhetero narrative closet. Even if they're 'unfeminine' in their heroism, hypermuscular in their construction, or lesbian-identified in their sexual relations, nobody wonders whether they're women" (*Wonder Women*, x).

4. Barbarella's relationship to the blind and impotent Pygar presents an interesting comparison to the character Luke, played by Jon Voight, in *Coming*

Home. Luke is a paraplegic Vietnam veteran with whom Fonda's character, Sally, has a satisfying sexual relationship, despite his impotence. Although the Luke-Sally coupling clearly validates the potential for women in a decentered male sexuality, the message in *Barbarella* is more ambiguous.

5. Zimmerman, "Paradise Found"; Kauffmann, "Stanley Kauffman on Films"; Adler, "Screen: Science + Sex = 'Barbarella,'" *New York Times,* October 12, 1968.

6. Fager, "Allegedly Satiric."

7. The post-sixties sexualizing of Fonda continues. TV Guide Network ranked her no. 17 on its 2010 list of "Film's Sexiest Women of All Time," calling *Barbarella* "an ode to Jane Fonda's sexuality . . . those legs were unreal." Marilyn Monroe was ranked no. 1.

8. See Andersen, *Citizen Jane,* 267.

9. Piercy, "Looking Good," 105. Fonda's statistics come from *Movie Life Yearbook (1963).*

10. Fonda's sultry and seductive roles in *Circle of Love* (1964) and *The Game Is Over* (1966) are similarly cited in Haddad-Garcia, *Films of Jane Fonda,* 108, 127, as a case for the eroticization of her legacy. But these films develop adult and sophisticated themes of sexuality, employing European motifs that devalue the kind of gratuitous titillation that Hollywood banked from the careers of Monroe and Mansfield and their peers. *La Ronde (Circle of Love)* opened in New York with a giant billboard featuring a painting of a supposedly naked Fonda. Saying there was no such scene in the film, Fonda successfully sued to have the billboard removed (Herman and Downing, *Jane Fonda,* 52).

11. For perspective, a search for "spider woman" done at the same time (June 13, 2003) produced about fifty thousand links, though *Spider Woman* is an on-going comic series with a large following of young readers. The number of links produced by a search varies, and depends on when the search is done.

12. Andersen, *Citizen Jane,* 279. In *A War Remembered,* of the 1986 Time-Life series Vietnam Experience, army warrant officer Geoffrey M. Boehm is pictured in 1970 beside his bunk, which is decorated with *Playboy*-type pinups (but no Jane Fonda) (88). In the 1989 film *Born on the Fourth of July,* Ron Kovic's mother admonishes him for reading *Playboy,* not for watching *Barbarella.*

13. Haddad-Garcia, *Films of Jane Fonda.*

14. These were August 2006 postings at www.forum.grunt.com. I added the parentheses to OPgunny's posting to make sure his point is not lost.

Chapter 5. From Lysistrata

1. The anonymous translation of *Lysistrata* quoted in this chapter is available at the EServer Drama Collection at http://drama.eserver.org/plays/classical/aristophanes/lysistrata.txt.

2. In basic training during the Vietnam era, trainees were introduced to "Jody," the legendary boy back home who would steal the wife or girlfriend. "Forget her," drill sergeants would tell a despondent draftee, "Jody's got her now." Soldiers in Vietnam receiving what would have been called "Dear John" letters during World War II were said to have gotten "Jodied." Bell notes versions of Odysseus's homecoming in which Penelope has sex with all one hundred-plus suitors, thus producing Pan (*Women of Classical Mythology*, 348–51).

3. "The Power of Women" is fig. 15 in Smith, *Power of Women*.

4. Bartra, *Cage of Melancholy*, 154.

5. Theweleit, *Women, Floods, Bodies, History*. One Internet site (www.about famouspeople.com) says matter-of-factly, "Women spying for either the North or the South used their large hoop skirts to hide weapons, secret documents and other contraband, as well as other means."

6. Kane, *Spies for the Blue and Gray*, 47–49.

7. Kane, *Spies for the Blue and Gray*, 29. Kane also calls Boyd's "best pair of legs in the Confederacy" an "asset" for her undercover work (130).

8. Kane, *Spies for the Blue and Gray*, 18, 23–24.

9. The details in this and the following paragraphs are taken from Howe, *Mata Hari*, which is the most authoritative biography of Mata Hari, and an on-line piece, *The Story of Mata Hari* by Denise Noe at www.trutv.com/library/crime/terrorists_spies/spies/hari/1.html.

10. Fonda's first husband was the French filmmaker Roger Vadim, with whom she made *Barbarella*.

11. Bill Gallo, in "Jane, Don't Be Dumb," *New York Daily News*, August 1, 2005, writes, "Vietnam vets compare [Fonda] with Tokyo Rose."

12. Boylan, "Tokyo Rose."

13. Howe, *Mata Hari*, 65.

14. For a facsimile of the contract for the two-thousand-dollar interview, see Howe, *Mata Hari*, 68. Howe concludes that "no signal corpsman claimed to have referred to 'Tokyo Rose'" (64) and that the "sultry beauty" Ruth Haya-kawa "most nearly corresponds to the image of the legendary 'Tokyo Rose' siren" (220).

15. Howe, *Mata Hari*. The origin of Tokyo Rose mythology is thus notably similar to that of the myth of spat-upon Vietnam veterans. When the FBI asked to hear from World War II veterans who had heard Tokyo Rose, it almost certainly biased its results by inserting her into the memories of the men who responded. The *Chicago Tribune* columnist Bob Greene used a column in the early 1980s to ask to hear from Vietnam veterans who had been spat on, virtually ensuring that he would hear from scores of spittled men—which he did. Greene subsequently published a collection of those letters, thereby making a major contribution to the myth that I debunk in *Spitting Image*.

16. Howe, *Mata Hari*, 180.

17. Iva Toguri D'Aquino died in Chicago at age ninety on September 26, 2006 (Goldstein, "Iva Toguri D'Aquino").

18. With nothing more to go on than "It's the episode where Klinger eats a Jeep," Diana Antul, the Holy Cross College interlibrary loan librarian (and M*A*S*H fan), came up with "38 Across," for which I'm very grateful.

Chapter 6. Betel Nuts and Razor Blades

1. *The Visitors* was preceded by films portraying sexually violent Vietnam veterans. In *Motor Psycho* (1965), for example, Brahmin rapes and kills before being killed himself.

2. Between *The Visitors* (1972) and *Coming Home* (1978), *Captive* (1974) and *Black Sunday* (1977) developed the connections between war, sex, and violence.

3. The story reported by CNN in 1998 about U.S. Special Forces having used Sarin nerve gas to kill GIs who had defected to the North Vietnamese was based on veterans' memories that bundled images and themes that had no existence outside of movie theaters. I discuss the mythical quality of the CNN report in *CNN's Tailwind Tale*.

4. The implication, then, of the distinction between the rifle (for fighting) and the crotch (for fun) is that the two do not go together and that the former must now take priority over the latter. Likewise with the sergeant's wake-up call: before induction, the "time to rock" may have referred to a sexual experience, but in the military it refers to dropping self-pleasuring activity, putting one's socks on, and getting trained for war.

5. For the details of 25th Infantry Division in this and the following chapter I've used information of the division's Web site (www.25thida.com).

6. In late summer 1969, after a night on guard duty, I was awakened from my mid-morning slumber by our hooch boy, Lon: "Lemgee, Lemgee! Wake up. 181

You go Da Lat"—my-less-than official, but nonetheless accurate, notification that I was being reassigned from the 41st Artillery Headquarters near Phu Cat to, eventually, a small camp near Ban Me Thout.

7. Johnson, *Sorrows of Empire*, contends that base-building itself has the hegemonic effect of demonstrating the power of occupying countries over colonized people. Free cigarettes were commonly available to GIs.

8. In-country marriages were hard to arrange, involving U.S. military authority and civilian Vietnamese authority. Marriages sought after GIs returned to the United States and left the service were also complicated. The number of marriages that came out of the war is an elusive figure.

9. On the Internet, readers can find references to "Sin City," a supposed sex camp, run by the U.S. military, to which GIs could gain access by asking their first sergeant for a pass. Some veterans remember such a camp in An Khe, others Ban Me Thout. "Sin City" may have been contemporary vernacular for any cluster of bars and brothels with an ambiguous relationship to U.S. sanction.

10. Veterans' fantasies and exaggerations of sex in Vietnam have sometimes been taken too literally by writers. Enloe, *Does Khaki Become You?* (33–34), for example, uses Mark Baker's *Nam* as a primary source, despite its lack of documentation.

11. I was among the "five" in the story—or was it three?

12. Walker, *Women's Encyclopedia of Myths and Secrets*, has a cross-cultural survey of stories about women with dangerous vaginas. The "shrinking penis" condition is known as the "Genital Retraction Syndrome" in Western medical literature, the Koro Syndrome in Malay, and Suk Yeong in Cantonese (Al-Hmoud, "Koro-like Syndrome in a Jordanian Male"; Tseng et al., "Sociocultural Study of Koro Epidemics in Guangdong, China"). By some accounts, the societies that preexisted the current Vietnam were matriarchies (e.g., the legend of the Trung sisters), which, if true, would raise questions about the patriarchal origins of the spitting women.

13. For the "terrible mother" with a meat-eating fish in her vagina, see Neumann, *Great Mother*, 168.

14. U.S. Senate, *Study of the Problems Facing Vietnam Era Veterans*.

15. Wu, "McDonald's in Taipei" provides a good introduction to the Asian betel-nut culture. The author points out that public spitting of the juice is generally frowned on in modern, urban settings but that a recent resurgence of ethnic identity and interest in traditional culture has broadened the popularity of "chewing."

16. The text attributed to the Marine Corps leaders handbook was found at www.usssatyr.com/betel (retrieved November 24, 2009) but its authenticity cannot be verified.

17. "Betel Chewing in Myanmar (and Elsewhere)," posted December 3, 2005, Far Outliers, http://faroutliers.wordpress.com/.

18. Henderson, *Marine Sniper*, 99–100.

19. The "strategic hamlets" were an idea adopted from the CIA's war against communists in the Philippines and were known as "agrovilles" in the early years of the Diem government. For details, see the interview with Ngo Vinh Long in Appy, *Patriots*, 57. Unaware at the time of the strategic significance of MEDCAP missions, I helped transport building materials to a school near Bong Son, socialized with Montagnards near Ban Me Thout (while the medics inoculated their children), and helped with an English class in Phan Thiet.

20. Shultz, *Secret War against Hanoi*, has the best account of the war against the North.

21. Shultz, *Secret War against Hanoi*.

22. In 1969 an American organization, Women Strike for Peace, and the Canadian Voice of Women invited Vietnamese women to a meeting in Canada. The Vietnamese women told the North Americans that women "were superior [to men] in reconnaissance and spying because enemy [U.S.] soldiers didn't think the women were a threat, so they could come and go around enemy posts" ("Ellin," "Meeting Vietnamese Women").

23. Paranoia was also a cultural affect of pot smoking. Although the brass did police the use of marijuana; being a "head" came with the virtual obligation to be paranoid. Kuzmarov, *Myth of the Addicted Army* inquires into the myth and realities of GI drug use in Vietnam.

24. On guard duty during 1969, buddies and I sometimes rigged the path to our bunker with warning devises that would be tripped by an officer sneaking up from behind to catch us for some minor rule violation. The term *fraggings* is derived from hand grenades that fragment into small pieces of metal when they explode. Hand grenades were sometimes used by GIs as weapons against officers but *fragging* came to refer to other forms of violence as well.

25. The film *Berkeley in the Sixties* (1990) is very effective at showing the continuity between the opposition to the McCarthyism of the 1950s and the social movements of the 1960s.

26. Hunt, *Turning*, has the best account of government infiltration of VVAW. 183

27. Jamail, in *Will to Resist*, writes about the climate of paranoia surrounding GI resistance to the war in Iraq. Fearing that their antiwar blogs will be monitored by the brass, he says, they write on-line while "looking over their shoulders."

28. Turner, *Even the Women Must Fight*, 28–35.

29. Turner, *Even the Women Must Fight*, 31.

30. Turner, *Even the Women Must Fight*, 35. James Daly, taken prisoner in the South, recalls seeing, and even having some interaction with, North Vietnamese women working on the Ho Chi Minh trail during his transport from the South to Hanoi (Daly and Bergman, *Black Prisoner of War*).

31. For the photographs of the housewife, member of the "Soldiers' Mothers" organization, and "skilled women propagandists," see Burchett, *Vietnam*, 34, 40, 65, respectively. For a discussion of Chi Kinh, see 164–66; for Blossom and Lissom's story, see 45. Burchett, *Grasshoppers and Elephants*, portrays most Viet Cong women as support workers or participants in nonviolent resistance, such as lying in front of bulldozers to stop the razing of their homes and fields. But one of Burchett's sources, Vo An Bao, told him about Vo Thi Phoung, who "headed a band of women armed with jungle knives which several times ambushed puppet patrols." "Puppet patrols" refers to troops of the government of South Vietnam, not U.S. troops—although there may have been U.S. "advisers" on those patrols who would have then experienced combat with the Viet Cong women.

32. Eisen, *Women and Revolution in Viet Nam*, 106. Eisen's material on the role of the women in the war is condensed in chap. 7.

33. Herr, *Dispatches*, cites Hasford, *Short-Timers*, for his truth-telling. Herr also collaborated on *Full Metal Jacket*.

34. I have reproduced the spelling and grammar as it appeared on the Internet.

35. "Ellin," "Meeting Vietnamese Women."

36. As a member of the *Insurgent*'s editorial collective in 1975, I would have participated in choosing graphics for that issue.

Chapter 7. Workout Jane

1. Boyer and Morais, *Labor's Untold Story*, 19–20.

2. After World War II, "sole survivor" status was limited to children whose parent had died in military service.

3. See Appy, *Working-Class War*, 28–38. Appy credits Hershey's "channeling manpower by deferment" for the ample supply of teachers, engineers, and

scientists "essential to the national interests" (36). After deferments for college and then two years for teaching math, I lost my appeal for continued deferment to my Plymouth County, Iowa, draft board in the spring of 1968 that I was more useful to the country as a teacher than a soldier. I was inducted in July.

4. Referring to one study, Appy says half of the workers who favored immediate withdrawal of troops from Vietnam also opposed the antiwar movement (Working-Class War, 41).

5. In Right-Wing Populism in America, Berlet and Lyons develop the concept of "producerism" (6–7, 348–49).

6. The conclave of rabbis in a Prague cemetery refers to the manifesto of anti-Semitic and white-supremacist movements Protocols of the Elders of Zion, a compendium of fictional writings that alleges a Jewish conspiracy to dominate the world through the control of ideas and money; in some versions, a rabbinical cabal meets in a Prague cemetery every hundred years to plot the takeover. Ridgeway, Blood in the Face sketches the history of the Protocols and their importance to the rightist movements of the 1980s in the United States.

7. The Peace Palace at The Hague opened in 1913 and was supported with funds from Andrew Carnegie to house the International Court of Justice. The court became the forerunner of the League of Nations and today is affiliated with the United Nations.

8. Tremoglie, "Red Queen of 'Peace.'"

9. Trumbo, Johnny Got His Gun. Blacklisted from Hollywood in the 1950s, Trumbo wrote under pseudonyms that won him, posthumously, an Academy Award. He gained popularity among antiwar activists during the Vietnam-war era for Johnny Got His Gun, which he helped turn into a film in 1971.

10. In the March 5 edition of Newsweek, the columnist Shana Alexander, remarking about the uniformity of the prisoners' claims of loyalty and patriotism, adds, "One wondered if they had not been brainwashed more in the twenty hours on the plane home than in all the years in camp" (32).

11. Complaints about the employment rate for Vietnam veterans may have distorted the reality. By law, employers were required to take draftees back when they returned from service and some employers went out of their way to hire Vietnam veterans. The energy crisis of the mid-1970s and the collapse of manufacturing in the early 1980s did hit the age cohort of Vietnam veterans hard, but memories that the labor market discriminated against veterans are probably apocryphal.

12. "P.O.W.s on Trial," *Winter Soldier*, July 1973, 12. The issue of class and rank within the POW population is developed more thoroughly in chapter 3.

13. For the front-page report on the New York City parade, see Robert McFadden, "Thousands Here Honor Vietnam Veterans," *New York Times*, April 1, 1973.

14. Sampley, "Hanoi Jane."

15. Zeiger responded to my inquiry about Sampley's claims in a September 20, 2007, e-mail message.

16. The details on the founding of Fonda's workout business come from Fonda, *My Life So Far*, chap. 15.

17. Fonda, *My Life So Far*, 394.

18. Mary Wollstonecraft recognized the centrality of economic independence to other forms of women's status in 1792 when she wrote *The Vindication of the Rights of Women*. Virginia Wolff reasserted the point in 1929 with *A Room of One's Own*.

19. See Faludi, *Terror Dream*, chaps. 3 and 4. The following paragraphs also draw on Faludi.

Chapter 8. Making Trope

1. The critical treatment of Fonda by POWs does not begin until 1989 with books by Everett Alvarez and Gerald Coffee. Over the next two years, four more POW autobiographies appear in which Fonda is portrayed negatively. In an article published in the *Seattle Times*, February 14, 2004, under the headline "Vietnam's Echoes Reverberating for Bush and Kerry," David Jackson and Michelle Mittelstadt write, "Fonda's visit to Hanoi in 1972 . . . earned her the lasting scorn of many Vietnam veterans who dubbed her 'Hanoi Jane.' " And, according to Sean French, "Veterans and their families still believed [in the 1980s] that President Nixon should have executed her when he had the chance" (*Jane Fonda*, 18).

2. See Kiernan, *Jane*, 347. Since *Newsweek* reported that "Hanoi Rose" was used on that occasion, it is possible that Kiernan took some license to recraft the phrase into "Hanoi Jane." It is also possible that Kiernan saw placards that newspaper reporters missed or did not report. Or, Kiernan may have simply coined "Hanoi Jane," but I have never been able to locate him to confirm that. In looking for a two-word phrase in newspapers one can never be sure that it was not missed.

3. Research claims to have found "the first" of anything have to be taken as provisional. In this instance, my saying that the 1973 use of "Hanoi Jane" in

American Opinion was the first does not mean that I prove that it was not used earlier someplace else. It just means that I have not found anything earlier.

4. Myra MacPherson, "Hayden and Fonda Back on the Road Again," *Washington Post*, September 27, 1979, D1. A twelve-minute on-line video titled *Documentary: How "Hanoi Jane" Fonda Got Her Name* (http://video.google.com/videoplay?docid=834009741378360o317#) offers a set of still photographs loosely themed as images of the war in Vietnam and Fonda's antiwar activism. The voice-over is her giving a speech to (apparently) an American audience after her return from Hanoi. Toward the end of the tape, a series of postcard-like captions runs in the following sequence: "She incited the protesters and rioters in the U.S."; "Her actions caused the torture and death of many Americans and allies"; "Now, in 2007, Jane Fonda officially sheds her 'Hanoi Jane' moniker"; "She has joined the jihadis who wage war in the civilized world"; "Jihad Jane. Do not let Jihad Jane and her comrades spit on our troops this time."

5. Russo is introduced in chapter 1.

6. With Mary Hershberger, I obtained two hundred pages of Fonda's FBI files from the Southern California office of the American Civil Liberties Union, which contains the documents referred to here. Tom Hayden's papers at the Southern California Library provide further documentation that the FBI thought of his and Fonda's activities as New Left.

7. According to George and Wilcox, DePugh's "most fertile recruiting grounds were among fringe elements—the John Birch Society, radical tax protesters, the Ku Klux Klan, and neo-Nazi organizations such as the National States Rights party," and Birch literature was what moved DePugh to form the Minutemen in 1960 (*Nazis, Communists, Klansmen, and Others on the Fringe*, 292, 275).

8. I have not been able to confirm the Coffin quotation.

9. As late as April 2007, there were claims that U.S. POWs were still held in Vietnam, posted at greasyonline.com, April 13, 2007.

10. A few weeks later, I came back to the VFW hall to return the materials Zyko lent to me. When I met him in the downstairs barroom, he was cold and accusatory. Having learned that I was the author of *The Spitting Image*, he indicated that I had not been fully forthcoming with him and others about what my "agenda" was. I did not hesitate when he offered to show me to my car and escort me to the I-84 on-ramp.

11. A major preoccupation of the National Security Center (NSC) in the closing decades of the twentieth century was the security of the Panama Canal,

which the United States was due to turn over to the Panamanians in 2000. Supporting its fears with references to the Birch newspaper, the *New American*, the NSC averred that the release of U.S. control would open the door to Chinese Communist control of the canal. The NSC founder and administrator was Richard A. Delgaudio, a former national administrator for Young Americans for Freedom who would later head the ultra-right-wing Legal Affairs Council, which raised money to defend the Iran-Contra conspirator Oliver North. Delgaudio's book *China Doll: Clinton, Gore and the Selling of the U.S. Presidency* was co-authored by Roger Canfield, a writer for the Birch newspaper, and published by the Birch-friendly U.S. Intelligence Council.

12. The North Vietnamese support for the fall 1969 moratorium actions was reported in the press and led to Vice President Spiro Agnew's denunciation of the antiwar movement for refusing to dissociate itself from Hanoi and to his signature "effete corps" label (Homer Bigart, "Dissension in City," *New York Times*, October 16, 1969; Marjorie Hunter, "Agnew Says 'Effete Snobs' Incited War Moratorium," *New York Times*, October 20, 1969).

13. Schmitz and Thompson quote Scheer as saying, "Richard Nixon wants to Americanize the world. But dig it. If Richard Nixon Americanizes the world, then America's children will become Viet Cong, and we shall be warriors in the process."

14. Hershberger, *Jane Fonda's War*, fleshes out the details of the legal matters surrounding Fonda's trip, and Holzer and Holzer, *"Aid and Comfort,"* revived those issues years later.

15. Hofstadter, *Paranoid Style in American Politics*.

16. Capell is the author of the 1974 volume *Henry Kissinger: Soviet Agent*.

17. The real name of "La Pasionaria" was Dolores Ibarruri.

18. King, *Lyndon LaRouche*. Many people remember the LaRouche followers at tables in airports during the late 1970s and early 1980s, and individuals involved in left-wing movements sometimes recall the rough physical tactics NCLC toughs used to break up their meetings. The documentation of LaRouche's use of Fonda is surprisingly light, although I found the Lawrence Felix Kramer Papers, at Brown University's John Hay Library, to be useful.

19. Emery's discussion of the "tiny pieces of paper" legend can be accessed at http://urbanlegends.about.com/library/aal 10399.htm. Attempts to access the original piece circulated by Dougherty at WorldNetDaily.com have not been successful. The second-person voice in which they are told begs their attribution.

20. Benge was interviewed for *The War Remembered*, a volume in the 1986 Time-Life series, The Vietnam Experience. He makes no mention of Fonda in that interview, although most of it is devoted to his time in captivity in South Vietnam before arriving at Hao Lo prison in Hanoi. In a long and friendly interview with me in July 2003, Benge was rambling and elusive on the details and sources of the "little pieces of paper" story.

21. Holzer explains in the introduction why he wrote the book. In the acknowledgments, he recognizes Ayn Rand as a "friend and mentor."

22. As Internet users might imagine, there was a lot of redundancy in that collection.

23. The candidate himself delivered a parody of military correctness with the words "Reporting for duty" accompanied by a boyish salute to the Democratic Party National Convention, a way of signaling to his television audience that his relationship to the armed services was nuanced by the totality his experience in the war and later opposition to it.

24. Schwartz, "Collective Amnesia."

Chapter 9. Jane Fonda

1. MacPherson, "Hayden & Fonda: Back on the Road Again," *Washington Post*, September 27, 1979, style section; Harris, "Baghdad Jane," *Observer* (London), July 31, 2005. Holzer writes, "Jane Fonda's desperate psychological need to overcome early parental rejection, to acquire a sense of identity and self esteem, and to fill her empty value system, caused her, first, to become an antiwar militant, and then to journey to wartime North Vietnam" (Holzer and Holzer, *Aid and Comfort*, 11).

2. Herman and Downing, *Jane Fonda*, 95–132.

3. That the attack on Hart came from within the Democratic Party proves only that that party's Right is as amenable to the use of character assassination as is the Republican Party. Hillary Clinton's attacks on Barack Obama's masculinity during the 2008 primary campaign—"He can't close the deal"—suggest that conservative Democrats have not forsaken the tactic.

4. Although she does not theorize it this way, Mary Hershberger, in *Traveling to Vietnam*, points out that Fonda was more likely to criticize herself for having played Barbarella than were others.

5. For the interviews, see Aarons and Ridenour, "Playboy Interview: Jane Fonda and Tom Hayden"; and Jong, "Jane Fonda."

6. As this book goes to press in 2010, few people, including those on the antiwar Left, seem to have an accurate sense of Fonda's relationship to her past.

7. Collier, *Fondas*, 28. Collier describes Henry as a "populist liberal" like his father. Syndicalism is the Italian term for unionism that in the 1920s of the United States was associated with anarchism and the Industrial Workers of the World, an organization popular with immigrant workers. In 1977, Massachusetts governor Michael Dukakis apologized for the state's failure of justice in the Sacco and Vanzetti case.

8. Hayden expressed the hope that "if an actor was going to be president, it would be Henry Fonda rather than Ronald Reagan" (*Reunion*, 473).

9. In their effort to denigrate Jane, some conservatives appear to rewrite the scripts for the roles her father played. In 1994 Jasper Garrison posted the following comment at www.smartfellowspress.com/Invisible/Chapter 8: "[Jane is] Henry Fonda's daughter. He was the embodiment of the American ideal: young Abe Lincoln, The Grapes of Wrath, Mr. Roberts—solid American values." In 2002 Mario Ragucci said at www.allnurses.com/forums/f112/hanoi-jane-we-honoring-traitor: "Henry had starred in some movie that left him in the eyes of the 40's generation everything manly, noble, honest and worthwhile in America. And his traitor daughter shoved it in his face."

10. Fonda, *My Life So Far*, 68. While recounting her father's objection to McCarthyism, Jane Fonda expressed puzzlement that he did not openly support its victims—puzzlement that inadvertently, perhaps, validates the more left-wing figure he otherwise cut in his professional and personal life.

11. Collier, *Fondas*, 144; Hayden, *Reunion*, 447.

12. Herman and Downing are the most strident on this point, writing that Fonda fulfilled her need for "parental love and family security . . . by becoming the erotic child-woman of Vadim's imagination." (*Jane Fonda*, 46).

13. French, *Jane Fonda*, 54.

14. See Collier, *Fondas*, 145–46; and Fonda, *My Life So Far*, 193–95.

15. Perrin tells his own story in *G.I. Resister*.

16. In her memoir *My Life So Far*, Fonda notes that she surrounded herself with a new "family" of activists in 1969 and then sarcastically comments, "They were, of course, all men" (218). Continuing in the next paragraph, she says she "*did* manage to marry men who were good fathers and provide the surrogate adult support" she needed.

17. See *My Life So Far*, chap. 5, for Fonda's account of *Klute*; the term "hooking" is hers (254).

18. See *My Life So Far*, 272–78, for Fonda's account of FTA and Levy's role in its founding. Levy can be seen in the 2006 documentary *Sir! No Sir!*

19. Hayden, *Reunion*, 445.

20. The penchant among conservatives for putting their enemies into hierarchical constructions that they then gender is evident in the creations of "Mr. Jane Fonda," appellations for Ted Turner and John Kerry, as well as Hayden. All can be found on the Internet. A particularly vile version of the Tom-submits-to-Jane interpretation, found at http://sexandpoliticsandscreedsandattitude .blogspot.com/2009/04/clive-james.html, implies that Hayden abided the political costs of association with the pariah Hanoi Jane as the price for access to her money. As is often true with Internet postings, it is not clear in this instance who is writing to whom and when.

21. Schonfeld, *Me and Ted against the World*, 8–9; Fonda, *My Life So Far*, 492.

22. Fonda, *My Life So Far*, 505, 508, 511.

23. The McManuses' view that "we had it won" is the soft version of the thesis that we did not lose the war, which might be more commonly voiced forty years after the war than before. At the spring 2009 meeting of the Organization of American Historians, a panelist on a session about the legacies of the war commented on the loss of the war, only to be met with fusillade of objection from audience members holding the hard-line position that it was not lost. Prados, *Vietnam*, restates the more conventional understanding.

BIBLIOGRAPHY

Aarons, Leroy F., and Ron Ridenour. "Playboy Interview: Jane Fonda and Tom Hayden." *Playboy*, April 1974, 67.

Alexander, Shana. "Prisoners of Peace." *Newsweek*, March 5, 1973.

Al-Hmoud, N. "Koro-like Syndrome in a Jordanian Male." *Mediterranean Health Journal* 5, no. 3 (1999): 611–13.

Allen-Mills, Tony. "Right Rallies to Halt McCain." *Times* (London), February 3, 2008.

Alvarez, Everett, Jr., and Anthony S. Pitch. *Chained Eagle*. New York: Donald Fine, 1989.

Amnesty International. *Report on Torture*. New York: Farrar, Straus and Giroux, 1975.

Andersen, Christopher. *Citizen Jane: The Turbulent Life of Jane Fonda*. New York: Henry Holt, 1990.

Anderson, Benedict. *Imagined Communities: Reflections of the Origin and Spread of Nationalism*. London: Verso, 1991.

Anton, Frank. *Why Didn't You Get Me Out? Betrayal in the Viet Cong Death Camps; The Truth about Heroes, Traitors, and Those Left Behind*. Arlington, TX: Summit, 1997.

Appy, Christian G. *Patriots: The Vietnam War Remembered from All Sides*. New York: Viking, 2003.

———. *Working-Class War: American Combat Soldiers and Vietnam*. Chapel Hill: University of North Carolina Press, 1993.

Axtell, James. "The White Indians of Colonial America." *William and Mary Quarterly*, 3d ser., 32 (1975): 55–88.

Baker, Mark. *Nam: The Vietnam War in the Words of the Soldiers Who Fought There*. New York: Berkley Books, 1981.

Bartra, Roger. *The Cage of Melancholy: Identity and Metamorphosis in the Mexican Character*. New Brunswick, NJ: Rutgers University Press, 1992.

Baty, S. Paige. *American Monroe: The Making of a Body Politic*. Berkeley and Los Angeles: University of California Press, 1995.

Bell, Robert. *Women of Classical Mythology*. New York: Oxford University Press, 1991.

Berlet, Chip, and Matthew L. Lyons. *Right-Wing Populism in America: Too Close for Comfort.* New York: Guilford Press, 2000.

Boyer, Paul. *When Time Shall Be No More: Prophecy Belief in Modern American Culture.* Cambridge: Harvard University Press, 1992.

Boyer, Richard O., and Herbert M. Morais. *Labor's Untold Story.* New York: United Electrical, Radio & Machine Workers of America, 1955.

Boylan, John. "Tokyo Rose: A Common Myth?" *History News Network,* December 11, 2001.

Burchett, Wilfred. *Grasshoppers and Elephants: Why Viet Nam Fell: The Viet Cong Account of the Last 55 Days of the War.* New York: Urizen Books, 1977.

———. *Vietnam: Inside Story of the Guerilla War.* New York: International, 1965.

Burkett, B. G., and Glenna Whitley. *Stolen Valor: How the Vietnam Generation Was Robbed of Its Heroes and Its History.* Dallas, TX: Verity, 1998.

Capell, Frank A. "Entertainment: There Is a Movement Stage Left." *American Opinion,* May 1973, 81.

———. *Henry Kissinger: Soviet Agent.* Zarephath, NJ: Herald of Freedom, 1974.

Chesley, Larry. *Seven Years in Hanoi: A POW Tells His Story.* Salt Lake City: Bookcraft, 1973.

Clinton, James W. *The Loyal Opposition: Americans in North Vietnam, 1965–1972.* Niwot: University Press of Colorado, 1995.

Collier, Peter. *The Fondas: A Hollywood Dynasty.* New York: G. P. Putnam, 1991.

Cortwright, David. *Soldiers in Revolt.* New York: Anchor, 1975.

Cumings, Bruce. *North Korea: Another Country.* New York: New Press, 2004.

Daly, James A., and Lee Bergman. *Black Prisoner of War: A Conscientious Objector's Vietnam Memoir.* Lawrence: University Press of Kansas, 2000. First published in 1975 by Bobbs-Merrill, under the title *A Hero's Welcome.*

DeMille, Nelson. *Charm School.* New York: Warner Books, 1988.

Edgar Bundy Ministries. *Betraying America: The Jane Fonda–Tom Hayden Axis; A Documented Report.* Wheaton, IL: Church League of America, n.d.

Eisen, Arlene. *Women and Revolution in Viet Nam.* London: Zed Books, 1984.

"Ellin." "Meeting Vietnamese Women." *Goodbye to All That,* c. 1969.

Emerson, Gloria. *War Torn: Stories of War from the Women Reporters Who Covered Vietnam.* New York: Random House, 2002.

Enloe, Cynthia. *Does Khaki Become You? The Militarization of Women's Lives.* Boston: South End Press, 1983.

Fager, Charles E. "Allegedly Satiric: *Barbarella.*" *Christian Century,* February 12, 1969, 238.

Faludi, Susan. *Terror Dream: Fear and Fantasy in Post 9/11 America*. New York: Metropolitan Books, 2007.

Feola, Christopher J. "The Americans Who Fought on the Other Side." *New York Folklore* 15, nos. 1–2 (1989).

Fonda, Jane. *Jane Fonda's Workout Book*. New York: Simon and Schuster, 1981.

———. *My Life So Far*. New York: Random House, 2005.

Forest, Jean-Claude. *Barbarella*. New York: Grove Press, 1966.

Franklin, H. Bruce. *M.I.A. or Mythmaking in America: How and Why the Belief in Live POWs Possessed a Nation*. New York: Lawrence Hill Books, 1992.

———. *Vietnam and Other American Fantasies*. Amherst, MA: University of Massachusetts Press, 2000.

French, Sean. *Jane Fonda*. London: Pavilion Books, 1997.

Freud. Sigmund. *Three Essays on Sexuality*. New York: Basic Books, 2000.

Gaither, Ralph. *With God in a P.O.W. Camp*. Nashville, TN: Broadman Press, 1973.

George, John, and Laird Wilcox. *Nazis, Communists, Klansmen, and Others on the Fringe: Political Extremism in America*. Buffalo, NY: Prometheus Books, 1992.

Gibson, James William. *Warrior Dreams: Violence and Manhood in Post-Vietnam America*. New York: Hill and Wang, 1994.

Goldstein, Richard. "Iva Toguri D'Aquino, Known as Tokyo Rose and Later Convicted of Treason, Dies at 90." *New York Times*, September 28, 2006, sec. C.

Grant, Zalin. *Survivors*. New York: W. W. Norton, 1975.

Greene, Felix. *The Enemy: What Every American Should Know about Imperialism*. New York: Vintage, 1971.

Griffin, David. *The New Pearl Harbor: Disturbing Questions about the Bush Administration and 9/11*. Northampton, MA: Olive Branch Press, 2004.

Gruner, Elliott. *Prisoners of Culture: Representing the Vietnam POW*. New Brunswick, NJ: Rutgers University Press, 1993.

Guarino, Larry. *A P.O.W.'s Story: 2801 Days in Hanoi*. New York: Ivy Books, 1990.

Hackworth, David H. *Defending America: Peter Arnett: American True and Blue?* July 14, 1998. http://www.hackworth.com/14jul98.html.

Haddad-Garcia, George. *The Films of Jane Fonda*. Secaucus, NJ: Citadel Press, 1981.

Hasford, Gustav. *The Short-Timers*. New York: Harper & Row, 1979.

Hayden, Tom. *Reunion: A Memoir*. New York: Collier Books/Macmillian, 1988.

Henderson, Charles. *Marine Sniper*. New York: Berkley, 1986.

Herman, Gary, and David Downing. *Jane Fonda: All American Anti-Heroine*. New York: Quick Fox, 1980.

Herr, Michael. *Dispatches*. New York: Basic Books, 1991.

Hershberger, Mary. *Jane Fonda's War*. New York: New Press, 2005.

———. *Traveling to Vietnam: American Peace Activists and the War*. Syracuse, NY: Syracuse University Press, 1998.

Hill, Lee. *A Grand Guy: The Art and Life of Terry Southern*. New York: HarperCollins, 2001.

Hodgkinson, Will. "Joan Baez: 'I was right 40 years ago and I am right now!' " *Times Online* (UK), August 29, 2008.

Hoffer, Thomas W., and Lawrence W. Lichty. "Republic of Vietnam (South Vietnam)." In *Broadcasting in Asia and the Pacific: A Continental Survey of Radio and Television*, ed. John A. Lent. Philadelphia: Temple University Press, 1978.

Hofstadter, Richard. *The Paranoid Style in American Politics and Other Essays*. New York: Alfred A. Knopf, 1965.

Holzer, Henry, and Erika Holzer. *"Aid and Comfort": Jane Fonda in North Vietnam*. Jefferson, NC: McFarland, 2002.

Horowitz, David. *The Professors: The 101 Most Dangerous Academics in America*. Washington, DC: Regnery, 2006.

Howe, Russell Warren. *Mata Hari: The True Story*. New York: Dodd, Mead, 1986.

Howes, Craig. *Voices of the Vietnam POWs: Witnesses to Their Fight*. New York: Oxford University Press, 1993.

Hubbell, John G. *P.O.W.: A Definitive History of the American Prisoner-of-War Experience in Vietnam, 1964–1973*. New York: Reader's Digest Press, 1976.

Hunt, Andrew. *The Turning: A History of Vietnam Veterans against the War*. New York: New York University Press, 2001.

Jamail, Dahl. *The Will to Resist: Soldiers Who Refuse to Fight in Iraq and Afghanistan*. Chicago: Haymarket Books, 2009.

Jeffords, Susan. *The Remasculinization of America: Gender and the Vietnam War*. Bloomington: Indiana University Press, 1989.

Jensen, Jay R. *Six Years in Hell: A Returned Vietnam POW Views Captivity, Country, and the Future*. Orcutt, CA: Publications of Worth, 1974.

Jensen-Stevenson, Monika. *Spite House: The Last Secret of the War in Vietnam*. New York: Avon, 1997.

Jensen-Stevenson, Monika, and William Stevenson. *Kiss the Boys Goodby: How the United States Betrayed Its Own POWs in Vietnam*. New York: Dutton, 1990.

Jhally, Sut. *Dreamlands: Desire, Sex, and Power.* Amherst, MA: Media Education Projects. Video, 1995.

Johnson, Chalmers A. *The Sorrows of Empire: Militarism, Secrecy, and the End of the Republic.* New York: Metropolitan Books, 2004.

Jong, Erica. "Jane Fonda: An Interview by Erica Jong." *Ladies' Home Journal,* April 1984, 32.

Kane, Harnett T. *Spies for the Blue and Gray.* Garden City, NY: Hanover House, 1954.

Karnow, Stanley. *Vietnam, a History: The First Complete Account of Vietnam at War.* New York: Viking, 1983.

Kauffmann, Stanley. "Stanley Kauffman on Films: Three for Fun." *New Republic,* November 9, 1968, 22.

Kelly, Michael. "The Road to Paranoia." *New Yorker,* June 9, 1995.

Kiernan, Thomas. *Jane: An Intimate Biography of Jane Fonda.* New York: G. P. Putnam, 1973.

King, Dennis. *Lyndon LaRouche and the New American Fascism.* New York: Doubleday, 1989.

Kinney, Katherine. "Hanoi Jane and Other Treasons: Women and the Editing of the 1960s." *Women's Studies* 32 (June 2003): 371.

Kuzmarov, Jeremy. *The Myth of the Addicted Army.* Amherst: University of Massachusetts Press, 2009.

Ladies' Home Journal. *100 Most Important Women of the Twentieth Century.* Des Moines, IO: Ladies' Home Journal Books, 1998.

Lembcke, Jerry. *CNN's Tailwind Tale: Inside Vietnam's Last Great Myth.* Lanham, MD: Rowman & Littlefield, 2003.

———. *The Spitting Image: Myth, Memory, and the Legacy of Vietnam.* New York: New York University Press, 1998.

Lewes, James. *Protest and Survive: Underground GI Newspapers during the Vietnam War.* New York: Praeger, 2003

Lipset, Seymour Martin. *The Politics of Unreason.* Chicago: University of Chicago Press, 1978.

MacArthur, John R. *Second Front: Censorship and Propaganda in the Gulf War.* New York: Hill and Wang, 1992.

McCain, John. *Faith of My Fathers.* With Mark Salter. New York: Random House, 1999.

McDaniel, Eugene B. *Before Honor: One Man's Spiritual Journey into the Darkness of a Communist Prison (Before Honor Is Humility—Proverbs 18:12).* New York: A. J. Holman, 1975.

McEldowney, Carol Cohen. *Hanoi Journal 1967*. Edited by Suzanne Kelley McCormack and Elizabeth R. Mock. Amherst: University of Massachusetts Press, 2007.

Moser, Richard. *The New Winter Soldiers: GI and Veteran Dissent during the Vietnam Era*. New Brunswick, NJ: Rutgers University Press, 1996.

Neumann, Erich. *The Great Mother*. Trans. Ralph Mannheim. Princeton: Princeton University Press, 1963.

O'Brien, Tim. *Going After Cacciato*. New York: Dell, 1975.

Page, Tim. *Another Vietnam: Pictures of the War from the Other Side*. New York: National Geographic, 2002.

Parks, Lisa. "Bringing *Barbarella* Down to Earth: The Astronaut and Feminine Sexuality in the 1960s." In *Swinging Single: Representing Sexuality in the 1960s*, ed. Hilary Radner and Moya Luckett, 253–76. Minneapolis: University of Minnesota Press, 1999.

Patrick, Robert. "The War Over Jane Fonda." In *Contra/Diction: New Queer Male Fiction*, ed. Brett Josef Grubisic, 281–92. Vancouver: Arsenal Pulp Press, 1998.

Perlstein, Rick. *Nixonland: The Rise of a President and the Fracturing of America*. New York: Scribner, 2008.

Perrin, Dick. *G.I. Resister: The Story of How One American and His Family Fought the War in Vietnam*. Bloomington, IN: Trafford, 2006.

Peters, Edward. *Torture*. Oxford: Basil Blackwell, 1985.

Piercy, Marge. "Looking Good." In *All the Available Light: A Marilyn Monroe Reader*, ed. Yona Zeldis McDonough, 103–8. New York: Simon & Schuster, Touchstone, 2002.

Prados, John. *Vietnam: The History of an Unwinnable War, 1945–1975*. Lawrence: University Press of Kansas, 2009.

Rand, Ayn. *Atlas Shrugged*. 1957; repr., New York: Plume, 1999.

———. *Fountainhead*. 1943; repr., New York: Plume, 1999.

Ridgeway, James. *Blood in the Face: The Ku Klux Klan, Aryan Nations, Nazi Skinheads, and the Rise of a New White Culture*. New York: Thunder's Mouth Press, 1990.

Risner, Robinson. *The Passing of the Night: My Seven Years as a Prisoner of the North Vietnamese*. New York: Random House, 1973.

Robinson, Lillian S. *Wonder Women: Feminisms and Superheroes*. London: Taylor and Francis, 2004.

Rochester, Stuart, and Frederick Kiley. *Honor Bound: American Prisoners of War in Southeast Asia, 1961–1973*. Annapolis, MD: Naval Institute Press, 1999.

Ruthven, Malise. *Torture: The Grand Conspiracy.* London: Weidenfeld and Nicolson, 1978.

Salisbury, Harrison. *Behind the Lines: Hanoi.* New York: Harper & Row, 1967.

Sampley, Ted. "Hanoi Jane: Yesterday's Communist Revolutionary; She's Today's Rich Capitalist." *U.S. Veteran Dispatch,* October–December 1996. http://www.usvetdsp.com/story8.htm.

Scarry, Elaine. *The Body in Pain: The Making and Unmaking of the World.* New York: Oxford University Press, 1985.

Schanberg, Sydney. "McCain and the POW Cover-up." *Nation,* September 17, 2008.

Schmitz, Hon. John G., F. Thompson, and R. H. Zion. *The Viet Cong Front in the United States.* Belmont, MA: Western Islands, n.d.

Schonfeld, Reese. *Me and Ted against the World: The Unauthorized Story of the Founding of CNN.* New York: HarperCollins, 2001.

Schwartz, Barry. "Collective Amnesia and the Symbolic Power of Oneness: The Strange Apotheosis of Rosa Parks." Paper presented at the annual meeting of the American Sociological Association, New York, 2007.

Shultz, Richard H., Jr. *The Secret War against Hanoi: Kennedy's and Johnson's Use of Spies, Saboteurs, and Covert Warriors in North Vietnam.* New York: HarperCollins, 1999.

Smith, George E. *P.O.W.: Two Years with the Viet Cong.* Berkeley, CA: Ramparts Press, 1971.

Smith, Susan. *The Power of Women: A Topos in Medieval Art and Literature.* Philadelphia: University of Pennsylvania Press, 1995.

Soley, Lawrence, and J. S. Nichols. *Clandestine Radio Broadcasting: A Study of Revolutionary and Counterrevolutionary Electronic Communication.* New York: Praeger, 1987.

Stockdale, Jim, and Sybil Stockdale. *In Love and War.* Revised and updated from the 1984 edition. Annapolis, MD: Naval Institute Press, 1990.

Strong, Pauline Turner. *Captive Selves, Captivating Others: The Politics and Poetics of Colonial American Captivity Narratives.* Boulder, CO: Westview Press, 1999.

Sturken, Marita. *Tangled Memories: The Vietnam War, the Aids Epidemic, and the Politics of Remembering.* Berkeley and Los Angeles: University of California Press, 1997.

Theweleit, Klaus. *Women, Floods, Bodies, History.* Vol. 1 of *Male Fantasies.* Minneapolis: University of Minnesota Press, 1987.

Tremoglie, Michael P. "Red Queen of 'Peace.' " *Frontpagemag.com*, December 11, 2002. http://www.frontpagemag.com/readArticle.aspx?ARTID=20730.

Trumbo, Dalton. *Johnny Got His Gun*. New York: J. B. Lippincott, 1939.

Tseng, W. S., K. M. Mo, J. Hsu, L. S. Li, L. W. Ou, C. Q. Chen, and D. W. Jiang. "A Sociocultural Study of Koro Epidemics in Guangdong, China." *American Journal of Psychiatry* 145 (1988): 1538–43.

Turner, Karen Gottschang. *Even the Women Must Fight: Memories of War from North Vietnam*. With Phan Thanh Hao. New York: Wiley, 1998.

U.S. Senate. *A Study of the Problems Facing Vietnam Era Veterans on their Readjustment to Civilian Life*. Washington, DC: U.S. Government Printing Office, 1972.

Vadim, Roger. *Bardot, Deneuve, Fonda/Roger Vadim*. Translated from the French by Melinda Camber Porter. New York: Simon and Schuster, 1986.

Walker, Barbara. *The Women's Encyclopedia of Myths and Secrets*. San Francisco: Harper, 1983.

Wollstonecraft, Mary. *A Vindication of the Rights of Women*. New York: Penguin Classics, 2004. Originally published in 1792.

Woolf, Virginia. *A Room of One's Own*. Fort Washington, PA: Harvest Books, 2005. Originally published in 1929.

Wu, David Y. H. "McDonald's in Taipei: Hamburgers, Betel Nuts, and National Identity." In *Golden Arches East: McDonald's in East Asia*, ed. James L. Watson, 111–35. Stanford, CA: Stanford University Press, 1997.

Wyatt, Barbara Powers, ed. *We Came Home*. Toluca Lake, CA: P.O.W. Publications, 1977.

Young, Marilyn B. *The Vietnam Wars: 1945–1990*. New York: Harper Perennial, 1991.

Zaretsky, Natasha. *No Direction Home: The American Family and the Fear of National Decline*. Durham: University of North Carolina Press, 2007.

Zimmerman, Paul. "Paradise Found." *Newsweek*, October 21, 1968, 99.

Zinn, Howard. *A People's History of the United States: 1492–Present*. New York: HarperCollins, Perennial, 2005.

INDEX

JERRY LEMBCKE is the author of six books including *The Spitting Image: Myth, Memory, and the Legacy of Vietnam* and *CNN's Tailwind Tale: Inside Vietnam's Last Great Myth*. His opinion pieces have appeared in the *Boston Globe*, *San Francisco Chronicle*, *Newsday*, and the *National Catholic Reporter*. Lembcke has appeared on several NPR programs including *On the Media*. The 2006 film *Sir! No Sir!* featured his book *The Spitting Image*. Lembcke grew up in northwest Iowa and received degrees from Augustana College, the University of Northern Colorado, and the University of Oregon. He was drafted in 1968 and served as a chaplain's assistant with the 41st Artillery Group in Vietnam. He is currently associate professor of sociology at Holy Cross College in Worcester, Massachusetts.

DATE DUE